Sylvia Barbara Soberton

Golden Age Ladies
Women Who Shaped the Courts of Henry VIII and Francis I

Golden Age Ladies

Women Who Shaped the Courts of Henry VIII and Francis I

Copyright © Sylvia Barbara Soberton 2016

The right of Sylvia Barbara Soberton to be identified as the Author of the Work has been asserted by her in accordance with the Copyright, Designs and Patents Act 1988.

All rights reserved. No part of this publication may be reproduced, stored in a retrieval system, or transmitted, in any form or by any means without the prior written permission of the publisher, nor be otherwise circulated in any form of binding or cover other than in which it is published and without a similar condition being imposed on the subsequent purchaser.

ISBN-13: 978-1532707551
ISBN-10: 153270755X

Contents

Introduction 1
Chapter 1 A mother's hope 11
Chapter 2 Queens, wives, widows 27
Chapter 3 The White Queen's mourning 37
Chapter 4 Scandalous marriage 41
Chapter 5 "Plain and badly lame" 54
Chapter 6 "Governess without restraint" 70
Chapter 7 Golden Queens 82
Chapter 8 The end of an era 102
Chapter 9 "To see and to be seen" 110
Chapter 10 Won and lost causes 128
Chapter 11 Love and loss 140
Chapter 12 "More French than a Frenchwoman born" 149
Chapter 13 "Devil in a woman's dress" 165
Chapter 14 "Ruined and lost" 176
Chapter 15 "It is not the custom in France" 193
Chapter 16 "Annoyed and humiliated" 202
Chapter 17 "Lightness of a woman" 217
Chapter 18 The peace-making Queen 230
Chapter 19 The Dauphine among enemies 237
Chapter 20 "Silly, poor woman" 247

Chapter 21 "She had not deserved such treatment" 262

Chapter 22 "The King is dead, long live the new mistress!" 272

Picture section 281

Select Bibliography 299

Acknowledgments 308

About the Author 310

INTRODUCTION

Henry VIII and Francis I are the most recognizable monarchs who ruled in sixteenth-century Europe. Their courts were so splendid that in 1515 the Venetian diplomat Niccolo Sagudino remarked that "two such courts as those of France and England have not been witnessed for the last fifty years"; both were centres of learning, art and patronage but also fierce rivalry and intrigues.[1]

Henry and Francis gained their thrones within a few years of each other and at relatively young ages: Henry in 1509 at seventeen, Francis in 1515 at twenty-one. They shared not only similar ages, but also interests in art, women and warfare. Their rivalry was legendary; Henry always quizzed ambassadors about Francis and had a lifelong ambition of subduing France and adding it to the English crown. The diplomatic relations between the two countries were underlined with a personal love-hate relationship between two monarchs thirsting for glory.

Yet somewhere behind the scenes, while Henry and Francis were busying themselves with seeking military glory and new love conquests, their women—mother, sisters, wives and mistresses—were trying to make their own marks on the court. They had to be strong if they wanted to make it in a man's world. They lived on the brink of the golden age of the European Renaissance and witnessed social and religious upheavals as the medieval world they knew crumbled to dust, replacing the old with the new.

Mary Tudor, Henry VIII's younger sister, shocked her contemporaries when she married for love after her first husband, King Louis XII, Francis's predecessor, died unexpectedly at the age of fifty-two. Brought up at the French court while serving Queen Claude, Francis's wife, Anne Boleyn took the English court by storm upon her return and changed the course of history when she refused to become Henry VIII's mistress.

Louise of Savoy, Francis I's mother, became regent during his notable absences and is remembered as one of the most admired women of her era. Margaret of Alençon, Francis's erudite sister, was known as one of the most learned women of her age, her advice often sought by ambassadors and visitors. Queen Eleanor, Charles V's sister, struggled to find her place at the French court after her marriage to Francis I in 1531, finding a formidable rival to his heart in the person of Anne de Pisseleu, who exerted more influence than any royal mistress before her. Witnessing the warring political factions at court, the young Catherine de Medici, humiliated by her husband's relationship with Diane de Poitiers, learned how to navigate the murky waters of courtly intrigue to emerge as the leading force on the international stage of sixteenth-century Europe.

This book tells these women's stories against the backdrop of the legendary rivalry between Henry VIII and Francis I, with a focus on their private lives and the sacrifices they had to make to survive at the Tudor and Valois courts.

Cast of Characters

The Court of Henry VIII

The King's wives and children:

Katharine of Aragon: Henry's first wife. Their marriage was annulled and Katharine banished from court.

Princess Mary: Their only child. She was later bastardised and degraded to the position of Lady Mary.

Anne Boleyn: Henry's second wife. She was executed on trumped-up charges of adultery, incest and high treason.

Princess Elizabeth: Their only child. Like her half sister Mary, she was bastardised after her mother's disgrace.

Jane Seymour: Henry's third wife. She died two weeks after delivering the longed-for male heir.

Prince Edward: Their only child. He succeeded his father after Henry VIII's death in 1547 as Edward VI.

Anne of Cleves: Henry's fourth wife. She was a German princess whose marriage to Henry VIII lasted for only six months.

Katherine Howard: Henry's fifth wife. She was executed after the King learned about her past and discovered her alleged adultery with one of the gentlemen of the Privy Chamber.

Katherine Parr: The sixth and final wife of Henry VIII.

Other relatives:

Mary Tudor: Henry's favourite younger sister. She married Louis XII, King of France.

Charles Brandon, Duke of Suffolk: Mary Tudor's second husband and Henry VIII's best friend.

Henry Fitzroy, Duke of Richmond: Henry VIII's illegitimate but acknowledged son.

Genealogical Table: Henry VIII and His Family

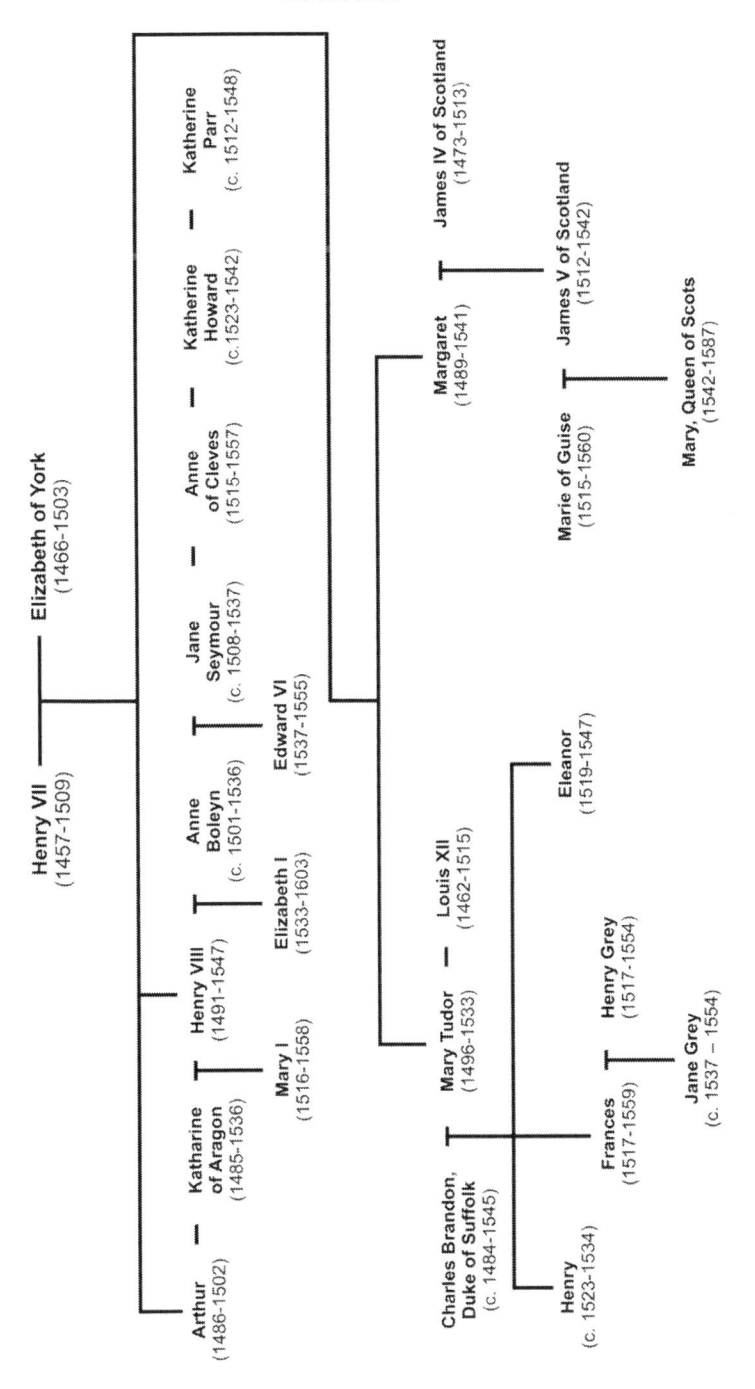

Introduction

- Henry VII (1457-1509) — Elizabeth of York (1466-1503)
  - Arthur (1486-1502) — Katharine of Aragon (1485-1536)
  - Henry VIII (1491-1547)
    - = Katharine of Aragon (1485-1536) → Mary I (1516-1558)
    - = Anne Boleyn (c. 1501-1536) → Elizabeth I (1533-1603)
    - = Jane Seymour (c. 1508-1537) → Edward VI (1537-1555)
    - = Anne of Cleves (1515-1557)
    - = Katherine Howard (c. 1523-1542)
    - = Katherine Parr (c. 1512-1548)
  - Margaret (1489-1541) — James IV of Scotland (1473-1513)
    - James V of Scotland (1512-1542) — Marie of Guise (1515-1560)
      - Mary, Queen of Scots (1542-1587)
  - Mary Tudor (1496-1533)
    - = Louis XII (1462-1515)
    - = Charles Brandon, Duke of Suffolk (c. 1484-1545)
      - Henry (c. 1523-1534)
      - Frances (1517-1559) — Henry Grey (1517-1554)
        - Jane Grey (c. 1537 – 1554)
      - Eleanor (1519-1547)

5

The Court of Francis I

The King's wives and children:

Claude of France: Francis's first wife and mother of his heirs.

Louise: Their first child. She died at the age of two in 1517.

Charlotte: Their second child. She died at the age of eight in 1524.

Dauphin Francis: Their third child and heir. He died unexpectedly in 1536.

Henri: Their fourth child. He succeeded his father as Henri II.

Madeleine: Their fifth child. She married James V of Scotland and died in 1537 at the age of sixteen.

Charles: Their sixth child. He died in 1545 at the age of twenty-three. He was Francis's favourite son.

Marguerite: Their seventh child. She outlived her parents. She married Emmanuel Philibert, Duke of Savoy, and had one son by him.

Eleanor of Portugal: Francis's second wife, known also as Eleanor of Austria. She was the sister of Francis's archenemy, Charles V.

Other relatives and court members:

Louise of Savoy: Francis's mother. She served as regent during his absences. She and her children were referred to as "the Trinity", and she herself styled Francis "my Caesar".

Margaret of Alençon: Francis's sister and friend, known later as Queen of Navarre.

Henri d'Albret: Margaret's second husband and father of her child.

Jeanne d'Albret: Margaret's only daughter and Francis's niece.

Louis XII: Francis's father-in-law, who appointed him heir to the throne.

Françoise de Foix: Francis's first officially appointed royal mistress.

Anne de Pisseleu: Francis's second officially appointed royal mistress.

Catherine de Medici: Francis's daughter-in-law, wife of his second son Henri.

Diane de Poitiers: Mistress of Francis's son Henri.

Nicolas d'Estouteville: The only recorded illegitimate child of Francis I, born in 1545.

Anne de Montmorency: Influential member of the court. He was named Grand Master of France, charged with the supervision of the royal household and the King's private service. He was later appointed Constable of France.

Genealogical Table: Francis I and His Family

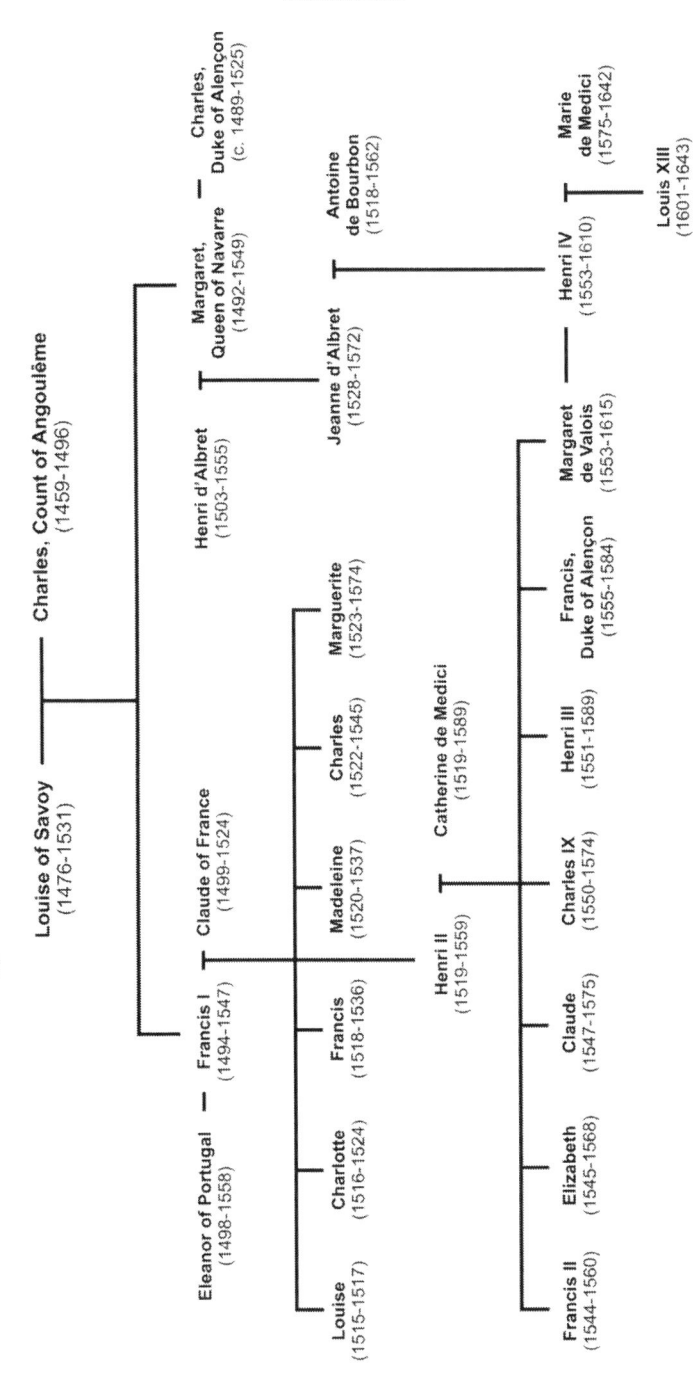

- Charles, Count of Angoulême (1459-1496) — Louise of Savoy (1476-1531)
  - Francis I (1494-1547) — Claude of France (1499-1524)
    - Louise (1515-1517)
    - Charlotte (1516-1524)
    - Francis (1518-1536)
    - Henri II (1519-1559) — Catherine de Medici (1519-1589)
      - Francis II (1544-1560)
      - Elizabeth (1545-1568)
      - Claude (1547-1575)
      - Charles IX (1550-1574)
      - Henri III (1551-1589)
      - Margaret de Valois (1553-1615) — Henri IV (1553-1610) — Marie de Medici (1575-1642)
        - Louis XIII (1601-1643)
      - Francis, Duke of Alençon (1555-1584)
    - Madeleine (1520-1537)
    - Charles (1522-1545)
    - Marguerite (1523-1574)
  - Francis I — Eleanor of Portugal (1498-1558)
  - Margaret, Queen of Navarre (1492-1549) — Charles, Duke of Alençon (c. 1489-1525)
  - Margaret, Queen of Navarre — Henri d'Albret (1503-1555)
    - Jeanne d'Albret (1528-1572) — Antoine de Bourbon (1518-1562)
      - Henri IV (1553-1610)

9

NOTES

[1] *Letters and Papers, Foreign and Domestic, Henry VIII,* Volume 2, 1515-1518, n. 410.

CHAPTER 1
A MOTHER'S HOPE

"I was born at Pont-d'Ain on 11 September 1476 at 5:24 p.m.", recorded Louise of Savoy humbly in her *Journal* written several years after her son acceded the throne. Her birth, in hindsight, was a momentous event because without her there would be no Francis I or the golden age of France he ushered in.[1] At the moment of her birth, however, no one could have ever predicted that this infant girl would play such an important role on the political stage of Europe.

Women, especially those of high rank, were expected to provide their husbands with male heirs to continue their lineage into the next generation. Boys were always welcomed with honours while girls were usually greeted with a mixture of relief and disappointment; relief if a mother survived, disappointment that she bore a girl. Louise of Savoy was the first child born to her parents, Philip, Count of Bresse, and Margaret of Bourbon. No one recorded their reaction to the birth of a baby daughter, but if we consider the example of one of their contemporaries, we may at least get closer to the fifteenth century's opinion of children. The childbearing experience of Marie of Valois, the illegitimate daughter of King Charles VII, throws more light upon a medieval French noblewoman's attitude towards her duties. In February 1464, Marie wrote a touching letter to her husband wherein she announced that she gave birth to a beautiful and healthy baby boy. "It seems to me that you ought to praise me very heartily because I have given you two such fine sons one after the other", she mused before adding poignantly, "If it had been a girl, I should have said everything bad in the world about it, on account of the trouble I had, but because it is a son, I should be ashamed to complain of that".[2] In her later life, Louise of Savoy held similar views and felt that a woman proved her worth when she delivered a son.

Louise's life changed dramatically when her mother died of consumption in 1483. Fortunately for Louise, her aunt was the celebrated Anne of Beaujeu, who took the girl under her wing and placed her, at the behest of Louise's father, in the royal household. A daughter of King Louis XI, Anne of Beaujeu was every inch as learned and ambitious as her father, the cunning Louis XI, who appointed her an unofficial regent during the minority of her brother, the thirteen-year-old Charles VIII. Louis called Anne "the least foolish of women" since he believed that "there are no wise women" in the world; this was the highest form of compliment this King could pay to his daughter. Anne took the reins of government and became a political authority to be reckoned with in a country where Salic law prevented women from assuming the crown.

A mother's hope

Two generations later, the courtly historian Pierre de Bourdeille, seigneur de Brantôme, wrote that her court was "very fine and grand". Despite many political duties, Anne of Beaujeu took it upon herself to educate young girls of noble families. Brantôme recorded that "there were no ladies or daughters of great houses in her time who did not receive lessons from her".[3] Anne had a broad knowledge of manners, court etiquette and politics of court life that she wanted to impart on her young charges, who were more than eager to learn from the most influential woman of their day.

Sometime in 1497, Anne sat down to write *Lessons for My Daughter*, a teaching manual originally intended for her only daughter, Suzanne.[4] The book was printed in 1504 and became one of the most important handbooks for young girls at the French court. It is certain that Anne's advice for her daughter, who was about eight years old when her mother started composing the lessons, were intended for all young girls who, like Suzanne, were raised to become the leading luminaries of the court. The advice can be grouped into two categories. There were light instructions pertaining to courtly etiquette—say your prayers each morning, pay attention while in church, dress warmly in cold weather, avoid making faces—while others instructed how to be a good wife and mistress of the household.[5]

Once a year, on New Year's Day, Anne of Beaujeu gave her charges eighty livres each to buy a court gown of crimson satin; it was probably during this time that Louise learned how to be thrifty and spend her resources wisely.[6] Whereas Louise was but a poor relative of Madame la Grande, as Anne of Beaujeu was called by her courtiers, there was a girl who was pampered from the time of her first arrival at court. Margaret of Austria, daughter of the Holy Roman Emperor Maximilian, was served by ninety ladies-in-waiting and dined on silver tableware. Born in 1480, Margaret was engaged to Charles VIII when she was three and lived at the French court until her engagement was broken off and she was forced to leave France after the young King repudiated her to marry Anne of Brittany. Margaret and Louise would make history together one day.

Louise of Savoy spent about five years in Anne of Beaujeu's school for girls, where she thrived in the refined, elegant and pious courtly atmosphere. In 1488, when Anne of Beaujeu arranged a match for her niece, Louise's childhood came to an end. She was to marry Charles, Count of Angoulême, the great-grandson of Charles V of France and a man seventeen years Louise's senior. Afraid of her marital duties, Louise unburdened herself to her father, whose letter to his second wife reveals how Louise—and certainly many other girls in her situation—felt about her impending marriage to a much older man. "My daughter says", wrote Philip of Bresse, "she is still too narrow, and she does not know whether she might die of it; so much so that she asks every day how big and how long his thing is, and whether it is as big and long as her arm". Philip dismissed his daughter's worries with a little bit of humorous banter, informing his wife that Louise's fears showed that "she is already itching to be at the business of you other old married women".[7]

Twelve was the minimum age at which a woman could be married. This was called the age of consent and meant that a girl was able to become a wife in the carnal sense. Sometimes, when a girl was believed to have been too young or too undeveloped for her age, the consummation of her marriage was deferred. Two years after her marriage, the fourteen-year-old Countess of Angoulême went on a pilgrimage to the castle of Plessis-lez-Tours, where the Italian hermit Francis of Paola, believed to have worked miracles, was residing. This hermit was often consulted by women who desired his divine assistance for producing children, and many heirs and heiresses were named after him.

Louise seems way too young to have been worried about childlessness at this age, but not after we consider the circumstances she found herself in. When she arrived in her husband's household, she discovered that he kept two mistresses, Antoinette de Polignac and Jeanne Comte, who had already borne him children. Instead of making a scene, the young Louise not only accepted her husband's mistresses but befriended them.

It was not unusual for a medieval woman to accept her husband's infidelities. In fact, in an age when marriages were mostly arranged for political or financial gain, contemporary thought endorsed such demeanour. In her best-selling manual for women, the fourteenth-century writer Christine de Pizan advised wives what to do if their husbands were unfaithful:

"Suppose that the husband, of whatever class he may be, has extremely perverse and rude behaviour. Suppose he is unloving towards his wife or strays into a love affair with some other woman. If the wife cannot remedy the situation, she must put up with all this and dissimulate wisely, pretending that she does not notice it and that she truly does not know anything about it. As a prudent woman, she will think, 'If you speak to him harshly, you will gain nothing, and if he leads you a bad life, you will be kicking against the spur; he will perhaps leave you, and people will mock you all the more and believe shame and dishonour, and it may be still worse for you. You must live and die with him whatever he is like."[8]

Louise accepted her lot and earned her husband's respect, but she never forgot that Francis of Paola promised her on that pilgrimage that she would bear a son who would one day become King. The longed-for male heir was born on 12

September 1494 and was named Francis, in honour of the hermit who predicted his birth. Louise recorded this event in her *Journal,* a document written with the benefit of hindsight several years after the described events:

"Francis, by the Grace of God, King of France, my pacific Caesar, took his first sight of the light of day at Cognac, about ten hours after midday 1494, the 12th day of September".[9]

Francis was Louise's second child. A daughter, Margaret, was born "in the year 1492, on the 11th day of April, at two o'clock in the morning".[10] Yet it was Francis who dominated entries in Louise's *Journal* and about whose future she was very anxious. Whenever the robust and athletic young Francis was in trouble, Louise trembled. On 25 January 1502, he was carried off by his mount. Louise recorded that:

"My King, my Lord, my Caesar and my son, was run away with across the fields, near Amboise, on a palfrey which had been given him by the Marshal of Gié, and so great was the danger that those who were present thought it irreparable. But God, the Protector of widows and the Defender of orphans, foreseeing the future, would not forsake me, knowing that if an accident had so suddenly robbed me of my love, I should have been too miserable to endure it."[11]

Similar accidents repeated throughout Francis's youth, and each time Louise suffered with her beloved son. Whether Francis of Paola truly foretold that Francis would become King may never be known for a fact, but harbouring such a hope was not unreasonable in her circumstances and soon became Louise's fixation.[12] Louise's husband was a first cousin of Louis, Duke of Orléans, and stood in direct line for the throne of France. The reason they were considered possible candidates for the throne was that King Charles VIII had no male heirs, and according to Salic law, only men could inherit the crown.

Louise's marriage to Charles of Angoulême was harmonious, and when the count fell sick during the winter of 1495, Louise rushed to his bedside and nursed him devotedly for more than a month before he died. "The first day of the year 1496", the entry in her *Journal* says, "I lost my husband".[13] This is a very laconic description of Charles's death; a more touching and no less accurate glimpse of Louise we find in a chronicle of a man who knew her and her husband very well. Jean de St Gelais, who lived in the couple's household, reported that Louise attended her dying spouse "day and night as tenderly and humanely as the poorest wife might nurse her husband".[14]

Charles's place in the succession was taken by his and Louise's son, Francis, who became known as Francis of Angoulême and later as the Duke of Valois. Yet Francis's accession to the throne was by no means sure. King Charles VIII died childless in 1498 in one of the strangest accidents of the era: the King was walking through the Chateau of Amboise when he struck his head on a low stone doorframe and died nine hours later.[15] The twenty-seven-year-old King was succeeded by Louis, Duke of Orléans, the cousin of Louise of Savoy's late husband, who assumed the throne as Louis XII.

The new King was married to Charles VIII's younger sister, Joan of France. Louis resented his marriage from the beginning because he was well aware that Joan's father, Louis XI, wished to extinguish his rival's dynasty through this unfortunate match. Joan was deformed from birth, and her father fancied that the children born to Louis and Joan "will not cost them much to rear".[16] This effectively meant that Louis XI believed that Joan's infirmity would prevent her, as it truly did, from bearing children. Louis XII eventually won annulment of his fruitless marriage and married Anne of Brittany, Charles VIII's widow. Anne was Duchess of Brittany in her own right, and the marriage agreement between her and her first husband stipulated that if Anne was widowed without having produced a son, the King's successor should marry her to keep the duchy of Brittany—a coveted prize—under French authority.

A son born to Louis XII and Anne of Brittany would deprive Louise of Savoy's boy of his royal inheritance, and for several long years, Francis's right to the throne hung in the balance. Anne, only eight months older than Louise, was in her early twenties when she became Queen of France for the second time, and it was reasonable to assume that she would be able to provide her husband with an heir to the throne. While married to Charles VIII, she had given birth to three sons successively, albeit only one, Charles Orland, lived past infancy, but he died at the age of three after contracting measles.[17]

Louise followed Anne of Brittany's childbearing history, littered with miscarriages and stillbirths, with unabashed curiosity, detailing each pregnancy and its outcome in her *Journal*. Anne's first child by Louis, Claude, was born in Louise's castle of Romorantin on 13 October 1499 at 8:54 p.m. The little princess would become one of the most important members of Louise's immediate family, and her birth too was scrupulously recorded in the *Journal*. With each of Anne of Brittany's failed pregnancies and dead infants, Louise's precious son's chances to inherit the crown became more and more real.

Soon, Anne and Louise became bitter rivals. Louis XII showed great affection for the widowed Louise and her children and invited them to his court early in the reign. The contemporary observer remarked that:

"My said lord the King received the party benignly and graciously, with honour befitting his nearest relatives on the paternal side. He gave the said lady lodgings in his castle at

Chinon, over his own chamber, where he went to visit her frequently in most familiar fashion. As for the children, he (the King) did not know how to show them favour enough; for, had he been their father, he could not have made more of them. And certes, there were few children to equal them in any rank of life; as, for their years, they were so accomplished, that it was pleasant and delightsome even to look at them".[18]

Soon the King decided that Louise should take up residence at the castle of Blois, so that "her children might be reared and educated at the same palace which he had spent his earliest years".[19] However, about a week later, he changed his mind and decided to send Louise, Francis and Margaret to the castle of Amboise with Pierre de Rohan, Marshal of Gié, as their custodian.

The castle of Amboise was one of the most luxurious royal residences of the time and would become one of Francis's favourites. To Louis XII, the castle invoked too many memories of his predecessor, Charles VIII, who had additions made to Amboise both before and after his Italian expedition, and this is why Louis decided to lodge Francis there. Charles's war campaign in Naples had a profound impact on the King's attitude towards the arts and architecture, and he wished Amboise's gardens and interiors to resemble what he saw in Italy.

To the young and impressionable Francis, Amboise was his first taste of luxury and the Italianate style he would later introduce to his own castles in the Loire valley. By 1495, Charles VIII had arranged the transport of 43 tons of works of art from Italy straight to Amboise. These included 130 exquisite tapestries, 172 carpets and 1140 volumes from the famous library of the Aragon kings of Naples, as well as paintings and furniture.[20] Surrounded by Italian style at Amboise as he was growing up, Francis developed a strong desire to accumulate Italian paintings and sculptures and venture on a war campaign there himself one day.

As the Queen's childbearing years were running out, Louise of Savoy was growing in confidence because Louis XII and his subjects started accepting Francis of Angoulême as the heir to the throne. Both Louis XII and Louise of Savoy understood that if Francis was to become King, he should take Louis XII's daughter Claude as his wife.

From the moment of her birth in 1499 until 1510, when the Queen gave birth to another daughter, Claude was the only child in the royal nursery and, as the King's eldest daughter, the pivot of his matrimonial diplomacy. Although she inherited a physical deformity from her mother—Anne was lame in one leg and used high heel shoes to disguise this infirmity—Claude was a desirable match not only because she was the King's daughter but also because she stood to inherit the duchy of Brittany from

A mother's hope

her mother. Additionally, her dowry was comprised of the French claims to Asti, Milan, Genoa and Naples. In other words, Claude of France was one of the wealthiest heiresses of her day.

The princess's mother, Anne of Brittany, planned to marry Claude to Charles of Luxembourg—the future Holy Roman Emperor Charles V—because she wanted the duchy of Brittany to preserve its independence from France. Louis XII had other plans, however. In April 1500, when Claude was but four months old, her father swore a secret oath nullifying any marriage contracted by his daughter save only to Francis of Angoulême. This happened behind Anne of Brittany's back because she strongly opposed the match.

The Queen opposed Claude's match to Francis because there was no love lost between Anne of Brittany and Francis's mother, Louise of Savoy. According to the sixteenth-century court historian Brantôme, the Queen "mortally hated Madame d'Angoulême" because their tempers were "quite unlike and not agreeing together".[21] The Queen also hated the thought that Francis was to become the next King because she believed that she was able to have more children herself.[22]

Others seemed all too ready to accept that Queen Anne would never have a son, and in 1506, the Assembly of Notables pleaded with Louis XII for a marriage between Francis and Claude. Two years later, Louise proudly recorded that marriage "de praesenti", wherein the couple verbally claimed each other in the present time, took place between Francis and Claude on 22 May 1507 in the palace of Plessis-lez-Tours. Over a year later, the fourteen-year-old Francis was invited to take up permanent residence at court as Louis XII's heir presumptive. Although happy that her son was now formally recognized as the King's heir, Louise, somewhat bitterly, recorded in her *Journal* that on 3 August 1508 "my son went away from Amboise to be a courtier and left me all alone".[23]

Although numerous pregnancies and miscarriages sapped her strength, Anne of Brittany never gave up. In 1508, after another miscarriage, the royal couple went on a pilgrimage to the church of St Maurice in Angers, a city famous for its flourishing cult of St René, patron of those seeking male offspring.[24] On 29 October 1510, the Queen gave birth to another daughter, Renée, who—although slightly disfigured—lived past infancy and was a healthy and lively child. Two years later, the birth of a stillborn son spelled the end of Anne of Brittany's childbearing years and ensured the crown's passing to Louise of Savoy's son. This last pregnancy of the Queen's was, in hindsight, so important to Louise that she recorded it—with an outburst of discernible glee—in her *Journal*:

"On 21 January, St Agnes's day, at Blois, Anne, Queen of France, had a son, but he could not impede the exaltation of my Caesar, for he lacked the breath of life. At that time I was at

Amboise in my room, and the poor gentleman, who served my son and myself with such humble and loyal perseverance, brought me the news".[25]

Despite so many pregnancies, miscarriages and stillbirths, Anne of Brittany generally enjoyed good health, but this all changed in late 1513. She suffered from attacks of what one of her contemporaries called "gravel" and died on 9 January 1514 from a kidney stone, aged thirty-seven.[26] Almost immediately after Anne's death, rumours that Louis XII, "who had no sons", would remarry started to swirl at court and abroad.[27]

To Louise and Francis, this new development potentially spelled disaster. When everyone learned that the King's new bride was only eighteen years old, a wave of disbelief swept through France, but Louis was bent on remarrying and siring male heirs with his new wife. Her name was Mary Tudor, and she was the younger sister of Henry VIII, King of England.

NOTES

[1] *Journal de Louise de Savoie*, p. 87.
[2] Frank Hamel, *The Lady of Beauty (Agnes Sorel)*, p. 287.
[3] Pierre de Bourdeille, seigneur de Brantôme, *The Book of the Ladies*, p. 218.

[4] The original title was *Les enseignements d'Anne de France a sa fille Suzanne de Bourbon* (*Anne de France's instructions for her daughter Suzanne de Bourbon*).
[5] Sharon L. Jansen, *Anne of France's Lessons for my Daughter*, p. 9.
[6] R. de Maulde La Clavière, *Louise de Savoie et François Ier: trente ans de jeunesse (1485-1515)*, p. 9.
[7] Pauline Matarasso, *Queen's Mate*, p. 39.
[8] Christine de Pizan, *The Treasure of the City of Ladies*, p. 38.
[9] *Journal de Louise de Savoie*, p. 87.
[10] Ibid.
[11] Ibid., p.88.
[12] In *Queen's Mate*, a triple biography of Anne of Beaujeu, Anne of Brittany and Louise of Savoy, Pauline Matarasso expressed her scepticism about the prophecy's existence. See Matarasso, p. 113.
[13] *Journal de Louise de Savoie*, p. 87.
[14] R.J.Knecht, *Francis I*, p. 2.
[15] Philip de Commines, *The Memoirs of Philip de Commines*, pp. 283-284.
[16] Kathleen Wellman, *Queens and Mistresses of Renaissance France*, p. 84.
[17] Philip de Commines, *The Memoirs of Philip de Commines*, Volume 2, p. 112
[18] Martha Walker Freer, *The Life of Marguerite d'Angoulême*, Volume 1, p. 13.
[19] Ibid.
[20] Colum Hourihane, *The Grove Encyclopedia of Medieval Art and Architecture*, Volume 2, p. 228.
[21] Pierre de Bourdeille, seigneur de Brantôme, *The Book of the Ladies*, p. 39.
[22] Ibid.
[23] *Journal de Louise de Savoie*, p. 87.
[24] Michael Alan Anderson, *St. Anne in Renaissance Music: Devotion and Politics*, pp. 162-165.
[25] *Journal de Louise de Savoie*, p. 87.
[26] Robert III de La Marck, seigneur de Fleuranges, *Mémoires du maréchal de Florange, dit le Jeune Adventureaux*, Volume 1, p. 147.
[27] *Calendar of State Papers Relating To English Affairs in the Archives of Venice*, Volume 2, n. 367.

CHAPTER 2
QUEENS, WIVES, WIDOWS

With the death of Anne of Brittany, the last obstacle standing in the way of Francis of Angoulême's marriage to Claude of France disappeared and, it seemed, also paved the way towards Francis's kingship. The Queen's death caused a series of gleeful entries in Louise of Savoy's *Journal*. These entries, permeated with a sense of triumph, show Louise and Francis at the highest points of their hopes for the future. The Queen's death meant that there would be no little dauphin coming into the world to interpose himself between Francis and the throne.

On 11 January 1514, two days after Anne of Brittany's passing, Louise and Francis set out from Cognac to Angoulême, into which town they made an official entry. Louise was travelling by litter, and her son walked by her side. The entry in Louise's *Journal* captures her feelings at that triumphant moment: "My son, showing the love he bore me, wished to go on foot and kept me good company".[1]

In the meantime, the royal court was plunged into mourning. Louis XII, who enjoyed a loving relationship with Anne of Brittany, ordered that the whole court should dress in black for mourning, and even the foreign ambassadors were not exempt from this command. When the King decided to allow his daughter Claude to marry Francis on 18 May 1514, the newlyweds too were ordered to appear in sombre black during the wedding ceremony. Brantôme recorded that:

"When he [Louis XII] gave his daughter to Monsieur d'Angoulême, afterwards King Francis, mourning was not left off by him or his Court; and the day of the espousals in the church of Saint-Germain-en-Laye, the bridegroom and bride were vestured and clothed in black cloth, honestly cut in mourning shape, for the death of the said Queen, Madame Anne of Brittany, mother of the bride, in presence of the King, her father, accompanied by the princes of the blood and noble seigneurs and prelates, princesses, dames and demoiselles, all clothed in black cloth made in mourning shape."[2]

Francis was confident that now, with Anne of Brittany dead and having the King's daughter as his wife, nothing could stand between himself and the crown. "Even if the King should commit the folly of marrying again", he was heard saying, "he will not live for long: any son he may have would be a child. This would necessitate regency, and in accordance with the constitution, the regent would be me".[3]

This confidence was misplaced, however. Although Louis XII was now fifty-two and ailing, he realized that he could still sire male heirs if he remarried. His new bride, the eighteen-year-old sister of King Henry VIII of England, Mary Tudor, was young enough to bear a son and thus threaten the position of Francis of Angoulême. Louise of Savoy was afraid that a son borne by the young Queen would supersede her son in the line of succession. Louise bitterly observed in her *Journal* that on 22 September 1514, Louis XII, "exceedingly old and weak", departed to Paris in order to greet his "young wife, Queen Mary".[4]

The young Mary overawed foreign dignitaries, who unanimously heaped praises upon her. One of the Venetian ambassadors wrote to Antonio Triulzi, Bishop of Asti, that Mary was "very beautiful and of sufficiently tall stature" although she appeared rather pale. This, the Venetian thought, was more because of "the tossing of the sea and from her fright", although he also opined that her eyebrows and eyes were too light. She looked very flattering in French dress, he added, and was "extremely courteous and well mannered".[5] The Venetian was not the only one who thought Mary Tudor was beautiful. "I think I never saw a more charming creature", wrote Gerard de Pleine, one of the ambassadors of Archduchess Margaret of Savoy. He also added:

"She is very graceful. Her deportment in dancing and conversation is as pleasing as you could desire. There is nothing gloomy or melancholy about her."[6]

Upon her arrival in France, one of the chroniclers reported that "the said lady is very beautiful, honest and joyous, and takes pleasure in all entertainments."[7] Aged fifty-two, Louis XII was an old man by the standards of his epoch, but it seemed that his bride was able to look past his age and infirmity. Shortly before the wedding, the Venetian ambassador remarked that Mary "does not mind that the King of France is a gouty old man . . . and she herself a young and beautiful damsel".[8]

Indeed, Mary revelled in being the centre of attention and basked in her husband's favour. Louis, clearly enamoured, could not refrain from kissing his beautiful young wife in public. Soon after her arrival, the King made preparations for the Mass in his own private suite, where Mary made a ceremonious entry in the morning. Louis doffed his bonnet while Mary sank to her knees in a deep curtsy, "whereupon His Majesty kissed her". When the treasurer of France presented Louis with a rich necklace "in which were set two beautiful jewels", the King ceremoniously "placed it round the Queen's neck".[9] Louis kissed Mary twice more during the Mass, and then they each departed separately to their own private apartments to eat and rest.

In the evening, Mary "arrayed herself in the French fashion", and the nobility of both realms reassembled to enjoy "banqueting, dancing and making good cheer" until the evening, when Louis XII's eldest daughter, Claude, now Duchess of Brittany, drew Mary Tudor away from the entertainment "to go and sleep with the King". The next morning, Louis XII emerged from his bedchamber and boasted that "thrice last night did he cross the river and would have done more had he so desired."[10] "Crossing the river" was a subtle allusion to consummating his marriage to Mary Tudor. Another contemporary observer, Robert de la Marck, seigneur de Fleuranges, reported that the King "claimed that he had done marvels" in his bedchamber.[11]

This all worried Louise of Savoy and her ambitious son. In her *Journal*, Louise recorded that the "amorous wedding" took place at ten in the morning, and in the evening the royal couple "went to bed together".[12] Louise of Savoy was not the only one who found it hard to accept the new situation. The King's daughter Claude was also disappointed with her father's decision to remarry. Louis XII had endangered his daughter's elevation to queenship, but what hurt Claude the most was the fact that he betrayed her mother's memory. According to Robert de la Marck, Claude "was greatly distressed, for her mother had been dead only a short while, and now she was obliged to serve her [Mary Tudor] as she had formerly served the Queen her mother".[13] Claude had shared an exceptionally close relationship with her late mother. Although, as a royal princess, she was looked after by an array of governesses from her early childhood, Anne of Brittany had taken a keen interest in her daughter's upbringing and exchanged letters with her on a regular basis. Her mother's death was a huge blow for Claude, who was now left with few friends.

Anne of Brittany had entrusted both of her daughters to the care of the woman she never loved, Louise of Savoy, knowing that as her eldest child's prospective mother-in-law, Louise was the best choice as a guardian and mentor. A somewhat exculpatory entry in Louise's *Journal* reveals how she felt about this task. She fulfilled it honourably, she claimed. "Everyone knows it", Louise insisted, "truth recognizes it; experience proves it; moreover, common report proclaims it".[14]

Although Louis XII boasted of his success in the marital bed, the King's health started to deteriorate soon after his wedding. He changed his unruffled lifestyle for Mary, who enjoyed pastimes such as dancing and hunting. Contemporary observers condemned her youth and blamed her for exerting ruinous influence on her husband's health. Mary Tudor's beauty and stamina fascinated her aging husband, who was very eager to please her and keep up with her. Robert de la Marck wrote about a malicious pamphlet circulating in France at the time, according to which the King of England had sent the King of France a young filly to gallop him off to hell or to heaven.[15]

Mary was well aware of her husband's ill health. On 13 October, the English ambassadors in France wrote to Henry VIII that Louis XII suffered from the renewed attack of gout and was confined to his bed. Mary, they assured, "was continually with him, of whom he made as much as she reported to us herself, as it is possible for any man to make of a lady".[16] Indeed, Louis was very generous towards Mary. Although he upset her by dismissing her attendants, including her longtime servant and confidante "Mother Guildford", he found means of consoling her. The English ambassadors reported that each day Louis gave Mary expensive jewels, including "a ruby two inches and a half long, and as big as a man's finger, hanging by two chains of gold at every end" and "a great diamond tablet with a great round pearl hanging by it". But this was not everything. Every day, they wrote, Louis presented Mary with "rings with stones of great estimation".[17] Although hurt by the fact that her favoured attendants were dismissed, Mary reciprocated with displays of wifely obedience and affection.

When Charles Brandon, Duke of Suffolk, was invited to an audience with the royal couple, he saw the bedridden Louis XII "and the Queen sitting by his bedside".[18] When the King's health improved, he was able to confirm that his new wife was to be crowned and anointed without any further delay. On 3 November 1514, Louise of Savoy recorded in her *Journal* that she arrived to the Basilica of St Denis to greet the young Queen, who was crowned two days later. Francis was prominent during the ceremony, leading Mary to the choir on the right side of the high altar where she was to be anointed. According to the English ambassadors:

"And first the Queen's Grace knelt before the altar in a place prepared therefore, and there the said Cardinal of Pree anointed her, and after delivered her the sceptre in her right hand, and the verge of the hand of Justice in her left hand; and after that he put a ring upon her finger, and fourthly he set the crown on her head, which done, the said Duke of Brittany [Francis] led her up a stage made on the left side of the altar, directly before us, where she was set in a chair under a throne, and the said Duke stood behind her holding the crown from her head to ease her of the weight thereof; and then began the high Mass sung by the said Cardinal, whereat the Queen offered, and after Agnus Dei she received the sacrament and, Mass done, she departed to Palace, and we to our lodgings to our dinners".[19]

Francis kept displaying kindness towards the new Queen because he had certain reasons to remain hopeful about his future. "I am sure", he confided in his friend, "unless I have been well and truly deceived, that the King and Queen cannot possibly have any children—something which would be greatly to my disadvantage if they did".[20] Despite this, Francis instructed his wife and the Queen's lady-in-waiting, Madame d'Aumont, to sleep inside Mary Tudor's chamber and keep him informed about the goings-on in the royal bedchamber.

NOTES

[1] *Journal de Louise de Savoie*, p. 87.
[2] Pierre de Bourdeille, seigneur de Brantôme, *The Book of the Ladies*, p. 38.
[3] R.J.Knecht, *Francis I*, p. 10.
[4] *Journal de Louise de Savoie*, p. 89.
[5] *Calendar of State Papers Relating To English Affairs in the Archives of Venice*, Volume 2, 1509-1519, n. 508.
[6] Ibid., Preface to Volume 1.
[7] Hippolyte Cocheris, *Entrées de Marie D'Angleterre*, p. 7.
[8] *Letters and Papers, Foreign and Domestic, Henry VIII*, Volume 1, 1509-1514, n. 3151.
[9] *Calendar of State Papers and Manuscripts, Relating to English Affairs, Existing in the Archives and Collections of Venice and in the Other Libraries of Northern Italy*, Volume 2, n. 508.
[10] Ibid.
[11] Erin A. Sadlack, *The French Queen's Letters*, p. 70.
[12] *Journal de Louise de Savoie*, p. 89.
[13] Robert III de La Marck, seigneur de Fleuranges, *Mémoires du maréchal de Florange, dit le Jeune Adventureaux*, Volume 1, p. 158.
[14] *Journal de Louise de Savoie*, p. 89.
[15] Erin A. Sadlack, *The French Queen's Letters*, p. 74.
[16] Henry Ellis, *Original Letters Illustrative of English History,* 2nd series, Volume 1, pp. 240-241.
[17] Ibid.
[18] Ibid.
[19] Henry Ellis, *Original Letters Illustrative of English History,* 2nd series, Volume 1, p. 250-258.

[20] Robert III de La Marck, seigneur de Fleuranges, *Mémoires du maréchal de Florange, dit le Jeune Adventureaux*, Volume 2, p. 160.

CHAPTER 3
THE WHITE QUEEN'S MOURNING

According to Robert de la Marck, seigneur de Fleuranges, during the winter of 1514, Louis XII "took lodgings at Tournelles in Paris because it had the best climate, and also he did not feel very strong, because he had desired to be a pleasing companion with his wife; but he deceived himself, as he was not the man for it... inasmuch as he had for a long time been very sick, particularly with gout, and for five or six years he had thought that he would die of it... because he was given up by the doctors, and he lived on a very strict diet which he broke when he was with his wife; and the doctors told him that if he continued, he would die from his pleasure".[1]

Indeed, Louis "died of his pleasure" on 1 January 1515. According to the English chronicler Raphael Holinshed, the King "so fervently loved Mary that he gave himself over to behold too much her excellent beauty bearing then eighteen years of age, nothing considering the proportion of his own years, nor his decayed complexion; so that he fell into the rage of fever, which drawing to it a sudden flux, overcame in one instant his life".[2] After eighty-two days of being Queen of France, Mary Tudor was now a widow. Louis XII's death meant that Louise of Savoy's golden boy, Francis, was now King, but there was one last issue to resolve before he could put a crown on his head. The etiquette required that a dowager Queen retired from public view for one month after her royal husband's death. The most important reason behind this custom was determining whether the Queen was pregnant. Should she prove to be with child, there would be no king until the birth.

Mary Tudor now became "la Reine Blanche" or "the White Queen", wearing white mourning gowns and retiring to a darkened chamber lit only by candlelight in the Hôtel de Cluny. At the Hôtel de Cluny, the young widow was allowed to receive guests. Francis of Angoulême "visited her often" and acted with "all possible kindness" towards her.[3] The Venetian ambassador reported that Francis "went every day to visit the Queen Dowager, who was sorrowful, lamenting much the death of her husband".[4] Three weeks into her confinement, Francis broached the delicate matter of the Queen's pregnancy and asked Mary directly "if he could consider himself King because he knew not whether she was pregnant or not." Mary answered that "he might and that she knew of no other King than he, for she had no idea of having any offspring that could prevent".[5] Francis was thus proclaimed King.

Several decades later, Pierre de Bourdeille, seigneur de Brantôme, who wrote extensively about French royal women in the sixteenth century, asserted that Mary Tudor aimed at becoming Queen Mother and pretended to have been with child, using "linen wrappages" to pad her body.[6] This deception failed when Francis of Angoulême's mother, Louise of Savoy, had Mary "so well watched and examined by physicians and midwives that her wrappages and clouts being noted, she was found out and baulked in her design, and instead of being Queen Mother was incontinently sent back to her own country".[7] Brantôme also claimed that Mary and Francis fell in love while Louis XII was still alive and that the couple was close to consummating their relationship, but Francis was stopped by Monsieur de Grignaux, a respected member of the court, who pointed out that Mary, "keen and cunning as she is", wanted only to use Francis in order to beget a son.[8]

What are we to make of this? Brantôme was not a contemporary, but his grandmother was attached to the courts of Anne of Beaujeu and Margaret of Angoulême, Francis's sister. According to Kathleen Wellman, Brantôme's link to the royal family—his aunt was Louis XII's goddaughter—gave him "access to documents that no longer exist", although his reports "are important but not completely credible".[9] In Mary Tudor's case, however, Brantôme reported that the story of her alleged deception was repeated as court gossip.[10] Mary herself had no reason to pretend that she was with child because she was eager to return to England and marry Charles Brandon, the man she loved before she became Louis XII's spouse. Furthermore, there were rumours that she might have still been a virgin.[11]

NOTES

[1] Walter C. Richardson, *Mary Tudor*, p. 125.
[2] Raphael Holinshed, *Holinshed's Chronicles of England, Scotland and Ireland*, Volume 3, p. 610.
[3] Erin A. Sadlack, *The French Queen's Letters*, p. 93.
[4] *Calendar of State Papers, Venice,* Volume 2, 1509-1519, n. 573, 574.
[5] Mary Anne Everett Green, *Lives of the Princesses of England: From the Norman Conquest,* Volume 5, p. 78.
[6] Brantôme, *Lives of Fair and Gallant Ladies*, Volume 2, p. 253.
[7] Ibid., p. 254.
[8] Ibid., p. 252.
[9] Kathleen Wellman, *Queens and Mistresses of Renaissance France*, p. 376, n. 39.
[10] One of the contemporary memoirists asserted that Francis's wife, Claude, and the newly appointed lady of honour, Madame d'Aumont, were to sleep inside Mary Tudor's chamber and keep an eye on her, but this was while Louis XII was still alive and clearly not connected to Brantôme's story of Mary's allegedly pretended pregnancy. Robert III de La Marck, seigneur de Fleuranges, *Mémoires du maréchal de Florange, dit le Jeune Adventureaux*, Volume 2, p. 160.
[11] *Letters and Papers, Foreign and Domestic, Henry VIII,* Volume 2, 1515-1518, n. 26.

CHAPTER 4
SCANDALOUS MARRIAGE

As a royal widow, Mary Tudor was once again swiftly pushed into the marriage market. At nineteen, she was young and "the most attractive and beautiful woman ever seen".[1] Anyone who controlled her—in this case it was Francis I, the new King of France—could use her for his political advantage. Thomas Wolsey, the Archbishop of York and Henry VIII's closest adviser, was very well aware of this fact when he wrote to the Dowager Queen Mary that "if any motion of marriage or other thing fortune to be made unto you, in no wise give hearing to the same". Mary's reply was courteous but assertive. She thanked the well-willing Wolsey for his "good lessons" but objected to his lack of confidence in her own judgment: "My Lord, I trust the King, my brother, and you will not reckon in me such childhood".

She was not naïve, and she had already decided that she would not become any man's pawn this time around. In fact, she was well aware that Henry VIII and Wolsey, although two friendly souls, underestimated her potential. She informed them both that she would marry "where my mind is". Henry VIII knew very well what it entailed, and Mary did not hesitate to remind her brother about a promise he made her before she left for France three months earlier. Always the realist, Mary was aware that sooner or later the sickly French King would die and she would become a widow. She already had plans for her prospective widowhood and, to make sure that her plans would come true, she extracted a promise from her brother:

"Sir, I beseech Your Grace that you will keep all the promises that you promised me when I took my leave of you by the waterside. Sir, Your Grace knoweth well that I did marry for your pleasure at this time, and now I trust you will suffer me to marry as me liketh for to do . . . wherefore I beseech Your Grace to be a good Lord and brother unto me".[2]

In the same letter, Mary threatened that if she would be pressured to marry for political reasons again, she would rather join a nunnery than relent. The young Queen Dowager surely did not entertain any such thought; she was way too pretty and lively to waste away in a convent, and she knew it. She only hoped that her brother would prove to be the chivalrous King he always styled himself to be and honour his promises. A convent, she knew, was not an option because "I think Your Grace would be very sorry . . . and all your realm", but it was a nice way of showing her elder brother how determined she was to get what she wanted, and she wanted Charles Brandon.

Henry knew that his younger sister was in love with Charles Brandon, his boon companion, friend and the man he created the Duke of Suffolk only recently and against murmurs at court. Charles Brandon's family was staunchly devoted to the Tudors; his own father, William, was killed while holding Henry VII's banner at the battle of Bosworth in 1485. Raised at court, Charles Brandon became Henry VIII's constant companion, confidante and close friend. They enjoyed the same pastimes and excelled in them, and both loved women and surrounded themselves with the same friends. Brandon was not only "a very handsome man" but also "one of the chief noblemen of England".[3] Even foreign dignitaries were aware that Brandon was like "a second King", and his graces were well worth cultivating because "it is he who does and undoes".[4] Wherever Henry went, Brandon was right by his side. No wonder, then, that the King's younger sister fell in love with this energetic man some twelve years her senior, who was always present in her life, and now wanted to become his wife.

Whereas Mary was free to remarry, Charles Brandon's marital history was littered with discarded brides and children of dubious legitimacy. He first pre-contracted himself to Anne Browne, with whom he had a daughter also named Anne. If consummated, pre-contract was as binding as marriage but should have been followed by a formal church ceremony. Brandon, however, discarded Anne Browne and went on to marry her aunt, Margaret Neville, a wealthy widow in her early forties. This, no doubt, was a marriage of convenience for

Brandon, who was some twenty years younger than his new bride. "In this country, young men marry old ladies", wrote the Venetian ambassador, Sebastiano Giustiniani, pointing out that "here, for instance, is the Duke of Suffolk, who at nineteen married a lady for her wealth . . . old enough to be his mother".[5]

What happened next is not entirely clear. The only sure thing is that Brandon decided to discard Margaret Neville. One source says that he had obtained a divorce from her citing his consummated pre-contract with Anne Browne, whereas another claims that there was no pre-contract with Anne Browne when he married Lady Neville, and thus no legal ground for the divorce existed.[6] In any case, Brandon promptly returned to Anne Browne and had one more daughter by her before she died in 1510.

Motivated by financial profit yet again, Brandon soon became engaged to a child bride, Elizabeth Grey, Viscountess Lisle, but there never was a marriage contracted between the two due to Elizabeth's tender age.

In the autumn of 1513, Brandon made flirtatious overtures to the Archduchess Margaret of Savoy, daughter of Emperor Maximilian. During the meeting in Tournai, Brandon snatched a ring from the archduchess's finger, as was the romantic custom in England, but the archduchess playfully scorned him by calling him a "thief", and thus let him know that

Scandalous marriage

she would never agree to marry him.[7] It was already well known that Brandon's marital situation was somewhat murky. Mary Tudor either chose to ignore Charles Brandon's past commitments or was unaware of their extent. During one of Francis I's visits to the Hôtel de Cluny, where she still resided as the mournful Queen Dowager, Mary told him that she was in love with Charles Brandon and desired to marry him. Francis promised to be the gallant of romantic tradition and play the couple's advocate.

When Brandon had his first audience with Francis on 3 February 1515, after arriving at the head of the English embassy to France, Francis greeted him with these words: "My Lord of Suffolk, so it is that there is a bruit in this my realm, that you are come to marry with the Queen, your Master's sister". At first, Brandon tried to deny this, writing to Wolsey:

"I answered and said that I trusted His Grace would not reckon so great a folly in me, to come into a strange realm and to marry a Queen of the realm, without his knowledge, and without authority from the King my master to him, and that they both might be content."[8]

Francis stopped teasing Brandon when he told him that Mary had revealed "her heart's desire" to him and used a certain password that only Mary could have known. Francis assured the surprised Brandon that "I shall never fail unto you, but to help and advance this matter betwixt her and you, with as good will as I would for mine own self".[9] Brandon was clearly overwhelmed by the speed of events and begged Wolsey to send him his precious advice. Wolsey wrote back immediately, declaring that he showed the contents of his letter to Henry VIII, who appeared to have been perfectly happy with the way Charles Brandon handled the conversation with Francis I.

On 4 February 1515, Charles headed to meet the Queen Dowager Mary at the Hôtel de Cluny. She was distraught and, crying incessantly, she told Charles that if he would not marry her within four days, she would never be his. The reason why she was so distraught was that two English friars visited her and told her that if she returned to England unwed, the King's council would never allow her to marry Charles Brandon. Fearing that the friars were sent by someone of Henry VIII's Privy Council to warn her, she decided to constrain Brandon "to break such promises as he made Your Grace". She had also heard from various French nobles that her brother planned to marry her off to Charles of Castile, and she would "rather be torn to pieces" than go to Flanders.[10] She threatened Brandon that if he refused to marry her immediately, he would lose her forever because she would not return to England with him.

Brandon was in a quandary because he promised Henry that he would not woo Mary while in France.[11] "I never saw a woman so weep", he wrote to his King, confessing that he and Mary married in secret because this was the only way to calm her fears. On 5 March 1515, Brandon wrote to Wolsey:

"My Lord, so it is that when I came to Paris, I heard many things which put me in great fear, and so did the Queen both; and the Queen would never let me be in rest till I had granted her to be married. And so to be plain with you, I have married her heartily and have lain with her, insomuch that I fear me lest she be with child".[12]

It now dawned on the couple that Mary might be pregnant and they should have a second, public wedding before their journey to England. "My Lord", Brandon implored Wolsey, "at the reverence of God help that I may be married as I go out of France, openly, for many things of which I will advertise [inform] you by mine next letters. Give me your advice whether the French King and his mother shall write again to the King for this open marriage; seeing that this privy marriage is done, and that I think none otherwise but that she is with child".[13] Whether Mary was mistaken about her condition, suffered a miscarriage or purposely misled Charles will never be known for sure. The couple's first child, Frances, was not born until 1517.

According to Robert de la Marck, Francis I was not happy about this secret marriage and burst into rage when he learned about it. "I did not think you had been so base", he confronted Brandon, "and if I chose to do my duty, I should, this very hour, have your head taken off your shoulders".[14] The reason behind Francis I's rage is obvious. When he agreed to intercede with Henry VIII on their behalf, the French King thought about the future and did not expect that Mary and Charles would be so bold as to break the etiquette that required a royal widow to wait at least a year before she contracted a new marriage. The unseemly haste felt like an assault on the memory of Louis XII.

Mary, on the other hand, had a different story to tell. She informed Francis about her love for Charles Brandon not because she needed his assistance but because she was "in extreme pain and annoyance" caused by "such suit as the French King made unto me, not according with mine own honour". So she told him everything because she feared that if she would keep this from his knowledge, he would not treat Brandon well and renew his "former malfantasy and suits".[15] Whether Francis truly molested Mary with importunate insinuations will never be known for a fact, but several decades later, courtly gossip had it that Francis had been in love with Mary and eager to consummate his match with her.[16] Some clue to Francis I's feelings about Mary is found in a little acidic comment he inscribed on a sketch of the Queen Dowager in the *Album d'Aix*: "More dirty than queenly".[17] Despite this, Francis agreed to a public wedding ceremony and appeared as a guest of honour. His mother, with thinly veiled scorn, recorded in her *Journal* that on "Saturday the last day of March, the Duke of Suffolk, a person of low estate whom Henry VIII had sent as ambassador to the King, married Mary of England".[18]

Louise of Savoy was not alone in pouring scorn upon Charles Brandon. He had been long disparaged in England as an upstart and "not of a very noble lineage". When he was elevated to a dukedom in early 1514, everyone sneered at how "the King has recently turned that new duke from a stable boy into a nobleman", referring to Brandon's earlier post as Henry VIII's Master of the Horse.[19] Now this freshly created Duke of Suffolk presumed to marry the King's own sister without his royal master's consent.

Henry VIII was displeased not only because Brandon went behind his back and married his sister but also because he broke his promise to him. Mary seemed to be firm in her purpose, boldly informing Henry that she would rather beg for his mercy than beg his council to allow her to marry the man she loved. Her political instinct proved to be correct because the moment her marriage became public knowledge, all of the leading councillors in England, except Wolsey, demanded to either put Charles Brandon to death or imprison him. Mary was eager to defend her new husband's honour and informed her brother that she was solely responsible for this hasty match: "I have affixed and clearly determined myself to marry with him; and the same I assure you hath proceeded only of mine own mind, without any request or labour of my said Lord of Suffolk, or any other person".[20]

Both Mary and Charles knew that there was only one way to appease Henry VIII. The King loved money and jewels, and Mary immediately sent him the most expensive piece of jewellery she received from Louis XII, "the Mirror of Naples". It was a diamond with a great pearl, and it was later said that Francis I "was sore displeased at the loss of the diamond called 'the Mirror of Naples'".[21] Unabashed, Mary promised her brother she would ship more luxurious jewels and plate to England, but the French King strongly disagreed and contested her right to the gold and jewels Louis XII had given her, claiming they were a gift to the Queen of France and therefore should remain within his realm. The English countered that the late King had given them to Mary, who had a right to keep them. Trying to outwit the English, Francis replied that if this was indeed so, Mary should also be responsible for part of the debts Louis incurred while they were married. In the end, the two sides were able to reach a compromise; Mary was allowed to keep half the jewels and gold, provided that she acknowledged them as a gift from Francis, not as property she was entitled to own. Still, when Mary left France on 16 April 1515, Francis, who held a grudge, gave her only four paltry rings as a parting gift.[22]

Scandalous marriage

On 2 May 1515, the Queen Dowager set her foot in England. Nine days later, Mary and Charles agreed in writing to return Mary's dowry to Henry VIII, to give him all of her remaining plate and jewellery and to pay him £24,000 to cover the expenses of her first marriage. They were officially married at Greenwich Palace on 13 May 1515. Chronicler Edward Hall recorded that:

"Against this marriage many men grudged, and said that it was a great loss to the realm that she was not married to the Prince of Castile: but the wisest sort was content, considering that if she had been married again out of the realm, she should have carried much riches with her; and now she brought every year into the realm 9,000 or 10,000 marks."[23]

Mary may well have been content because, as a widow, she attained the status of feme sole, an independent woman who did not have to ask her brother to remarry. Charles Brandon was the one who risked the most as Henry VIII's subject. Before they crossed the Channel, Brandon was in danger of his life while staying in Calais. "The Duke of Suffolk did not dare to leave the King of England's house", wrote one of the paid spymasters, "as he would have been killed by the people for marrying Queen Mary".[24] Mary Tudor, on the other hand, arrived home victorious. Although she departed from France leaving a bitter aftertaste of scandal behind her, she had it all: she had become Queen, tasted the mystique of monarchy and married for the second time for love rather than for political gain. She was Queen of France for a mere eighty-two days, but she decided that she would be known in England as "the French Queen" rather than "Duchess of Suffolk". She had committed a mésalliance, true, but she was too vain to accept a lower title. She would forever remain the Queen Dowager of France and pride herself in this title.

NOTES

[1] *Calendar of State Papers Relating To English Affairs in the Archives of Venice*, Volume 2, 1509-1519, n. 600.
[2] Mary Anne Everett Wood, *Letters of Royal and Illustrious Ladies of Great Britain*, Volume 1, p. 188.
[3] *Calendar of State Papers Relating To English Affairs in the Archives of Venice*, Volume 2, 1509-1519, n. 464.
[4] *Letters and Papers, Foreign and Domestic, Henry VIII*, Volume 1, 1509-1514, n. 2171.
[5] Walter C. Richardson, *Mary Tudor*, p. 164.
[6] Mortimer Levine, *A "Letter" on the Elizabethan Succession Question, 1566*, p. 23.
[7] Eric Ives, *The Life and Death of Anne Boleyn*, p. 26.
[8] Mary Anne Everett Wood, *Letters of Royal and Illustrious Ladies of Great Britain*, Volume 1, p. 195.
[9] Ibid., p. 196.
[10] Ibid., pp. 200-201.
[11] When Brandon could not console her, the duke agreed to marry her in France if Mary could get Henry's permission "or else I durst not because I had made unto Your Grace such a promise". *Letters and Papers, Foreign and Domestic, Henry VIII*, Volume 2, 1515-1518, n. 80.
[12] *Letters and Papers, Foreign and Domestic, Henry VIII*, Volume 2, 1515-1518, n. 224.
[13] Walter C. Richardson, *Mary Tudor*, p. 173.

[14] Mary Anne Everett Green, *Lives of the Princesses of England: From the Norman Conquest*, Volume 5, p. 90.
[15] Ibid., p. 86.
[16] As discussed in Chapter 3.
[17] "Pleus sale que royne". This phrase is usually translated into English as "More dirty than queenly". In 1863, the French scholar Étienne Antoine Benoit Rouard pointed out that it is difficult to unequivocally interpret this phrase and offered another version rendered into modern French as: "Plus folle que royne", because an 's' resembles an 'f' in Francis I's handwriting. It could be thus translated into English as "More foolish than queenly" or, alternatively, "More fool than a Queen". Rouard, *François Ier chez Mme De Boisy*, p. 34.
[18] *Journal de Louise de Savoie*, p. 89.
[19] Alison Weir, *Henry VIII: King and Court*, p. 168.
[20] Mary Anne Everett Wood, *Letters of Royal and Illustrious Ladies of Great Britain*, Volume 1, p. 205.
[21] *Letters and Papers, Foreign and Domestic, Henry VIII*, Volume 2, 1515-1518, n. 343.
[22] Ibid.
[23] Edward Hall, *Hall's Chronicle*, p. 582.
[24] *Letters and Papers, Foreign and Domestic, Henry VIII*, Volume 2, 1515-1518, n. 399.

CHAPTER 5
"PLAIN AND BADLY LAME"

When Francis I assumed the throne in January 1515, he was twenty-one years old. The English chronicler Raphael Holinshed captured the feeling of high expectations surrounding Francis's accession:

"The world had such a hope in his virtues, and such an opinion of his magnanimity and such a concept of his judgement and wit, that everyone confessed that of very long time there was none raised up to the crown with a greater expectation. He was made the more agreeable to the fancies of men by the consideration of his age, bearing then but two and twenty years; his excellent features and proportion of body, by his great liberality, and general humanity, together with the ripe knowledge he had in many things. But especially he pleased greatly the nobility, to whom he transferred many singular and great favours."[1]

Six months earlier, Francis had married Louis XII's elder daughter, the fifteen-year-old Madame Claude, Duchess of Brittany, who was already believed to have been pregnant.[2] As Holinshed explained, Francis "was preferred to the succession of the kingdom before the daughters [Claude and Renée] of the dead King by virtue and disposition of the Salic law, a law very ancient in the realm of France, which excluded from the royal dignity all women".[3]

Claude's thoughts touching the preferment of her husband's claim over hers are not recorded, but we may assume that she was content with the role of a royal consort because she had been groomed to become one from her early childhood. At the same time, she was well aware of her importance and the political implications of her marriage to Francis. Despite being Queen of France, Claude was simultaneously Duchess of Brittany in her own right and sought to assume her own independent political role as such.[4] Yet Claude also knew that despite her importance as Louis XII's daughter, she must prove her worth by giving birth to a male heir, a duty her mother never fulfilled.

The importance of becoming the mother of a son was emphasized in the epitaph composed to honour Anne of Brittany after her death: "I married King Louis XII, wearing the crown of the French, with whom I had only two daughters".[5] Claude knew that being wife of the King meant nothing as long as she was not a mother of his sons; her own father repudiated his first barren and deformed wife to marry Claude's mother, and the pope made no qualms about helping him do it. Luckily for Claude, she was pregnant when Francis became King.

When the English ambassadors, with Charles Brandon as the leading envoy, arrived to France in early February 1515, they visited the new Queen and tried to learn whether she was with child. "There is no truth in the rumour that the French Queen, that now is, is with child", they reported to Henry VIII, adding that her physicians did not believe she was pregnant, "and also, at our being there, we saw no great appearance thereof". Cunningly, the ambassadors offered her congratulations in Henry VIII's name, saying that "we showed her that Your Grace was right glad and joyous that she was with child", but Claude replied that "it was not so as yet".[6] Claude was either not sure of her condition or she deliberately misled the English ambassadors because she was indeed pregnant at the time, and her first child was born six months later.

Other ambassadors seemed to have had the correct information. One of the early descriptions of Claude was recorded by Mercurino di Gattinara, the Italian statesman who had an audience with her on 15 February 1515. Gattinara reported that Claude's face resembled that of her late mother, Anne of Brittany. She was also "very small and strangely corpulent" and, he added poignantly, "already very big".[7] Gattinara expressed his concern about Claude's delivery, pointing out that she would have problems to bring forth the child if it would be as strong as its father, Francis I.[8] Like her mother, Claude suffered from certain malformations that gave rise to fears about her childbearing capabilities. She was "small in stature, plain and badly lame in both hips", but was said to be "very cultivated, generous and pious".[9]

Claude's name was linked to that of Francis I from her early childhood, and although she was the best match for the future King, some people opposed it on the basis of Claude's frail physique. Pierre de Rohan, Marshal of Gié, told Louise of Savoy that he would rather see her son "married to a simple shepherdess of this kingdom than to Madame Claude because the misfortune is such that Madame Claude is deformed in body and unable to bear children".[10] When she became pregnant, most people assumed that she would die while giving birth. According to one English observer, rumour had it that even the pope alleged that "the French asserted the present Queen would die in childbed".[11] Claude eventually proved her critics wrong, giving birth to seven children during the period from 1515 to 1524. Historian Simone Bertière calculated that Claude was pregnant 63 of the 122 months of her reign.[12] These frequent pregnancies took their toll on the Queen's fragile health, and she could not attend her husband's court and play a ceremonial role as often as etiquette required.

At the same time, Claude was neither neglected by her husband nor living in some kind of self-imposed seclusion spent on rounds of religious observances, as implied by some historians.[13] Quite the contrary. The Italian visitor Antonio de Beatis was impressed with Francis's demonstrations of love and respect towards Claude. He was said to hold his wife "in such honour and respect that when in France and with her he has never failed to sleep with her each night".[14] At the same time, however, Francis did keep an official mistress, Françoise de Foix, countess of Châteaubriant, who served as the chief Lady of Honour—the highest and most lucrative post—in the Queen's household.[15]

Francis and Claude were a mismatched couple. The King was tall, athletic and full of energy. Antonio de Beatis wrote:

"The King is very tall, well featured and has a pleasant disposition, cheerful and most engaging, though he has a large nose, and in the opinion of many, including Monsignor, his legs are too thin for so big a body."[16]

Francis's big nose and thin legs were notorious throughout Europe. Edward Hall, the English chronicler, described him as "a goodly prince, stately of countenance, merry of cheer, brown coloured, great eyes, high nosed, big lipped, fair breasted and shoulders, small legs and long feet".[17] When Francis ascended the throne in 1515, he was young and thirsting for glory, just as Henry VIII was when he became King six years earlier. The fact that the two monarchs were young—Henry was three years Francis's senior—fuelled their rivalry. The two Kings displayed keen interest in one another's appearance and political undertakings and were often compared against each other by foreign ambassadors. The amicable relations between Henry and Francis were established when Henry's sister, Mary Tudor, arrived in France in October 1514. Francis, as Louis XII's heir, took an active part in celebrations and fetes honouring Mary, and the two men indulged in exchanging letters and compliments through the ambassadors of their countries. Francis, then Duke of Brittany, professed admiration for Henry VIII's "active courage in feats of arms". "My Lord, I assure you", wrote the English ambassador, "this Prince can speak well and wisely".[18]

Henry had six years of experience in ruling when Francis became King on 1 January 1515, and so he decided to take a patronising approach towards the fellow monarch. On 2 February 1515, Francis admitted a group of three English ambassadors to his presence. One of them, Nicholas West, made a Latin oration in which he congratulated Francis on his accession and then lectured him on the virtues which a King should possess and made efforts to persuade him to stick to these values.[19]

Henry VIII was very curious about Francis and decided to quiz the Venetian ambassador, Pietro Pasqualigo, who had recently come from France to England, about Francis's appearance. Addressing the ambassador in impeccable French, Henry invited him to a friendly conversation. "The King of France, is he as tall as I am?" Henry asked. There was "but little difference", Pasqualigo replied. "Is he as stout?" "He was not", was the answer. "What sort of legs has he?" This was the most important question of all because Henry was very fond of his muscular calves. When Pasqualigo replied that Francis's legs were "spare", Henry "opened the front of his doublet, and placing his hand on his thigh said: 'Look here and I have also a good calf to my leg'".[20] Henry was in the prime of his youth and made a strong impression on Pasqualigo, who reported that:

"The King is the handsomest potentate I ever set eyes on; above the usual height, with an extremely fine calf to his leg, his complexion very fair and bright, with auburn hair combed straight and short, in the French fashion, and a round face so very beautiful that it would become a pretty woman, his throat being rather long and thick. He was born 28th of June 1491, so he will enter his twenty-fifth year the month after next. He speaks French, English and Latin, and a little Italian; plays well on the lute and harpsichord, sings from book at sight, draws the bow with greater strength than any man in England and jousts marvellously."[21]

Henry's wife, on the other hand, was harshly described by the Venetian ambassadors as plain and unattractive. Katharine of Aragon was six years older than Henry VIII, and after six years of marriage, she still struggled to give Henry a son. Their "New Year's boy", Prince Henry, born on 1 January 1511, died after fifty-two days and left his parents grief-stricken. In the autumn of 1514, rumour had it that Henry contemplated repudiating Katharine "because he is unable to have children by her".[22] The rumour proved to have been unfounded, but Henry's doubts as to his marriage would resurface in the years to come.

Although she was always "richly attired" in the latest fashions of Spain, Burgundy and France, at thirty Katharine of Aragon was described as "rather ugly than otherwise" and presumably with child.[23] At this stage in their relationship, Henry VIII was still in love with Katharine, although he often strayed from the marital bed. His love affairs, however, were not as notorious as those of Francis I's, who kept Françoise de Foix as his maîtresse-en-titre, the officially designated royal mistress. Henry VIII conducted his liaisons in private out of respect for Katharine of Aragon, who was extremely jealous at first but learned how to shut her eyes and endure her husband's infidelities with silent dignity.

As to Queen Claude's reaction to Francis I's infidelities, little is known about her feelings. It was no great secret that

Francis's marriage to Claude was a purely political match, at least in the beginning, and the young man was in no hurry to share bed with his wife, deserting her soon after the wedding to join his mistress in Paris, where he spent two months. It was Admiral Bonnivet who took it upon himself to go after Francis and convince him to return to Claude and father a child on her.[24] Francis was fond of women, so much so that he compared a court without ladies to a "garden without beautiful flowers" and quadrupled the number of ladies-in-waiting in the Queen's service.[25] His view was similar to the one generally held in sixteenth-century Europe. In Baldassare Castiglione's *The Book of the Courtier*, a manual of courtly life, we read that:

"No court, however great it may be, can have in it adornment of splendour or gaiety, without ladies, nor can any Courtier be graceful or pleasing or brave, or perform any gallant feat of chivalry, unless moved by the society and by the love and pleasure of ladies: so, too, discussion about the Courtier is always very imperfect, unless by taking part therein the ladies add their touch of that grace wherewith they perfect Courtiership and adorn it."[26]

Francis made sure that his court was adorned with the most beautiful and best-dressed women in the kingdom. The King's wish to be surrounded by beautiful and expensively dressed ladies was a constant drainage on his finances—by the

"Plain and badly lame"

end of his reign, he was spending three times more on salaries for his female courtiers' than on building, according to the Venetian ambassador—but he was prepared to go to great lengths to achieve his purposes. In 1515, he wrote a letter to Isabella d'Este, Marchesa of Mantua—one of the leading political and cultural figures of the Italian Renaissance—to ask her to send him a fashion doll dressed in the most recent Italian garments so that the ladies of his court could copy her style.[27] He was also regularly paying for his female courtiers' wardrobes, displaying an extraordinary and unprecedented interest in their appearance.[28]

The French King was known as a notorious lover of female charms from the early years of his reign. Antonio de Beatis wrote that he was "a great womanizer", and many other dignitaries commented upon his "whoring", while Henry VIII heard that Francis was "not much attached to his Queen".[29] There is plenty of evidence that Queen Claude—although "of small stature and not beautiful"—took especial care of her appearance and wardrobe in order to keep up with her husband's exuberant court.[30] She dressed fashionably, often dazzling the foreign ambassadors with the quantity and size of jewels she wore as well as with the quality of materials she chose for her gowns.[31] She also displayed an interest in cosmetics, receiving three jars of scented hand cream from the fashionable Isabella d'Este.[32]

Just like her husband was aware that beautiful, erudite and well-dressed women reflected well on the entire court and helped to make an impression on foreign envoys, Claude was also eager to surround herself with her ladies-in-waiting. In doing so, she followed into her mother's footsteps. Anne of Brittany was, according to the testimony of Brantôme, "the first Queen to hold a great Court of ladies".[33] "Her suite was very large of ladies and young girls, for she refused none", he relates, "she even inquired of the noblemen of her Court whether they had daughters, and what they were, and asked to have them brought to her". Just like Anne of Beaujeu's court, Anne of Brittany's establishment "was a noble school for ladies; she had them taught and brought up wisely; and all, taking pattern by her, made themselves wise and virtuous".[34] In 1498, a total number of 253 servants peopled Anne of Brittany's household; by 1523, Claude had 285 servants, which means that she not only maintained but even surpassed the high standards set by her beloved mother.[35]

Although one author suggested that Claude's court was "run almost as a convent", there is no evidence to that effect.[36] Quite the contrary; Claude enjoyed reading romances and had a deep appreciation for poetry. Amongst her ladies-in-waiting was a noblewoman, Anne de Graville, the sole female French court poet of that period and a strong-minded individual who married her husband, Pierre de Balsac, against her father's

"Plain and badly lame"

wishes and eloped with him.[37] Claude requested poems and translations of Latin texts from Anne; *La Belle Dame sans Mercy* (*The Beautiful Lady without Mercy*), a re-adaptation of Alain Chartier's poem, and a historical romance, *Palamon and Arcita*. Both were dedicated to Queen Claude, whom Anne de Graville extolled beyond measure as her patroness.[38]

Just like Francis I in France, Henry VIII was also eager to impress foreign envoys with the beauty and eloquence of his wives' female companions. They were chosen for their beauty and high birth, but they also had to possess language skills. The language of the cultured at court was French and Latin, and Henry VIII insisted that the ladies selected to take part in banquets and masques to honour the foreign dignitaries should speak impeccable French. These ladies often made great impressions on ambassadors, who admired not only their beauty but also their language skills and apparel. In 1518 it was noticed that "lady maskers" spoke "good French" with the French ambassadors, "which delighted these gentlemen, to hear these ladies speak to them in their own tongue".[39] Nine years later, the Venetian ambassador admired "the ladies, whose various styles of beauty and apparel, enhanced by the brilliancy of the lights, caused me to think I was contemplating the choirs of angels".[40] These "angels" and "goddesses rather than human beings" were the leading luminaries of Henry VIII's court.[41] Naturally, the King selected his mistresses from among these young and charming damsels, but beauty was not the only factor in choosing a partner. Henry, who dabbled in composing music and poetry, paid much attention to women with similar skills. His first recorded long-term mistress, Elizabeth Blount, was said to excel all other ladies "in singing, dancing, and all goodly pastimes".[42]

The King's wife, Katharine of Aragon, seemed to enjoy watching her ladies dance in her chambers rather than dancing herself, but she was known for her impeccable sense of style, kindness and charity.[43] She was not the most beautiful of women—by the time she turned thirty, she was already corpulent as a result of numerous pregnancies—but she dazzled the spectators with her fashion choices. The oft-repeated notion that Katharine of Aragon wore unfashionable, sombre gowns stems partly from the much later religious propaganda that tried to contrast Katharine's piety with the pleasure-loving character of Henry VIII's second wife of evangelical interests, Anne Boleyn. Whereas Katharine may have worn "the habit of St Francis"—a penitential hair shirt—beneath her royal attire and knelt on the church floor without cushions, other evidence provides clues as to Katharine's undiminished interest in fashion.[44] Two miniatures painted before 1527 and firmly dating to her lifetime depict Katharine with low-cut décolletages, bejewelled headdresses and a rich amount of hair showing from under an Italian-styled headpiece.[45] Katharine favoured the fashions of her native Spain, but she also imported cloth and jewellery from Italy and the Netherlands. She liked to show off her long auburn hair, as clearly visible in the abovementioned miniature and in a description from the ambassador who saw locks of hair falling down over Katharine's shoulders in 1520.[46] There's also evidence that she was curious about the French fashions and ordered the English resident ambassador, Thomas Boleyn, to either describe or draw them so that her tailor could sew them for her.[47] Ordering the French gowns in 1520 served as preparation for the summit between Francis I and Henry VIII at the Field of the Cloth of Gold, a meeting that would go down in history as one of the costliest diplomatic deceptions of the sixteenth century.

NOTES

[1] Raphael Holinshed, *Holinshed's Chronicles of England, Scotland and Ireland*, Volume 3, p. 611.
[2] "They hope the Duchess of Britanny is with child" in *Letters and Papers, Foreign and Domestic, Henry VIII*, Volume 2, 1515-1518, n. 32.
[3] Raphael Holinshed, op.cit.
[4] Kathleen Wilson-Chevalier, *Claude de France: In Her Mother's Likeness, a Queen with Symbolic Clout?*, p. 127.
[5] Cynthia J. Brown, *Like Mother Like Daughter: The Blurring of Royal Imagery in Books for Anne de Bretagne and Claude de France*, p. 121.
[6] *Letters and Papers, Foreign and Domestic, Henry VIII*, Volume 2, 1515-1518, n. 139.
[7] *Négociations diplomatiques*, ed. Le Glay, Volume 2, p. 53.

[8] Ibid.
[9] *Travel Journal of Antonio de Beatis*, ed. J.R. Hale, p. 107
[10] Paul Lacroix, *Louis XII et Anne de Bretagne*, p. 306.
[11] *Letters and Papers, Foreign and Domestic, Henry VIII*, Volume 2, 1515-1518, n. 647.
[12] Simone Bertière, *Les Reines de France*, p. 205.
[13] There is no evidence to justify the statement that Claude "felt ill at ease at her husband's more exuberant court, where she was forced to suffer the indignity of a neglected wife". Josephine Wilkinson, *Anne Boleyn: The Young Queen To Be*, p. 35.
[14] *The Travel Journal of Antonio de Beatis*, ed. Hale, p. 107.
[15] *Officiers des Maisons des roys, reynes, enfans de France et de quelques princes du sang*, p. 313
[16] *The Travel Journal of Antonio de Beatis*, op.cit.
[17] Edward Hall, *Hall's Chronicle*, p. 610.
[18] *Letters and Papers, Foreign and Domestic, Henry VIII*, Volume 1, 1509-1514, n. 3342.
[19] *Letters and Papers, Foreign and Domestic, Henry VIII*, Volume 2, 1515-1518, n. 114.
[20] Ibid., n. 395, 411.
[21] Ibid.
[22] *Calendar of State Papers, Venice,* Volume 2, 1509-1519, n. 479.
[23] *Letters and Papers, Foreign and Domestic, Henry VIII*, Volume 2, 1515-1518, n. 410.
[24] Francis Ambrière, *Le favori de François Ier*, pp. 53, 54.
[25] Pierre de Bourdeille, seigneur de Brantôme, *Oeuvres complètes*, Volume 3, p.127. David Potter, *Politics and Faction at the Court of Francis I*, p. 130.
[26] Baldassare Castiglione, *The Book of the Courtier*, p. 174
[27] Yassana C. Croizat, *"Living Dolls": François Ier Dresses His Women*, pp. 94-130.
[28] Ibid.
[29] *Letters and Papers, Foreign and Domestic, Henry VIII*, Volume 2, 1515-1518, n. 4136.
[30] Ibid.
[31] Read more in Chapter 7.
[32] Yassana C. Croizat, op.cit.
[33] Pierre de Bourdeille, seigneur de Brantôme, *The Book of the Ladies*, pp. 29-30.
[34] Ibid.

[35] Caroline zum Kolk, *The Household of the Queen of France in the Sixteenth Century*, p. 10.
[36] Josephine Wilkinson, *Anne Boleyn: The Young Queen To Be*, p. 35.
[37] Diana Maury Robin, Anne R. Larsen, Carole Levin, *Encyclopedia of Women in the Renaissance*, pp. 173-174.
[38] Ingrid Akerlund, *Sixteenth Century French Women Writers*, p.55.
[39] Victoria Sylvia Evans, *Ladies-in-Waiting*, p. 12.
[40] *Calendar of State Papers Relating To English Affairs in the Archives of Venice*, Volume 4, 1527-1533, n. 105.
[41] Ibid.
[42] Victoria Sylvia Evans, op.cit.
[43] During the notorious divorce case, Katharine was chided by Henry's councillors for exhorting her ladies "to dance and pass time" instead of praying. She was also accused of showing "no pensiveness in her countenance, nor in her apparel, nor behaviour". *Letters and Papers, Foreign and Domestic, Henry VIII*, Volume 4, 1524-1530, n. 4981.
[44] Henry Clifford, *The Life of Jane Dormer, Duchess of Feria*, p. 73.
[45] Richard Walker, *Miniatures: 300 Years of the English Miniature*, p. 18.
[46] Read more in Chapter 7.
[47] Janet Arnold, *Queen Elizabeth's Wardrobe Unlock'd*, p. 113.

CHAPTER 6
"GOVERNESS WITHOUT RESTRAINT"

When a crown was firmly placed on Francis I's head on 25 January 1515, Louise of Savoy was overwhelmed with emotions, and she recorded them in her *Journal*:

"On the feast of St. Paul's conversion 1515, my son was anointed and consecrated in the Cathedral of Reims. For this I am indebted and obligated to God's mercy, through which I have been abundantly rewarded for all the trials and tribulations that I suffered in childhood and the flower of my youth. Humility has kept me company and patience had never abandoned me".[1]

It was noticed early in the reign that Louise "hath a great stroke in all matters with the King her son" and she quickly became a force to be reckoned with.[2] One of Francis's first orders was to reward his beloved mother and elevate her to the title of Duchess of Angoulême:

"Desiring to show respect to our very dear and very loved lady and mother, the Duchesse of Angoulême and Anjou; considering that while we remained under her care, government, and administration, she carefully and affectionately brought us up, and caused us to be well and diligently instructed in all good and virtuous morals, for which cause we therefore hold ourselves bound in honour and duty to impart and bestow upon her the highest honours and privileges of our realm".[3]

In addition, she also received the duchy of Anjou, the counties of Maine and Beaufort-en-Vallée and the barony of Amboise. Louise was now thirty-nine years old and as powerful and respected as she would ever be. By all accounts, she was also an attractive woman. In February 1515, Mercurino de Gattinara observed that she "seems much younger than she did four years ago".[4] She was "an unusually tall woman, still finely complexioned, very rubicund and lively" and looking young for her age.[5] Miniatures in her manuscripts often depict her disguised as Prudence dressed in a black velvet robe trimmed with fur and modestly closed at the neck.

Although Francis I waited for his coronation for almost his entire life to that point, the early days of his reign were filled not with matters of state but with pleasures. "The King's mode of life was as follows", wrote the Venetian ambassador Contarini, "he rises at eleven, hears Mass, then remains for two or three hours with his mother and afterwards visits his sweethearts or goes out hunting".[6] Young and thirsting for glory, Francis soon decided that he would assert himself as the powerful King by conquering Milan. Francis claimed the duchy of Milan in right of his descent from the Visconti dukes—his ancestor was Valentina Visconti—as well as through the fact that both his father and paternal grandfather held the title of the Duke of Milan. Francis's wife, Claude, was also descended from the same Visconti ancestor, providing a third claim. The duchy was the possession of the French monarchy for years; Louis XII established Milan as a French capital in Italy in 1500 but lost it to the Sforza family twelve years later. Now, Francis decided to reconquer the duchy and return triumphant.

The summer of 1515 saw a slow progress towards the city of Lyons. On the way from Chaumont to Amboise, the King ran a thorn into his leg, an accident that Louise of Savoy noted in her *Journal*. "He had much pain", she grievously remarked, "and I too, for true love forced me to suffer the same pain".[7] By 30 June, Francis was with Louise at her little chateau of Romorantin, from whence he departed to Lyons on 4 July 1515 at seven o'clock in the morning. In Lyons, Francis made last preparations for war and declared that "we have decided to leave the government of our realm to our well beloved and dear Lady Mother, the Duchess of Angoulême and Anjou, in whom we have entire and perfect confidence, who will, by her virtue and prudence, know how to acquit this trust".[8] Louise's first regency had thus commenced.

Whereas Louise was given the regency and started carving out a formidable presence at court, Francis's wife was barely noticeable in the early months of her husband's reign. Queen Claude did not take part in the King's coronation and did not accompany him to Lyons during the summer. The reason she was not present at Francis's coronation, according to Jean Barrillon, secretary of Chancellor Duprat, whose chronicle of the early reign of Francis I is invaluable, was because she was with child at the time. Also, the "heavily pregnant" Claude stayed behind in Amboise when on 29 June 1515 Francis slipped away quietly from the castle and left for Romorantin.[9]

The Queen's first child was born on 19 August 1515 while Francis was waging war in Italy. When he was informed that Claude had successfully given birth to a healthy daughter, he was disappointed because he was hoping for a son.[10] The King's mother, on the other hand, was content because the little princess was named Louise after her. Louise of Savoy recorded in her *Journal* that "Madame Louise, the eldest daughter of my son, was born in Amboise on 19 August 1515 at 10:47 in the morning".[11]

On 13 September 1515, Francis I won the battle against the Old Swiss Confederacy near the town of Marignano, some ten miles southeast of Milan. The victory was so spectacular that Marshal Gian Giacomo Trivulzio, veteran of every war waged for the past forty years, praised Marignano as the "battle of giants" and stated that compared to it, all previous battles in his lifetime had been like "children's games".[12] Back in France, Louise of Savoy was overwhelmed with joy after receiving letters from Francis. The entry in her *Journal* states that she went on foot to the shrine of Notre-Dame des Fontaines to give thanks for the victory and recommend to the care of the saints "him, whom I love better than myself, my boy, glorious and triumphant Caesar, subjugator of the Swiss".[13]

Louise's "triumphant Caesar" was back in France in January 1516, and Louise, together with her daughter, Margaret, and Queen Claude, started their progress towards Sisteron, where they were to be reunited with the King. The ecstatic entry in Louise's *Journal* captures her emotions perfectly:

"The thirteenth day of January, my son, returning from the battle with the Swiss, met me near Sisteron, in Provence on the banks of the Durance, at about six o'clock in the evening, and God knows that I, poor mother, was thankful to see my son safe and sound after all he had suffered and endured to serve the common good".[14]

Francis's triumphant return marked a new era for him and his family. He asserted himself as the major player on the international political stage and became a force to be reckoned with. When Henry VIII heard about the French King's victory at Marignano, he was shocked and refused to believe that Francis won, even though he received the news directly from the French King's mother. It was only after Francis sent a special envoy, Monsieur Bapaume, accompanied by a herald, that Henry had finally realized that his rival had truly triumphed. Bapaume's long despatch addressed to Louise of Savoy makes interesting reading. Bapaume visited Henry in Greenwich Palace on 6 November 1515 and, after making cordial recommendations on behalf of Francis I and Louise of Savoy, presented him with two letters written by the French King. Henry, Bapaume recorded with relish, "did not take any great pleasure in reading them; for it seemed, to look at him, as if tears would have burst from his eyes, so red were they from the pain he suffered in hearing and understanding the good news and prosperity of my master, who had advertised him thereof by his letters".[15]

The English King was devastated because Francis's impressive victory eclipsed what Henry had achieved in France two years earlier. On 16 August 1513, the English troops, backed by the imperial forces, won over the French army, but the victory was not spectacular because there was no pitched battle, and the French, taken by surprise and outmanoeuvred, galloped across the fields at Guingate, leaving only golden spurs glinting in the sun behind them. In fact, Henry VIII was not even there when his troops won because he was laying siege to the nearby town of Therouanne. Francis I, on the other hand, fought valiantly in the thick of the battle in Marignano, and his life was in danger, according to Jean Barrillon. Because so many Frenchmen died fighting for him, Francis vowed in a letter to his mother that never would anyone refer to the French army as "hares in armour" after their escape from the battlefield in 1513; the same escape that ensured Henry's victory at the Battle of the Spurs.[16]

Francis I now needed a male heir who would add lustre to his victory and ensure the succession. In January 1516, Henry VIII decided to brag about his wife's condition in a letter to Francis, writing boldly that Queen Katharine was pregnant and Francis "should put Queen Claude in the like situation".[17] In fact, Claude conceived again around that time. Katharine of Aragon gave birth to Princess Mary on 18 February 1516, crushing Henry's hopes for a male heir yet again. Putting a brave face on, Henry boasted that he and Katharine were still young and "if it was a daughter this time, by the grace of God the sons will follow".[18]

Four months later, Louise of Savoy recorded in her *Journal* that "my daughter Claude begun to feel within her body the first movement" of her baby.[19] Although the cessation of menstruation was one of many signs of pregnancy, in an age of no pregnancy tests, women were sure about their condition only after they felt their child's movement, called "quickening", a sign that the child was alive. Princess Charlotte, the second daughter of Francis and Claude, was born in Amboise on 23 October 1516.

The Queen proved that she was able to provide her husband with healthy children, although she was still under considerable pressure to produce a male heir. Nevertheless, Francis and his mother decided that, considering Claude's enormous popularity, she should be crowned. Claude's coronation took place on 10 May 1517 in the Basilica of St Denis. The Queen, wearing a cloak of blue velvet lined with ermine over her shoulders, dazzled the spectators with the richness of her clothes and jewels. On her head, she wore "the most expensive cape" sewn with little leaves of gold onto silver cloth given to her by her mother, Anne of Brittany. During the Mass when "Te Deum" was sung, Claude prostrated herself in front of the high altar, as was customary, and then knelt. She was anointed with holy oil on her forehead, chest and shoulders.

During the coronation festivities that stretched over three days, the Queen was celebrated as the "daughter of the most Christian King Louis XII of his name and of Madame Anne of Brittany, twice crowned Queen of France". On 9 May 1517, Claude paid respects to her deceased parents, visiting their tomb in the Basilica of St Denis "to pray and say orisons in great devotion and contemplation over the tomb and statue of her father and mother, and not without tears and lamentations".[20] Several stages with allegorical tableaux vivants, where actors re-enacted highly symbolic scenes, were erected along the Queen's entry route into Paris. Allusions to Claude's mother and her Breton ancestry were present in these scenes, but the Queen was upstaged in the final tableau, which featured a dialogue between St Louis and his mother, Blanche of Castile, emphasizing the relationship Francis I shared with his mother rather than with his wife.[21]

The relationship between Louise of Savoy and Claude of France has been long characterised as hostile, partly due to Brantôme's description in *The Book of the Ladies*—he claimed that Louise treated Claude harshly—as well as because of what we know about these two women's characters.[22] In 1525, Louise's forceful personality prompted the Venetian ambassador to describe her as "a most terrible woman" who he believed would treat Francis's second wife, Eleanor of Portugal, "like a servant wench".[23] Was this comment prompted by what the Venetians knew about Claude's treatment and they assumed Eleanor's would be no different, or was it because Louise was such a strong and formidable woman that they assumed Eleanor would be treated this way? It is impossible to reach a definite conclusion.

Considering the fact that Anne of Brittany and Louise of Savoy strongly disliked each other, it would be an educated guess that Louise transferred this animosity towards her rival's daughter, but it is also possible that the two women formed a close relationship because they lived in each other's company for most of their lives. Claude knew Louise her entire life, having been born in her castle of Romorantin and engaged to Francis from the age of six. The young Queen was "a person of few words", a rather shy and withdrawn young woman who lived in the shadow of her husband's lively mother, sister and glittering mistresses.[24] Perhaps this is the reason Claude was extremely popular with her subjects. The Venetian ambassador marvelled that Claude was "so universally loved, that it is impossible to describe or imagine greater affection". Francis and Louise, on the other hand, were "more unpopular all over France than words could express".[25]

It was easy for Louise to feel compassion towards this physically ailing girl who was her beloved son's wife. Entries in Louise's *Journal* are mostly dedicated to Francis, Claude and their children. Louise often called Claude "my daughter", but it is significant that the Queen's coronation was not among the events Louise wished to commemorate in her *Journal*. In fact, it seems that Louise perceived Claude as a royal baby maker, and all of the events in her *Journal* are either connected to Francis or his children by Claude. Claude as a separate entity made no appearance in the *Journal*; she was always defined by her role as Francis's wife and mother of his children. The fact that Louise later claimed that she had faithfully fulfilled her role of Claude's guardian, imposed on her by the late Anne of Brittany, and that "common report proclaims it" proves that she treated Claude honourably, or at least it appeared so in the public eye.[26] Foreign dignitaries noted the ever-present Louise accompanying both Francis and Claude. "She always accompanies her son and the Queen and plays the governess without restraint", reported one of the observers who was clearly impressed with Louise's personality and appearance.[27] Despite the fact that she was with Claude almost all the time, Louise never took precedence over the Queen, observing correct etiquette on all occasions. Although herself not a crowned Queen, Louise was treated as such by foreign ambassadors and other ruling families who recognized her key role at court and often referred to her, incorrectly, as "Queen Mother".[28] She would soon prove to be a skillful negotiator between her son and Henry VIII.

NOTES

[1] *Journal de Louise de Savoie*, p. 89.
[2] *Letters and Papers, Foreign and Domestic, Henry VIII*, Volume 2, 1515-1518, n. 105.
[3] Martha Walker Freer, *The Life of Marguerite D'Angoulême*, p. 78.

[4] *Letters and Papers, Foreign and Domestic, Henry VIII,* Volume 2, 1515-1518, n. 114.
[5] *The Travel Journal of Antonio de Beatis*, p. 108
[6] *Calendar of State Papers, Venice,* Volume 2, 1509-1525, n. 600.
[7] *Journal de Louise de Savoie*, p. 89.
[8] Dorothy Moulton Mayer, *The Great Regent*, p. 86.
[9] *Journal de Jean Barrillon, secrétaire du chancelier Duprat, 1515-1521,* Volume 1, p. 17, 64.
[10] Ibid.
[11] *Journal de Louise de Savoie*, p. 89.
[12] R.J. Knecht, *Francis I*, p. 47.
[13] *Journal de Louise de Savoie*, p. 90.
[14] Ibid.
[15] *Letters and Papers, Henry VIII,* Volume 2, Preface.
[16] Knecht, op.cit.
[17] *Calendar of State Papers, Venice,* Volume 2, 1509-1525, n. 680.
[18] Ibid., n. 691.
[19] *Journal de Louise de Savoie*, p. 90.
[20] Cynthia J. Brown, *The Queen's Library: Image-Making at the Court of Anne of Brittany, 1477-1514*, p. 55.
[21] Ibid., p. 58.
[22] Pierre de Bourdeille, seigneur de Brantôme, *The Book of the Ladies*, p. 219.
[23] *Calendar of State Papers, Venice,* Volume 3, 1525-1526, n. 1066.
[24] Ibid., Volume 2, 1509-1519, n. 1271.
[25] Sebastiano Giustiniani, *Four Years at the Court of Henry VIII*, Volume 2, p. 318.
[26] *Journal de Louise de Savoie*, p. 88.
[27] *The Travel Journal of Antonio de Beatis*, op.cit.
[28] *Letters and Papers, Foreign and Domestic, Henry VIII,* Volume 4, 1524-1530, n. 5704.

CHAPTER 7
GOLDEN QUEENS

In November 1517, Francis I went on a pilgrimage to St Martin at Tours to pray for a son. His wife, Queen Claude, was pregnant again and the King desired nothing more than to see succession established. Claude, too, desired a son and heir. Following the example of her mother-in-law, Claude made a vow that she would name her son Francis after Francis of Paola, the saint who once told Louise of Savoy that she would give birth to a son who would become King. If she had a son, the Queen vowed, she would make sure that Francis of Paola was canonised.

On 28 February 1518, the Queen finally gave birth to her first son, Dauphin Francis, which was the occasion for great rejoicings throughout the entire realm. Claude was so happy that she told the Venetian ambassadors that her son was "even more beautiful" than her husband the King. Francis rejoiced that the newly born dauphin was "the most beautiful and puissant child one could imagine and who would be the easiest to nourish".[1] Louise of Savoy, the proud grandmother, welcomed "the son of my son" with great joy.[2]

News of the birth of Francis I's son reached England quickly. Henry VIII's reaction was not recorded, but Thomas Wolsey viewed the birth as providential for Anglo-French relations. "The King of France has now got a son, and His Majesty here has a daughter", Wolsey told the Venetian ambassador, adding that he would unite the two nations through marriage.[3] This was a grand scheme and the crowning achievement of Wolsey's ambitions. He was always a Francophile and dedicated to establishing peace. This humble butcher's son grew from obscurity to become one of the most powerful and influential men at the court of Henry VIII. By 1515, he was made cardinal and chancellor, effectively becoming the King's right-hand man.

Sebastiano Giustiniani, the Venetian diplomat who spent four years at the Tudor court, was impressed with Wolsey, who was "about forty-six years old, very handsome, learned, extremely eloquent, of vast ability and indefatigable". Wolsey alone transacted business that "occupied all the magistracies, offices and councils of Venice, both civil and criminal" and he was good at it. He had a reputation of being "extremely just", and that is why the common people, especially the poor, loved him.[4] Nobles at court did not share this adoration, however. They perceived Wolsey as a greedy upstart who had overreached himself. Wolsey, it seems, felt that as long as he had Henry VIII on his side, all was well. He ruled "both the

King and the entire kingdom", wrote Giustiniani. The ambassador noticed a gradual change in the way Wolsey talked about business. "His Majesty will do so and so", he used to say but subsequently "forgetting himself", Wolsey commenced saying, "we shall do so and so", and towards the end of Giustiniani's stay at court, Wolsey "reached such a pitch" that always commenced by saying, "I shall do so and so."[5] Henry, it seemed, was satisfied with the way Wolsey conducted business because it meant that he had more time for his favourite pastimes.

Henry VIII and Francis I both agreed that the mutual alliance should be approved of and accepted the notion of the marriage between Princess Mary of England and Dauphin Francis of France. Both kings decided to send embassies to each other's courts. The French embassy to England arrived in the autumn of 1518. On 26 September, Henry VIII dressed "in very rich attire", formally received the ambassadors.[6] On 3 October 1518, the King swore to the Treaty of Universal Peace at St Paul's Cathedral during the Mass celebrated by the architect of the alliance, Cardinal Wolsey.

Two days later, Princess Mary was engaged to Dauphin Francis. It was a splendid ceremony. Mary, now two and a half years old, was dressed in a robe of cloth of gold with a black velvet cap perched on the top of her head and numerous jewels adorning her small person. She was a beautiful and vivacious child, living proof of the King's virility and the Queen's fertility. The ceremony took place in the Queen's chamber at Greenwich, although Katharine of Aragon was not very keen on the French alliance. Nevertheless, the royal couple had unanimously given their consent when the French ambassadors solemnly asked them if they approved of their daughter's match. Henry and Katharine watched as Cardinal Wolsey placed a small ring with a large diamond on Mary's tiny finger. The princess made everyone laugh heartily when she asked Guillame Bonnivet, the proxy groom who slipped the ring down over her second joint, whether he was the Dauphin of France because she wished to kiss him. After the ceremony was concluded, feasting and dancing continued into the late hours.

Amongst the conditions of the marriage alliance, the French insisted that Mary should be recognised as Henry VIII's heiress. Unlike in France, in England women were not debarred from succession, but England never really had a successful female ruler, and Henry was haunted by the memory of a dynastic conflict known in history as the Wars of the Roses. His father, Henry VII, won the crown in the Battle of Bosworth, defeating the Yorkist Richard III and establishing the Tudor dynasty. Henry VII merged the warring factions, Lancasters and Yorks, by marrying Princess Elizabeth of York. Their marriage produced several children, including an heir, Prince Arthur, and a "spare", the future Henry VIII. Prince Arthur married

Katharine of Aragon in 1501 but died several months after the wedding. Katharine was way too valuable a catch to be released and sent back to Spain, and she was trapped in England, where Henry VII treated her as a pawn on the political chessboard. After Henry VII's death, Henry VIII married her, claiming that he was fulfilling his father's deathbed wish. By 1518, Henry and Katharine had only one living child together, and the Queen was pregnant again. In the eighth month of her pregnancy, she went into premature labour, and on 9 November 1518 was delivered of a stillborn daughter.[7] This time Henry VIII was not the only one devastated because "never had the kingdom so anxiously desired anything as it did a prince". Had Henry known what the outcome of this pregnancy would be, he would never have allowed for Princess Mary's French match because, as Sebastiano Giustiniani reported, "the sole fear of this kingdom" was "that it may pass into the power of the French through this marriage".[8] This fear was understandable. If the King had no legitimate male heirs, any man who married his daughter could claim England through her. Henry could not come to terms with this thought. In fact, he found it hard to accept that he and his wife were unable to have male children. Although neither Henry nor Katharine were aware of it, the 1518 pregnancy was Katharine's last and marked the end of her childbearing years.

The French embassy left England on 11 October 1518, and now it was Henry VIII's turn to send his ambassadors to

France. Sebastiano Giustiniani noted that the four English ambassadors departed "with very great pomp, rather regal than ambassadorial, endeavouring in every respect to outvie the French ambassadors".[9] They reached France by 10 December 1518, and two days later they had their first audience with Francis I. On 16 December, the French King ratified the treaty of marriage between the Dauphin and Princess Mary.

After the formalities, there was time for pleasure. On 22 December 1518, a great banquet in honour of the English ambassadors was held in the medieval Bastille fortress dating back to the fourteenth century. The walls were hung with silver and gold brocade, the ceilings were decorated with gilt stars, signs and celestial planets to represent the heavens and the floors were covered with rich carpets. The massive space was lit by torches and chandeliers "throwing such a marvellous blaze of light on the starry ceiling, as to rival the sun".[10] Francis I's sister Margaret, Duchess of Alençon, sat on the King's left side during the entertainments. Queen Claude and Louise of Savoy observed the spectacle from one of the galleries near the King's dais. Claude was six months pregnant at the time, and this may well explain why she wasn't as prominent as her sister-in-law. Nevertheless, she cut a magnificent figure and overawed the foreign ambassadors with her rich clothes and jewellery. She was "sumptuously dressed with a necklace of innumerable very large pearls, in which sundry very valuable jewels were set".[11] The next day a tournament with banqueting and dancing took place. The Queen and the King's mother again observed everything from the gallery above. Claude yet again dazzled the spectators "dressed in a very rich gown of cloth of gold, lined with very beautiful sables, and a quantity of jewels on her head and neck, and around her waist, so that she quite sparkled".[12]

Early in 1519, England and France exchanged resident ambassadors for the first time in history. Previously, both kingdoms were exchanging embassies, but they were usually motivated by special events such as the marriage of Mary Tudor to Louis XII in 1514. By 1518, when amicable relations were re-established between the two countries, Henry VIII and Francis I decided that they should have ambassadors residing in their respective countries for longer periods of time. The first English ambassador to France in the winter of 1518 was Sir Thomas Boleyn, a skillful diplomat and linguist who had previously served as an ambassador at the court of Archduchess Margaret of Savoy in the Low Countries. Boleyn's despatches provide a valuable insight into life at Francis I's court and offer a clue to Queen Claude's health. Pregnant for the fourth time, in early 1519 Claude was "very sickly, worse than she has been in any former confinement".[13] This statement points to the fact that Claude's pregnancies were difficult. The young Queen gathered more weight with each successive pregnancy, and this put a considerable burden on her already strained body. In addition to uneven hips, Claude also suffered from scoliosis that deepened with each pregnancy.

On 11 March 1519, accompanied by her mother-in-law, the Queen went on a journey to St-Germain-en-Laye, where she was to give birth to her child, but she was taken ill on the way and was obliged to take temporary lodgings in the village of La Porte de Neuilly. That night Thomas Boleyn reported Claude was "in great danger", and the next morning various false reports spread first about her delivery of a son and then about her death.[14] By late March, Claude was able to finish her travel to St Germain-en-Laye. On 28 March 1519, Louise of Savoy led Thomas Boleyn by the hand to Claude's private chamber, where the pregnant Queen "was accompanied by fourteen or fifteen lords and gentlewomen, in a nightgown, and had nothing upon her head but only a kerchief, looking always her hour when she shall be brought to bed."[15] Three days later, on 31 March, the Queen gave birth to Henri, Duke of Orléans, named after Henry VIII.

While in England etiquette dictated that an expectant mother must withdraw from the public life about a month before the delivery date, the birth of a royal child in France was a public event and occurred with the nobility and male doctors awaiting news from the birthing chamber right at the door while midwives assisted the Queen. By the eighteenth century, this custom had evolved and royal birth became one of the chief courtly amusements, with nobility—both men and women— inside the birthing chamber observing the process from up close. The custom was banned only in 1778 when Queen Marie Antoinette almost died from the lack of fresh air caused by the fact that too many people gathered in her room when she was giving birth to her first child.

On 15 April 1519, Thomas Boleyn reported that a magnificent thanksgiving procession took place at court, "where went in the same King, the Lady his Mother, with all the lords and ladies of the court". The cause of this procession was "to honour the holy cord that our Lord was bound to the pillar with, and many other relics, which were sent to the Queen here from an abbey in Poytow [Poitou] and from divers other places, now when she was delivered of a child".[16] Religious objects were believed to ease the pain during labour and help to bring forth a healthy child. During this particular procession, the relics were revered, carried on a little cushion and placed on the high altar.

On 5 June 1519, Boleyn sponsored the infant duke in the name of Henry VIII during a magnificent christening. In the course of this grand ceremony, Thomas Boleyn presented a salt-spoon, cup and layer of gold to Queen Claude. Cardinal Wolsey sent a substantial sum of £100 to be distributed as baptismal gifts between the infant's nurse, rocker of his cradle and three gentlewomen of Queen Claude's privy chamber. The newfound amity between England and France opened the door for amiable relations between Queens Katharine and Claude. They started exchanging cordial letters, talking mostly about their children's well-being. One of Katharine of Aragon's letters to Claude survives and reads as follows:

> "My good sister and cousin,
>
> I have by your esquire of the stable received your good and affectionate letters, and I assure you that I have been much and very greatly consoled at having heard the good news, health, estate, and prosperity in which is my very dear and most beloved good son, and yours the dauphin. And believe what by your said esquire you will similarly hear, not only of the good health, estate, prosperity, and news of the King my husband, of me and of my daughter the princess, but also the affection, good will, and very great desire that the King my said lord and husband and I have to the good and continuance of the good love, friendship, and fraternal intelligence and alliance which now is between the two Kings our husbands, and their kingdoms, which I hold inseparable, and ever pray God that it may continue, which I desire above all things, and for my part shall exert myself for it as I have always done and shall do. However, I will cease writing you a longer letter, except praying you that from time to time I may be participant of your good news, and of those of my said son the dauphin. Also, if there be

any thing in which I could do you pleasure, I will do it with very good heart, as she who considers herself and wishes ever to continue,

> Your good sister and cousin,
>
> Katharine."[17]

Although the letter is pleasant, it lacks a personal touch and seems almost as if dictated by current politics. Katharine of Aragon was known to have been against the French alliance because, as a Spaniard, she was naturally inclined towards the league with her nephew Charles, King of Spain. The French alliance was against Charles's interests, and Katharine always felt bound to the members of her family. With her father's death in 1516, Katharine now chose to demonstrate her allegiance towards Charles, her sister's son. The first occasion to manifest her support occurred in 1519. After the Holy Roman Emperor Maximilian died on 12 January 1519, seven electors had the power to choose their next sovereign. Charles, as Maximilian's grandson, was the most serious among the contenders, but this didn't stop either Francis I or Henry VIII from competing for the title. Louise of Savoy, the French King's mother, even wrote letters and sent bribes to the electors in the hope of her son becoming the Holy Roman Emperor. Soon it became clear that Henry VIII stood no chance, and the real contest was between Charles and Francis. The Venetian ambassador observed that

Henry VIII favoured his wife's nephew but would rather see that neither Charles nor Francis won. When Charles was elected and became Charles V, Holy Roman Emperor, it was observed that Katharine of Aragon, "being a Spaniard, evinced satisfaction at the success of her nephew".[18]

Katharine of Aragon's political sympathies didn't escape the notice of Louise of Savoy, who was heavily involved in planning the upcoming meeting between Francis I and Henry VIII to facilitate their friendship. To demonstrate their unity, the two monarchs made a pact not to shave their beards before they met. This was motivated by Henry's desire to compete with Francis in everything, including personal appearance. "On hearing that Francis I wore a beard", wrote Sebastiano Giustiniani, Henry "allowed his to grow, and, as it is reddish, he has now got a beard which looks like gold".[19] Katharine of Aragon did not like the beard, and when Henry shaved it off, it caused an international incident. Louise of Savoy was quick to notice that it wasn't only because of Katharine's personal tastes that her husband was now clean shaven. When the English ambassador was quizzed about his master's beard, he insisted that "the Queen daily made him great insistence and desired him to put it off for her sake". Louise was not fooled. "Is not the Queen's Grace aunt to the King of Spain?" she slyly enquired. "Madame, he is her sister's son", was the reply. Louise suspected that Katharine begged Henry to shave the beard off because it was a symbol of his friendship with her son, but she chose to ignore this fact and announced that the love between Francis and Henry was "not in the beards, but in the hearts".[20] She was, nevertheless, open-eyed about the English Queen's actions. When Thomas Boleyn was replaced by Richard Wingfield, Louise asked him whether Katharine had "any great devotion to this assembly". The Queen was, in Wingfield's words, virtuous and wise, and had no other pleasure but to "follow all that she may think to stand with the King's pleasure".[21] Charles V's envoys begged to differ. "There is no doubt that the French interview is against the will of the Queen and of all the nobles", their report claimed.[22]

The meeting between Henry VIII and Francis I was set up, however, and there was little Katharine of Aragon could do to prevent it, but she could still do something else. Knowing that Charles V was sailing to Flanders, she wanted him to stop in England for a short visit and worked with Henry and Wolsey to arrange the meeting before leaving for France. The King was soon persuaded and even told Charles's envoys that in order to give him enough time to reach England before the intended meeting with Francis I, he wrote to the French King asking him to defer the interview until June or July without revealing the cause of the intended delay. Henry knew very well that postponement was out of the question since several months earlier Louise of Savoy had informed him that Queen Claude was expecting her fifth child in July, and Francis I was desirous to take her with him without endangering her health. The French King conceded to defer the meeting until 31 May but could not allow further delays because his wife would then be eight months gone with child and would not be able to travel at such an advanced state of pregnancy.[23]

The French Queen's pregnancy was not enough to persuade Henry VIII to stop asking for a delay. He claimed, somewhat ungallantly, that if Claude delivered her child during the meeting, she would have the honour of Henry and Katharine attending the infant's christening. This was unacceptable, and Francis "marvelled" at Henry's wish to have the meeting postponed, adding that "the time when the Queen may be present has been carefully calculated and cannot be put off for a month".[24] In the end, Charles V landed at Dover on 26 May 1520 and left four days later. Henry VIII and his entourage also set sail for France on the same day, arranging another meeting with Charles between Calais and Gravelines, which would follow the meeting with Francis I.

The meeting between Henry VIII and Francis I lasted from 7 until 20 June 1520 in the vale between the village of Guines, in the English pale of Calais, and the village of Ardres in neighbouring France. The city of tents and pavilions of cloth of gold was created on an empty plain, giving rise to the event's name: "Field of the Cloth of Gold". This forest of sumptuous structures glistened in the spring sunshine like liquid gold, although the particularly rainy and windy weather forced Francis I to give orders for pulling his tents down after only four days. Rumour had it that when Henry VIII was informed prior to the meeting of how luxurious Francis's tents were to be, he ordered construction of a sumptuous temporary palace with walls of timber painted to look like real brick. Inside the structure there were chambers hung with tapestries and silks inhabited by the royal family and Cardinal Wolsey.

Besides Henry VIII and Katharine of Aragon, Mary Tudor also came to the meeting. Despite the fact that she was married to Charles Brandon, she chose to emphasize her ties with the French court. Her chambers in Henry VIII's temporary palace were decorated with the letters *M* and *L*, standing for Mary and Louis, joined with golden knots, and hangings embroidered with porcupines, Louis XII's heraldic emblem. The same symbols were proudly displayed on Mary's litter.

Henry VIII and Francis I met for the first time on 7 June 1520. Comparisons between the two monarchs were drawn immediately, and one of the Venetian commentators wrote:

"In stature, beauty, grace, and address in jousting there is little difference between them, save that the King of France appears to me rather the taller, and the English King has rather the handsomer face and more feminine, though in truth they are two very fine men and have a splendid retinue."[25]

Francis's retinue was a riot of colour in gold and silver brocades, silks, velvets and satins. Henry's retinue was also superbly dressed and wearing massive gold chains. Visually, there was no great difference between the nations except for the fact that the French turned up in greater numbers. On 9 June, the two Kings and their companies jousted together during the "feat of arms". The next day being Sunday, the King of France went to dine at Guines with the English Queen, and the King of England came to dine at Ardres with the Queen of France. Francis danced with Anne Browne, who was the mistress of a Frenchman held in England as a hostage after the 1513 war campaign. She was described as "the handsomest in the company" and clearly captured the French King's attention.[26]

The jousts recommenced on 11 June when the Queens and their retinues arrived on the field in richly decorated litters. Katharine of Aragon arrived first, sitting in an open litter covered with crimson satin embroidered with gold. She was dressed in a gown of cloth of gold cut in the Spanish fashion, with tresses of hair cascading down her shoulders. She was accompanied by forty ladies-in-waiting on palfreys and thirty ladies accommodated in six chariots. There are several conflicting reports by Italian observers touching on the English ladies' appearance. Some of them claimed that the Englishwomen were "neither very handsome nor very graceful". The Venetians disparaged their typically English apparel, claiming that they "were not richly clad", while others claimed that the Queen's ladies were "well dressed but ugly".[27] Only one account, that of Governor Triulzi, claimed that the Englishwomen were "superbly arrayed" but not as good as the French ladies, who were unanimously praised for richness of their apparel and their physical charms.[28] They were "better arrayed and handsomer than the English", wearing gowns of stiff brocade and many costly jewels.[29] Queen Claude arrived in a litter of cloth of silver wrought with golden knots. She was correspondingly dressed in a cloth of silver gown and wore a necklace of precious stones. In stark contrast to the two Queens, Louise of Savoy—referred to as Madame—travelled in a litter covered with black velvet with "an infinite number of ladies" dressed in crimson velvet with sleeves slashed with cloth of gold.[30] Claude joined Katharine of Aragon on the observation balcony, and after exchanging greetings, they both took their seats upon a wooden stage to watch their husbands jousting at the tilt.

Jousting was a sport that both kings enjoyed and excelled at, although it was a dangerous and potentially deadly pastime. Jousting was the focal point of tournament, which in the Field of the Cloth of Gold also included fighting in the open field and combat on foot at the barriers. In the joust, two fully armoured knights would charge at each other with high speed on either side of a wooden barrier called the tilt, holding a lance in their right hands. They scored high points for breaking their lances against an opponent's body.

On 11 June, it was reported that Henry and Francis jousted for a little more than three hours and "bore themselves valiantly", especially Francis, who "shivered spears like reeds and never missed a stroke".[31] In one encounter, the English King's lance was splintered and his hand sprained. Six days later, on 16 June, Francis was stricken on the temple and eye, either from the spear's impact or his horse's loosened headpiece. He displayed his injuries in front of the Queens and his mother, riding without helmet with a black eye and a black patch.[32] In his *Chronicle*, Edward Hall asserted that Francis I's nose was broken, but this was probably an exaggeration since an injury like that would have been widely commented upon.[33]

The meeting ended on 23 June 1520, and, although both kings competed in manifesting fraternal love and respect towards each other, the Field of the Cloth of Gold went down in history as a costly deception, an illusion of peace between England and France. By 1522, Princess Mary's engagement to Dauphin Francis was over and a new fiancé—France's enemy, Charles V—was offered instead. The King of England was dazzled by Charles's proposal of the so-called "Great Enterprise", which assumed a joined attack on France. Henry VIII saw himself as the rightful King of France, under the claim first put forward by Edward III, who claimed the French throne in 1340 as the sororal nephew of the last direct Capetian, Charles IV. Edward and his heirs fought the Hundred Years War to enforce this claim and were briefly successful in the 1420s under Henry V and Henry VI, but the House of Valois, a cadet branch of the Capetian dynasty, was ultimately victorious and retained de facto control of France. Despite this, English monarchs continued to prominently call themselves Kings of France.[34] War with France hung in the air.

NOTES

[1] *Journal de Jean Barrillon,* Volume 2, p. 78.
[2] *Journal de Louise de Savoie,* p. 90.
[3] *Calendar of State Papers, Venice,* Volume 2, 1509-1519, n. 1019.
[4] Ibid., n. 1287.
[5] Ibid.
[6] Ibid., n. 1095.
[7] Ibid., n. 1103.
[8] Ibid.
[9] *Letters and Papers, Foreign and Domestic, Henry VIII,* Volume 2, 1515-1518, n. 4563.
[10] Sebastiano Giustiniani, *Four Years at the Court of Henry VIII,* Volume 2, p. 303.
[11] Ibid., p. 305.
[12] Ibid., p. 307.
[13] *Letters and Papers, Foreign and Domestic, Henry VIII,* Volume 3, 1519-1523, n. 111.

[14] Thomas Boleyn to Henry VIII, 14 March 1519, quoted in Elizabeth Benger, *Memoirs of the Life of Anne Boleyn, Queen of Henry VIII*, pp. 116-17.
[15] *Letters and Papers, Foreign and Domestic, Henry VIII*, Volume 3, 1519-1523, n. 189.
[16] Henry Ellis, *Original Letters*, Volume 1, p. 159.
[17] Mary Anne Everett Wood, *Letters of Royal and Illustrious Ladies*, Volume 1, pp. 238-240.
[18] Sebastiano Giustiniani, *Four Years at the Court of Henry VIII*, Volume 2, p. 316.
[19] Ibid., p. 312.
[20] *Letters and Papers, Foreign and Domestic, Henry VIII*, Volume 3, 1519-1523, n. 514.
[21] Ibid., n. 721.
[22] Ibid., Preface.
[23] *Letters and Papers, Foreign and Domestic, Henry VIII*, Volume 3, 1519-1523, n. 549, 681.
[24] Ibid., n. 725.
[25] *Calendar of State Papers, Venice,* Volume 3, 1520-1526, n. 80.
[26] Ibid., n. 50.
[27] Ibid., n. 81.
[28] Ibid., n. 80.
[29] Ibid.
[30] Ibid., n. 84.
[31] Ibid., n. 80.
[32] Ibid., n. 50.
[33] Joycelyne Gledhill Russell, *The Field of Cloth of Gold*, p. 135.
[34] This caused certain awkwardness during the Field of the Cloth of Gold when one of Henry's titles—that of the King of France—was read aloud.

CHAPTER 8
THE END OF AN ERA

The child Queen Claude was expecting in 1520, a daughter named Madeleine, was born on 10 August of that year. The Queen would go on to have two more children: a son, Charles, born on 22 January 1522, and a daughter, Marguerite, born on 23 June 1523. The Queen's firstborn daughter, Louise, died on 21 September 1517 at the age of two.[1] By the time Claude was twenty-three, she was a mother of six children and her health had already begun to deteriorate. Ambassadorial despatches yield evidence of the Queen's constantly ill health, referring to her sicknesses, physicians' visits and dangers of childbearing. Her physical defects—uneven hips, hunched back and obesity, increasing with each pregnancy—put her life at great risk. The first information of the serious illness that eventually killed Claude is hinted at in a letter written by Margaret, Duchess of Alençon, to her friend and spiritual guide, Guillaume Briçonnet, Bishop of Meaux, on 4 October 1523. The King's sister nursed Claude in her sickness and encouraged Briçonnet "to visit the Queen, who is gravely ill".[2]

In March 1524, a rumour circulated at court and abroad that Claude had died, "having been long sick of the French pox".[3] In the following months, she was spoken about as if she were already dead. For instance, in the instructions for his ambassador, Charles V included a proposal of marriage between his sister, Eleanor of Portugal, and Francis I in case of Claude's death, which seemed imminent at the time.[4] Indeed, the Queen expired on 26 July 1524, only three months shy of her twenty-fifth birthday.

What killed Claude of France? Was it the strain of constant childbearing coupled with her already weak physique, or was it something else? The court historian Brantôme blamed Claude's philandering husband for infecting her with syphilis, a disease that "shortened her days".[5] Whereas many French historians dismiss Brantôme's claim as mere gossip, rumours about Claude suffering from "the French pox", as syphilis was popularly called in the sixteenth century, abounded during the months leading up to her death. Many foreign ambassadors wrote that the young Queen "was said to be dying of the [great] pox".[6] In August 1524, Francis I was also rumoured to have been treated for this disease.[7] According to Robert de la Marck, the Queen was sick "for six or seven months" before her death, but in reality her health began to deteriorate in October 1523, which means that she was dying for nine months. Without descriptions of the Queen's symptoms, however, it is impossible to reach a conclusion touching the nature of her last illness.[8]

Francis I's reaction to his wife's death was a mixture of shock and grief. Although he had mistresses during his marriage, he nevertheless had strong feelings for the woman to whom he was married for nine years. In a letter to Guillaume Briçonnet, Francis I's sister, Margaret, wrote about his reaction to Claude's death:

"Perceiving that it could not long be averted, he mourned exceedingly, saying to Madame [their mother]: 'If my life could be given in exchange for hers, willingly would I surrender it. Never could I have believed that the bonds of marriage, confirmed by God, were so difficult to sever'. And so in tears we separated. Since, we have had no news how he fares, but I fear that he is burdened with heavy sorrow."[9]

The Queen's death plunged the entire nation into mourning. Robert de la Marck remarked that Francis grieved and rightly so because there never had been "a more honest princess on earth, nor one more beloved in all the world, and everyone, young and old, believed that if she had not gone to paradise, then few would go".[10] Apart from the King, his mother and sister were also heartbroken after the Queen's death. Louise of Savoy and Margaret of Alençon decided to leave Blois, where Claude was slowly sinking into her grave, trusting that she would still be alive upon their return. When Claude's health suddenly became worse, the royal trinity was summoned back to Blois. The King, himself sick and mobilising for war, made no attempt to reach Blois, having seen his wife in June, but Louise and Margaret decided to make their way back. Louise was very sick herself and was forced to gather her strength in Herbault, where she soon received the devastating news of the Queen's death.

In her letter to Guillaume Briçonnet, Margaret of Alençon wrote that Louise collapsed as a result of "unbelievable grief" she felt after Claude's death and started bleeding "as she had from terrible fever, from every part, and in such quantity and force that if it had continued, she would not have survived". Margaret went on to say that Louise separated with Claude "so unwillingly" and only "on the assurance the physicians gave that she would live above three months" and was rushing back to Blois not only to see her dying daughter-in-law but also to nurse her through sickness. Margaret's description of Louise of Savoy's reaction to Claude's death gives lie to claims that Louise treated her son's wife badly. In fact, Claude's death, and Louise's absence at her deathbed, plunged the unbreakable Madame Regent into a state of deep melancholy. Margaret was also devastated, although, as spiritually inclined as she was, she believed that the Queen departed in joy to paradise, and therefore there was no reason to despair. Her letter is the most detailed and accurate description of Queen Claude's last hours:

"Therefore, in this hour of tribulation, the contrary ought to be felt, considering that all mortal pains and labours are ended, and eternal repose secured to the soul of her whom God had given us for our Queen; of whom it may be truly said that none before her ever bestowed on the nation such fair and precious gifts: these are that exalted renown for virtue, grace, and goodness, with which she was so richly endowed, a face and person that none could wish more comely, and the boon which she has conferred on France of three sons and three daughters. To make a suitable ending to so virtuous a life, she (the Queen) has committed to the care of her only and much loved husband, the execution of her last will and testament, in which she has nominated him her sole executor, and bequeathed to him her duchy of Brittany, which is to revert at his decease to her eldest son; thus wisely perpetuating union and concord throughout the kingdom. She received the sacrament of confession, and retained her understanding and speech until the last, when she departed, as I believe, in joyous hope, leaving to her friends and relatives such deep affliction for her loss that I have great fears lest the health of Madame may suffer greatly..."[11]

Because Francis I was preparing for war, Claude was embalmed and temporarily laid to rest in the Saint-Calais Chapel in Blois. An air of sanctity surrounded the late Queen, whose body was said to have performed miracles.[12]

Claude's death was not the only tragedy that befell the French royal family in 1524. On 18 September, only two months after Claude, Madame Charlotte died of measles. Charlotte was the second daughter of Francis I to die during her father's lifetime, Madame Louise having died six years earlier. The eight-year-old Charlotte was her aunt's favourite, and Margaret of Alençon kept constant vigil by her niece's bed. Knowing that neither her brother nor her mother could cope with the knowledge of Charlotte's grave illness, Margaret decided to keep it secret until Charlotte's recovery, but she unburdened herself in a letter to Briçonnet:

"My sorrow is that it has pleased God to inflict upon Madame Charlotte so grievous a malady of fever and flux after her measles that I know not whether it may not be His good pleasure to take her to Himself without suffering her longer to taste the miseries of this world. As Madame [Louise of Savoy] is not yet strong enough to endure the smallest sorrow, I conceal this from her and from the King likewise, for you are aware that he has enough to think about elsewhere. Therefore, as upon me alone this care must fall, I ask the help of your fervent prayers that as the Almighty wills, so it may be done. I pray you not to grow weary in giving me that succour which my unbelief renders so necessary. I hope that ere messenger reaches you that she [Madame Charlotte] may be relieved from apprehension of death; or else may have attained that state which we all ought to desire rather than dread, but which grace can alone comprehend—that grace which especially with all her imperfections needs..."[13]

Louise of Savoy eventually learned about her granddaughter's death through the indiscretion of one of her servants and cried from dinner to supper, suffering "such intense and almost insupportable bodily pain" that Margaret, who came to comfort her mother, believed that she beheld "a soul wrapped in ecstasy of spiritual transport".[14] Francis I was equally inconsolable, but he said that he would rather die than wish his daughter back in this world against God's will. The deaths of his wife and daughter marked the end of a certain era for Francis. Although he would remarry in the years to come, he would have no more legitimate children. These two deaths, as it later turned out, were just a prelude to a series of tragedies that awaited the French King and his family.

NOTES

[1] *Journal de Jean Barrillon*, Volume 2, p. 108.
[2] Guillaume Briçonnet, Marguerite d'Angoulême, *Correspondance (1521-1524)*, Volume 2, p. 64.
[3] *Letters and Papers, Foreign and Domestic, Henry VIII*, Volume 4, 1524-1530, n. 155.
[4] *Calendar of State Papers, Spain*, Volume 2, 1509-1525, n. 650.
[5] Auguste Cullerier, *De quelle maladie est mort François Ier*, p. 11.
[6] *Calendar of State Papers, Spain*: Further Supplement To Volumes 1 and 2, entries for 30 March and 15 April 1524.

[7] *Letters and Papers, Foreign and Domestic, Henry VIII,* Volume 4, 1524-1530, n. 606.
[8] The seventeenth-century historian Scévole de Sainte-Marthe claimed that Claude suffered from a skin condition referred to as "une espèce de darte", which her doctors didn't know how to cure. Georges Touchard-Lafosse, *Histoire de Blois*, p. 154.
[9] François Génin, *Lettres de Marguerite d'Angoulême*, pp. 166-167.
[10] Robert de La Marck, seigneur de Fleuranges, *Mémoires du maréchal de Florange, dit le Jeune Adventureaux*, Volume 2, p. 148
[11] François Génin, *Lettres de Marguerite d'Angoulême*, op.cit.
[12] Read more in Chapter 10.
[13] H. Noel Williams, *The Pearl of Princesses: The Life of Marguerite d'Angoulême, Queen of Navarre*, p. 156.
[14] Ibid., p. 157.

CHAPTER 9
"TO SEE AND TO BE SEEN"

When Francis I departed on a war campaign for Italy, Louise of Savoy—appointed regent yet again—feared that her impetuous son "would advance too quickly before he assembled sufficient forces" and begged Anne de Montmorency to prevent any such action.[1] Louise's fears were justified. When she received news that the French army was disastrously defeated at Pavia and her son captured and taken prisoner of Charles V, she became hysterical but quickly regained her composure.

Among his first actions during his imprisonment, Francis I sought permission to write to his mother. In a heartfelt letter, he stated that "all things here remain to me naught save honour and life, which are safe". Knowing Louise of Savoy better than anyone else, Francis begged her not to despair but "to employ your usual prudence, for I cherish hope that in the end God will not forsake me; recommending your grandchildren and my children to your care . . ."[2] Louise's reply, couched in the language of motherly love and affection, was equally tender:

"Monseigneur,

I cannot make a better beginning to my letter than by praising God that He has been pleased to preserve your honour, your life, and your health; of which under your own hand you have been pleased to assure me. This news has been of such comfort to us in our tribulation that it cannot be sufficiently expressed; also that you are now in the hands of so worthy a man [Viceroy of Naples], who treats you so well. Monseigneur, hearing these things, and that it is your intention to endure with resignation the ills that God has inflicted upon you, I, for my part, likewise promise to bear this reverse as you hope and desire, in such manner, for the aid of your little children and the affairs of the kingdom, that I shall not be the occasion of greater grief to you. I beseech God, Monseigneur, to have you in His holy keeping, as prays with all her heart.

Your very humble and good mother and subject, Louise".[3]

While Louise of Savoy was devising plans to release her son from captivity, Henry VIII celebrated his rival's defeat. He was informed about the outcome of the battle on the morning of 9 March 1525. "Did you see the King of France in the hands of the Viceroy of Naples, as this letter testifies?" he quizzed the messenger. The messenger replied that he helped to disarm the French King, who was lying on the ground beneath his horse.

Francis was slightly wounded on the cheek and in the hand, but overall he was in good health. When Henry VIII learned that Richard de la Pole, known as "the White Rose", was killed in the battle, he had yet another reason to celebrate because de la Pole was the last Yorkist pretender to the Tudor throne. "All the enemies of England are gone", Henry shouted and ordered free wine to be distributed and bonfires to be lit across the country. He now wanted to proceed with his intended invasion of France to regain the ancient claim of the English Kings. Henry strongly opposed the idea that Francis should be ransomed, believing that "his line and succession ought to be abolished, removed and utterly extinct".[4] But to carve France into pieces, he needed the promised help of Charles V. This never materialized, and Charles entered the negotiations for the French King's release with Louise of Savoy. Henry, disappointed with Charles V, also decided to seek the French alliance, resulting in the Treaty of the More signed on 31 August 1525.

Louise of Savoy was unable to leave France in order to negotiate with Charles V in Spain, but she decided to send her recently widowed daughter, Margaret of Alençon, as an envoy extraordinaire to Charles V's court. After gathering her entourage and receiving a safe conduct from the emperor, Margaret set sail on 28 August 1525 and reached the outskirts of Madrid on 19 September. She found her brother in such a condition that she feared he might die soon because Francis was racked by fever, and even Charles V visited the French King's bedside to make sure he was well taken care of. The memoirist Guillaume du Bellay, who accompanied Margaret to Spain, later recalled that upon her arrival, the Duchess of Alençon "found the Emperor, who had come to visit him [Francis], not through any kindness towards him but, in my opinion, because he feared he might die, causing him to lose his prisoner, and the spoils of his victory".[5] Margaret nursed her beloved brother through what she believed was his last illness and had an altar set up in his chamber so that Mass could be said in his presence. Francis's condition was so serious that he received the last rites but eventually recovered and later claimed that "without her [Margaret], he would have died".[6]

Margaret had one aim when she came to Spain: to negotiate the peace treaty with Charles V and thus secure her brother's release as soon as possible. Two of the most rational proposals touched on Margaret's marriage to Charles and Francis's marriage to Charles's sister, Eleanor, as means of reconciliation for both monarchs. Shortly before her arrival, the English ambassadors to Charles V's court reported dismissively that Frenchmen who were already in Spain "are more fit than a woman to treat" and Margaret, "being young and a widow, comes, as Ovid says of women going to see a play, to see and to be seen, that, perhaps, the Emperor may like her". Furthermore, she might also "woo the Queen dowager of Portugal [Eleanor] for her brother, which no one else dares do without the Emperor's knowledge". Fearing that the two women might work together, the English ambassadors added that "as they are both young widows", Margaret "shall find good commodity in cackling with her [Eleanor] to advance her brother's matter, and if she finds her inclined thereto, they will help each other".[7] This "cackling" and Margaret's proposed marriage to the emperor was what worried the English ambassadors the most, but Henry VIII was of a very different opinion. Margaret, he informed his ambassadors in instructions dating to September 1525, went to Spain partly with Henry's connivance to save her brother, not to arrange her own marriage to Charles V. Her real aim, according to the English King, "is to persuade her brother not to give up anything derogatory to his crown or dignity". Henry now saw himself as the mediator who would help the French to release their King from captivity, but he was eager to make sure that the marriage between Francis I and the emperor's sister Eleanor would never take place. This marriage, Henry claimed, would not only bring no satisfaction to both sides, but, above all, it would impair Louise of Savoy's authority, as it later truly did.[8] These two September dispatches show a different side of Henry VIII. Unlike his ambassadors, who were clearly prone to see women in a misogynistic way, Henry had no doubts that both Louise of Savoy and Margaret of Alençon were as able politicians as men. He closed his letter of instructions by telling his ambassadors to stop questioning Louise of Savoy's authority to practice foreign policy.

Henry VIII was right. Margaret had no intention of marrying Charles V, and it remains speculative whether the emperor seriously considered her as a candidate for a wife. Although described as "rich, a widow, young and with a very large dowry", Margaret was already thirty-three years old, and, although married for fifteen years, she had no children by her late husband.[9] In her private correspondence, Margaret frequently made references to her "sterility" and bemoaned the fact that she had no children. The emperor, whose priority was to sire heirs, certainly saw Margaret's age and childlessness as obstacles. Furthermore, he knew how devoted Margaret was to her brother, and this meant that she would never be fully devoted to the imperial cause. What's more important, the two also did not like each other on a personal level. "I found him quite cold", Margaret informed Francis in October. "He drew me into his chamber, accompanied by a woman, but his remarks did not justify all this formality, for he put me off to consult with his council and said he would give me a reply today".[10] After this encounter, Charles took Margaret to introduce her to his sister, Eleanor.

Eleanor was twenty-seven, attractive and already somewhat acquainted with Francis I, her future husband. In July, the French King bribed his captor, Viceroy Charles de

Lannoy, to send a love letter to Eleanor. Francis played a chivalrous lover to perfection, and Eleanor, charmed with what she had heard about the French King, was overjoyed.[11] Eleanor was a woman who, deep down in her heart, dreamed about a romantic love match. As a teenager, she fell in love with Frederick of Bavaria, prince of the Palatinate, and pursued this relationship as if she controlled her own destiny. Charles had detected and broken off this match because he needed Eleanor for a more important dynastic union. He arranged Eleanor's marriage to Manuel, King of Portugal, who had been previously married to two of Eleanor's aunts. The marriage was purely political. Manuel was sickly and almost thirty years older than Eleanor. The marriage lasted for three years, during which Eleanor bore a son, who died shortly after birth, and a daughter, Infanta Maria, with whom Eleanor was separated when she returned to Spain after Manuel's death. Eleanor's name had been linked to Francis I's for several years prior to their engagement. If we are to believe what Henry VIII wrote in the instructions for his ambassadors to Charles's court, the French King entertained hopes of marrying Eleanor as early as February 1518, when his wife, Claude, was pregnant and it was believed she might die during childbirth. The following excerpt is interesting and worth quoting at some length:

"When the ambassadors have an opportunity of speaking to the King [Charles of Spain] alone, they shall tell him that Francis is not much attached to his Queen [Claude], who is of small stature and not beautiful, and as she is now with child there may be some danger in her delivery; on which account Francis, hearing of the singular beauty of the Lady Eleanor, Charles's eldest sister, and considering her prospects in relation to the succession of Spain, is endeavouring to prevent her being married into Portugal, that if his own Queen die he may marry her . . . The King [Henry VIII] therefore urges Charles to give up the French marriage, and ally himself without loss of time with the house of Portugal, or elsewhere, so that he may shortly have an heir."[12]

This report seems to have been Henry VIII's cunning way of dissuading Charles from the French alliance he was contemplating at the time. Death in childbirth was always a possibility, especially considering Queen Claude's ill health, and rumours about the risk of her death during labour circulated before she gave birth to her first child in 1515.[13] In 1518, however, Claude was pregnant for the third time and had successfully undergone two labours in the past; for Henry to claim that Francis was hoping for his wife's death in childbirth was merely a tactic to rush Charles into concluding the alliance with Portugal. Henry also cunningly exploited Francis's extramarital affairs to claim that he was not very devoted to his wife, but this was not the case. Francis had mistresses, but he treated Claude with utmost respect and knew that marriage to her was politically very important as she was the former King's daughter. Had there been no Salic law in France, Claude could have been Queen in her own right.

Shortly before Claude's death in the summer of 1524, Charles V, informed of her deteriorating health and slim chances of survival, hoped to arrange a match between Francis and Eleanor, but this plan came to nothing at the time because Francis was more interested in waging war against Charles than in concluding peace with him. This seems to be the ultimate proof that Henry VIII's intimations of 1518 were false; in choosing a wife, the French King was more interested in political advantages than personal tastes. Henry suggested that Francis was ready to marry Eleanor in 1518 chiefly because of her "singular beauty" as well as her place in the Spanish succession, but this was far from the truth, as later events clearly showed. This was the major difference between the two monarchs. Whereas Francis perceived marriages as purely political arrangements, Henry sought romantic love in each of his six marriages and selected his wives based on his feelings rather than political gain.[14] As we will shortly see, Henry was even ready to risk war to marry the woman he loved.

As to Eleanor of Portugal, she clearly hoped that her impending marriage to Francis I would prove to be a happy one, and she had every reason to believe her dream would come true. Not everyone was as enthusiastic, however. Charles

V used Eleanor as a pawn and, although he clearly considered her marriage to Francis a real possibility, around the time when Francis sent her a love letter, Charles told the French ambassador that he had no sister to offer Francis, "as the one he had belonged already to Monsieur de Bourbon".[15] Charles was referring to Eleanor's potential engagement to Charles III, Duke of Bourbon, who was the last of the great feudal lords to oppose Francis I.[16] Bourbon sent his agent, Monsieur de Lursi, to Toledo in the summer of 1525 to pick up all the rumours and news circulating at the imperial court. After Eleanor's audience with the French ambassador, Monsieur de Lursi came to visit her and "in a long discourse endeavoured to deter her from marrying the King of France". He used strong arguments to discourage Eleanor from marrying Francis and to dissipate her overly romantic view of him. He started by saying that "of the King personally, he neither would nor could speak evil, as he was a very gallant sovereign; but she must first of all remember that she would pass under the yoke of Madame the Regent, who was a most terrible woman, and would treat her like a servant wench".[17] We must take this remark with a touch of reserve because de Lursi's aim was to convince Eleanor that a match with Francis was not good for her.

Louise of Savoy was known as a resolute, prudent and energetic woman with a forceful personality; whether de Lursi's observation was exaggerated or at least partly based on what he knew about her treatment of Queen Claude is difficult to establish. Was he hinting that Louise would treat Eleanor badly because she herself once nurtured hope of marrying the Duke of Bourbon? The rumour once circulated at court that Louise of Savoy was Bourbon's mistress and intended to become his wife. The only evidence of any form of relationship between Louise and Bourbon was hinted at by the imperial ambassador Jean de Saint-Mauris, who wrote that "there is a great displeasure between the King Francis and the Duke of Bourbon, perhaps because he will not marry Madame the Regent, who loves him much".[18] Was de Lursi making it clear to Eleanor that Louise would try to revenge herself upon her because Bourbon preferred to marry the emperor's sister rather than the French King's mother? This we will never know, but it remains a tantalising possibility, reminding us that history is not only about dates and wars but about people like us, prone to all feelings known to humanity.

As if invoking Louise of Savoy's wrath wasn't enough, Monsieur de Lursi reminded Eleanor of what happened to the French King's first wife. Francis "had been and was much diseased with pox, which malady the late Queen caught from him and died of it". Furthermore, if Eleanor naively believed that Francis would be faithful to her, she was wrong because "the King's amorous temperament would always render her the most jealous woman in the world". These were the main points of de Lursi's discourse, although he also pointed out that any children Eleanor might have by Francis would follow the King's three sons, and the Dauphin would always look first to "aggrandize his other brothers" after the King's death. It was true, however, that if the King's sons were to die, Eleanor's children by Francis would inherit the Crown.

At the time, this all seemed like an excessively gloomy vision of Eleanor's future, but, as she was later to experience, her marriage was as unhappy as Monsieur de Lursi predicted. Monsieur de Lursi, however, was wrong if he believed that Eleanor had anything to say about her future marriage. Her destiny lay in the hands of her brother, and she was well aware of this fact. She might have dreamed about love and happiness, but she was never free to choose her husband. She concluded her interview with Monsieur de Lursi by telling him that "she meant to do whatever should be commanded her by the Emperor, her lord, whose will she would never dispute in anything".[19]

When Margaret of Alençon came to visit Eleanor on 3 October 1525, the two women clearly started their relationship on good footing. In a letter to her royal brother, Margaret related that she stayed with Eleanor "until quite late". Eleanor "spoke to me in terms of great friendliness", Margaret recorded and hoped that she could use Eleanor as a means of influencing her brother the emperor. Unfortunately, Charles never let his sister influence his opinions or political actions. Quite the contrary; it was Eleanor who had to obey him in everything. Sensing that the two women could bond, Charles wanted to prevent it and ordered his sister to depart for Guadalajara. "I think she goes more by obedience than by choice, for they keep her very much in subjection", was Margaret's observation.[20] The English ambassadors at Charles V's court remarked that Margaret was greatly disappointed by Eleanor's departure.[21]

Margaret's negotiations with Charles V reached a stumbling block when the emperor raised the question of Burgundy. The duchy had reverted to the French Crown when Charles the Bold died without male heirs in 1477 and Louis XI was recognized as its liege lord. Charles V, as the grandson of Charles the Bold's daughter Mary, Duchess of Burgundy, had always regarded the duchy as his lawful inheritance and was determined to recover it. The French were loath to lose Burgundy, and Margaret realised that she had reached a stalemate and had to return home.

Margaret was always honest, often to the point of annoying Charles. She found the Spaniards "unreasonable", and she described dealing with them as "painful". Charles, on the other hand, was tired of Margaret's manoeuvrings and was especially angry when he learned that she wanted to arrange her brother's escape. Charles was eager to see Margaret out of his country, and on 23 November 1525, he signed a safe conduct. She had to leave Spain by 31 January.[22] Margaret and Charles did not even have a final audience. Instead, Margaret wrote him a letter apologizing for not saying good-bye to him in person and expressing hope that the intended marriage of her brother and his sister would serve as a means of facilitating peace between the two monarchs. On her way home, she bombarded Francis with letters asking him to recall her and assuring that she did everything in her power to release him from captivity. She informed her brother that the emperor demanded Burgundy and refused a large ransom.

The French King's situation looked truly hopeless. Shortly before Margaret's departure, Francis drew up an edict of abdication, appointing the Dauphin as the new king and his mother as the regent. The edict was probably intended to rush Charles V into action because it also stipulated that the Dauphin should relinquish the throne if his father was able to return home. The plan failed, and the emperor made it clear he would always demand Burgundy. Finally, Louise of Savoy decided to accept Charles V's condition: she was prepared to lose Burgundy. Her son could not remain imprisoned, and, knowing Charles V's resolve, she feared Francis faced many more years of captivity. The King's son was too young to rule, and Louise, always the realist, knew that she was too weak to be a regent much longer. She believed it was pointless to fight for Burgundy while France needed its King.

Francis shared his mother's opinion. On 14 January 1526, he signed the Treaty of Madrid with the emperor, abandoning Burgundy along with his claims in Italy and Artois. He agreed to marry the emperor's sister, Eleanor, and hand over the Dauphin and his second son as hostages to ensure the fulfillment of the treaty. Francis demanded that Charles consent to his being set at liberty before the treaty's implementation, arguing that only he could convince his subjects to relinquish such a vast territory as Burgundy. The French King never intended to keep the promises he made, however, swearing an oath that he was compelled to submit by force.

On 20 January 1526, Francis I was betrothed to Eleanor of Portugal by proxy. He was still recovering from his illness; he had recently suffered from fever and was pale when the English ambassadors visited him eight days later. In mid-February, Francis and Charles met again, and the French King was taken to Illescas to finally meet Eleanor, his future bride. Eleanor was presented to Francis at the foot of the stairs ascending the great hall of the castle. She stood a step higher, having Germaine, Dowager Queen of Aragon, on her right and Don Hernandez Velasco, Constable of Castile, on her left. When Charles V introduced his sister to the French King, Eleanor tried to kneel and kiss his hand, but Francis, playing the role of a chivalrous gallant of courtly love tradition, stepped forward and insisted on embracing her as his wife. Giving her his hand, Francis then led Eleanor into the great hall, where four royal seats stood on a richly decorated dais. Francis and Eleanor sat together while Charles V placed Queen Germaine, his mistress, on his right. The four royal personages banqueted together, and the next day Eleanor, at the request of her brother, performed a Spanish dance in front of Francis.[23]

The news of the treaty reached France on 29 January 1526. Louise of Savoy ordered prayers and a procession to celebrate her son's delivery, but her joy was clouded by the fact that her two grandsons, Francis and Henri, were to be delivered to the emperor's court as hostages. On 1 February 1526, she set out for Blois. The English ambassador, Dr John Taylor, complained that the journey was especially difficult because "within two miles of Blois, the Loire had so increased that the whole country was flooded, and the wind was so ragious that no man might pass over without great danger". On 17 February, the ambassador dined with Dauphin Francis and his brother, Henri, and then visited Louise of Savoy in her private quarters. The King's mother, "though troubled with the gout in her hand", was preparing for further journey to Bayonne.[24] She was eager to be present at her son's homecoming and the transfer of her grandsons.

While travelling towards Bayonne, she learned that Francis reached the town on 10 March, but Louise did not arrive until five days later, exhausted and anxious. Dr Taylor reported that she "was in such great anxiety for the sending forth of the Dauphin and his brother, and for great desire to see the King her son, that she could attend to no other thing".[25] On 17 March 1526, on the Bidasoa River, at the French and Spanish border, the exchange of hostages took place. Francis I embraced his two eldest sons and promised them that he would soon bring them back home. In reality, it would be six years before the King saw his sons again.

NOTES

[1] Kathleen Wellman, *Queens and Mistresses of Renaissance France*, p. 139.
[2] H. Noel Williams, *The Pearl of Princesses: The Life of Marguerite d'Angoulême, Queen of Navarre*, p. 169.
[3] Ibid., 171.
[4] J.J. Scarisbrick, *Henry VIII*, pp. 136-139.
[5] Patricia Francis Cholakian, Rouben Charles Cholakian, *Marguerite de Navarre: Mother of the Renaissance*, p. 116.
[6] Pierre de Bourdeille, seigneur de Brantôme, *The Book of the Ladies*, p. 238.
[7] *Letters and Papers, Foreign and Domestic, Henry VIII, Volume 4*, 1524-1530, n. 1485.
[8] Ibid., n. 1628, 1655.
[9] Ibid., n. 1555.
[10] François Génin, *Lettres de Marguerite d'Angoulême*, p. 188.
[11] *Calendar of State Papers Relating To English Affairs in the Archives of Venice, Volume 3*, 1520-1526, n. 1063.
[12] *Letters and Papers, Foreign and Domestic, Henry VIII, Volume 2*, 1515-1518, n. 4136.
[13] Read more in Chapter 5.
[14] The only marriage Henry made out of political obligation was to Anne of Cleves. This union ended in disaster, as set out in Chapter 16.

[15] *Calendar of State Papers Relating To English Affairs in the Archives of Venice, Volume 3,* 1520-1526, n. 1066.

[16] As noticed by Kathleen Wellman in *Queens and Mistresses of the Renaissance France*, the tale of Bourbon's plot against the French King is "a complex tale of the accretion of power by a nobleman" (p. 134). Such a study would be a major undertaking in its own right and therefore falls beyond the scope of this book.

[17] *Calendar of State Papers Relating To English Affairs in the Archives of Venice, Volume 3,* 1520-1526, op.cit.

[18] Whether this was indeed the case remains speculative. Historians point out that this intriguing report was "not followed up on" as it would certainly have been, considering that it touched Madame the Regent's person. Kathleen Wellman, *Queens and Mistresses of the Renaissance France*, p. 135.

[19] *Calendar of State Papers Relating To English Affairs in the Archives of Venice, Volume 3,* 1520-1526, op.cit.

[20] François Génin, *Lettres de Marguerite d'Angoulême*, p. 189.

[21] *Letters and Papers, Foreign and Domestic, Henry VIII,* Volume 4, 1524-1530, n. 1799.

[22] Patricia F. Cholakian and Rouben C. Cholakian, *Marguerite de Navarre: Mother of the Renaissance*, pp. 121-122.

[23] M. Aimé Champollion-Figeac, *Captivité du Roi François Ier*, p. 504.

[24] *Letters and Papers, Foreign and Domestic, Henry VIII,* Volume 4, 1524-1530, n. 1999.

[25] Ibid., n. 2032.

CHAPTER 10
WON AND LOST CAUSES

When Francis I left Spain, Eleanor of Portugal believed that she would soon join him in France. At the end of January 1526, the French ambassador reported that Louise of Savoy was pleased at the deliverance of her son and his intended marriage to Eleanor, and that "she will be glad if the lady might be sent to Bayonne, and the marriage consummated immediately".[1] As it was soon to become apparent, Louise and the whole of France were to wait for the new Queen's arrival for several years.

Upon Francis I's return, it was agreed that when the principal conditions of the Treaty of Madrid had been fulfilled, Eleanor should bring her stepsons with her to France. By May 1526, Henry VIII was heard saying: "I marvel if the French King will have her [Eleanor], for there did run an evil bruit upon her. Howbeit, the possibility of succession that doth appear by her is great".[2] What "evil bruit" was circulating about Eleanor at the time Henry did not say, and in any case, Francis had already started manoeuvring to avoid the ratification of the Treaty of Madrid.

There was also the necessity of arranging a lavish funeral for his first wife, Queen Claude, whose embalmed body was still lying unburied in Blois, where it had been enclosed in a lead coffin and placed in the chapel of Saint-Calais.[3] A manuscript currently stored in Bibliothèque Abbé Grégoire in Blois contains a sketch of wax effigies of Queen Claude and Madame Charlotte lying in state on a richly decorated bed under a canopy of estate.[4] At the foot of the bed stands a bench with a tall cross. The Queen's effigy is shown with her hands clasped, wearing a sleeveless surcoat, a mantle furred with ermines and a crown, with a sceptre and a hand of justice lying freely on cushions alongside. Charlotte, with her hands clasped and hair loose, is lying next to her mother.

As beloved in death as she was in life, many people believed in Queen Claude's sanctity, and it was said that "the gentle lady performed miracles".[5] By 1526, fuelled by claims of posthumous miracles, the strength of Claude's cult caused several persons to carry offerings and candles to the chapel of Saint-Calais in Blois. There were people, including one woman claiming that Queen Claude had cured her from fever which had long tormented her, who "attested that they were cured and saved from some malady by her merits and intercessions".[6] How Francis I, his mother and sister viewed the claims of these supposed miracles remains unknown.[7]

Although Claude's death plunged him into deep mourning, at the time when her body was prepared to be moved to the Basilica of St Denis, Francis I was said to have been "occupying himself in his disports and passing the time in hunting".[8] Louise of Savoy informed the English ambassador John Clerk that she intended to be present "at the solemnity of the setting forward of the body of the said late Queen" to St Denis planned for 15 September 1526, but her sickness—probably another painful bout of gout—prevented her from attending. By 5 October, the cortege carrying the late Queen's body was already on its way to St Denis; she was finally buried there on 6 November 1526.[9] Claude's daughter, Charlotte, who died two months after the Queen, was buried that same day.[10]

Although Francis I was formally engaged to Charles V's sister, it was unthinkable that a man of his appetites should remain celibate, especially because it remained unclear whether the marriage to Eleanor would ever take place. Before Francis was captured in Pavia, he was romantically involved with Françoise de Foix, his official royal mistress, who often played a ceremonial role at court. But when he returned home, he was no longer interested in his mistress. Louise of Savoy, who always detested Françoise de Foix, decided to introduce her son to a teenaged Anne de Pisseleu, who captured the King's heart right away.

Whereas Françoise was famously dark, with her olive complexion and black hair, Anne was a pale, blue-eyed blond. Her beauty was highly praised, although the English ambassador remarked that he saw nothing remarkable about Anne's appearance.[11] Françoise could not understand why she had been set aside. She and Francis had previously engaged in writing verses to each other, and upon discovering the King's feelings for Anne, Françoise criticized his choice, writing that "the colour white should be scorned. . . but the dark complexion and the colour black is of high price and great value". The King did not appreciate his former sweetheart's interference and sharply replied: "If I had not held you so dear for the time I spent with you, I could say, 'rest in peace'". Françoise could only bitterly complain: "You have made a change from one who loved you so much to a strange Amie".[12] Yet it was Anne de Pisseleu who would hold the King's interest until his death twenty-one years later.

The King of France had no intention of honouring the stipulations of the Treaty of Madrid. "I shall take off my mask", he was heard saying to the English ambassadors. When the English special envoy, Thomas Cheyne, had an audience with Francis I on 9 April 1526, the King received him very graciously and went as far as to say that "his deliverance was due to his good brother and best friend, the King of England, for if any man had occasion to have been cruel against him, considering the war betwixt them and the time of his captivity, it was the King of England".[13] Henry VIII decided to use Francis I's gratitude to his advantage and offered him his own daughter, the ten-year-old Princess Mary, as a bride. This offer took Francis by surprise. "I pray you, repeat unto me none of all these matters", he told the English ambassadors. He praised Henry VIII's only daughter, telling the English ambassadors that:

"I know well enough her education, her form and fashion, her beauty and virtue, and what father and mother she cometh of, and how expedient and necessary it shall be for me and for my realm that I marry her. And I assure you for the same causes I have as great a mind to her as ever I had to any woman; but I must do my things as near as I can without displeasure of God and reproach of the world".[14]

Francis may have, perhaps, paused to think about all those years he and Henry were at odds. There was a time when the French King laughed at Henry's wife, Katharine of Aragon, and disparaged her for the lack of male heirs: "He [Henry] has an old deformed wife, while he himself is young and handsome".[15] Now, whatever his personal opinion of the English Queen—who was the aunt of his chief enemy, Charles V—Francis had to extoll her and heap praises upon her only daughter. Princess Mary, most recently engaged to Charles V, had been jilted when the emperor married his cousin, Isabella of Portugal, in March 1526.[16] But Francis was unwilling to enter marriage negotiations with England, claiming that he was pre-contracted to Eleanor of Portugal after all. But it soon became apparent that the English alliance was more profitable. Francis intended to send an embassy to Charles V's court and demand Eleanor be sent to France; if this was denied, Francis would marry whomever he pleased and, as Louise of Savoy remarked, "her son's mind had been for a long season clearly fixed upon the daughter of England as upon that thing that should be most profitable to both realms".[17] Despite this, both Louise and Francis knew that if they wanted to see the King's sons, they had to ally with the emperor. Francis made it clear that he would not marry Eleanor for her own sake, but only to recover his sons. He would marry not only the emperor's sister, he said, but even his mule if that guaranteed his sons' safe return to France. Eleanor, in the meantime, decided to make a statement and exchanged her widow's apparel for new clothes and started using the title of Queen of France.

The English ambassadors were afraid that Francis was merely tricking them. He liked Eleanor more than he wanted to admit, they claimed. John Clerk was told that when Francis was in Spain, "he seemed to have had great pleasure in Madame Eleanor's company, and to this day he speaks now and then very good and pleasant words of her".[18] Despite all this, Francis decided to abandon the imperial alliance and enter marriage negotiations with England.

It seems almost unbelievable that Henry VIII seriously considered giving his daughter to the French King. She was only eleven years old, and when the French ambassadors saw her in the spring of 1527, they concluded that she was "so thin, spare and small as to make it impossible for her to be married for the next three years".[19] Louise of Savoy, sensing that the marriage proposal might have been a trap to keep Francis out of the imperial alliance, suggested a solution that even the English ambassadors found shocking. If anyone believed that Princess Mary was too young to be married to the man twenty-two years her senior, Louise saw no danger because "she herself was married at eleven". She suggested that Francis I and Henry VIII should meet in Calais, where the marriage between her son and the English King's daughter should be solemnized. After the ceremony, Francis and Mary should consummate their match to ensure its validity; it didn't have to be a long consummation, it sufficed that Francis might "abide himself for an hour or less with the princess". Louise assured that her son was "a man of honour and discretion and would use no violence". This, Louise claimed, would be means of assuring that Francis was legally married to the English princess and Henry VIII could take her back to England "unto such time as she should be thought more able". The English ambassadors thought the proposal "very strange" and, indeed, such proceedings were unheard of even in the sixteenth century.[20]

Princess Mary, small and undeveloped for her age, was probably not menstruating and thus wasn't a fully grown woman in the eyes of her contemporaries. Although girls were allowed to marry at the age of twelve, sexual intercourse was advised to take place when a girl reached her sixteenth birthday. It stemmed from the belief that between twelve and sixteen, a girl was too young and too fragile to survive the perils of pregnancy and childbirth. Henry VIII's grandmother, Margaret Beaufort, was the best example of what happened to a girl when her marriage was consummated too early. She gave birth when she was only thirteen years old, and this traumatic experience left her damaged and unable to have more children by her successive husbands. Bishop Fisher, Margaret's friend and admirer, marvelled: "It seemed a miracle that of so little a personage anyone should have been born at all". Margaret had certainly believed so as well because many years later she ensured that her young and fragile granddaughter, Margaret Tudor, was not sent to be married to the King of Scotland too early, lest her much older husband would not wait for her to mature "but injure her, and endanger her health".[21] She would have certainly felt the same way about Princess Mary, who, like her grandmother and aunt, was small for her age. Princess Mary would have reached her twelfth birthday (the age of consent) on 18 February 1528, more than a year after the proposed consummation, and even this would not mean that she was able to have intercourse. Indeed, the English ambassadors who thought this proposal was outrageous were loath even to put it in writing. Needless to say that Henry VIII rejected it immediately, arguing that his daughter "was of tender age and there was plenty of time to talk about marrying her".[22]

The peace with France was nevertheless concluded on 30 April 1527, and it was agreed that Princess Mary would either marry King Francis or his second son, Henri, Duke of Orléans. It was also agreed that France and England would send a joint embassy to Charles V to negotiate for the release of Francis's sons and for the payment of the emperor's debts to Henry VIII. By February 1528, France and England had declared war on Charles V, who still insisted on his terms. The emperor tightened his grip on Francis's sons, sending them to a remote castle in Segovia and dismissing all of their French attendants except the Duke of Orléans's dwarf and tutor. Eleanor, hearing of her brother's treatment of her prospective stepsons, fell into melancholy and withdrew to a monastery for a time.[23]

On 3 August 1529, the Treaty of Cambrai was signed. Both Francis I and Charles V, unwilling to meet in person, sent two able women to negotiate. Louise of Savoy, as regent during her son's absences, met with her former sister-in-law,

Archduchess Margaret of Savoy, who acted as Regent of the Netherlands for her nephew, Charles V.[24] The treaty, known also as the Peace of the Ladies, put a temporary stop to the war between Francis I and Charles V. It was agreed that the French King's sons would be ransomed and escorted to France by Francis's fiancée, Eleanor.

After the treaty was signed, Louise of Savoy sent her representatives to Spain to check on her grandsons. Before they left France, Dauphin Francis and his brother, Henri, were cheerful and vivacious boys, but their characters changed significantly during imprisonment. They were held in a dank cell "which had neither tapestries nor hangings of any kind". The only window was wrought in iron bars and placed so high that the two boys could hardly enjoy fresh air and light.[25]

In July 1530, Dauphin Francis and Henri, Duke of Orléans, were escorted to France by Eleanor, the future wife of their father. The new Queen was presented to the court in a series of lavish ceremonies and celebrated by the French as the peacemaker. Her meeting with Francis I was described in the most glowing terms, and the King welcomed her with open arms:

"The meeting took place as was natural between two lovers. The marriage ceremony was then performed, Mass said, and the newly married couple retired to the nuptial chamber.

They have not quitted each other since, whether travelling or at home. The King and his subjects, high and low, spare no means of doing the Queen's pleasure, and no wonder, for it is impossible to possess more graceful manners, frankness, and sweet dignity than she has, at which all those who surround her are enchanted, saying that she is the real cause of this honourable peace."[26]

For the time being, Eleanor was happy, and her future by Francis I's side looked bright. But this was only an illusion, as she was soon to discover.

NOTES

[1] *Letters and Papers, Foreign and Domestic, Henry VIII,* Volume 4, 1524-1530, n. 1950.
[2] Ibid., n. 2215.
[3] Ibid, n. 2520. *Journal d'un bourgeois de Paris sous le règne de François Ier,* 1515-1536, p. 207.
[4] *Manuscrit des Funérailles de Claude de France et Charlotte sa Fille,* Blois-Agglopolys, Bibliothèque Abbé Grégoire, Fonds patrimonial, ms. 245.
[5] *Journal d'un bourgeois de Paris sous le règne de François Ier,* 1515-1536, p. 207.
[6] Ibid. See also Pierre de Bourdeille, seigneur de Brantôme, *The Book of the Ladies,* p. 220.
[7] Usually, claims of posthumous miracles constituted the prelude to processes of beatification and canonisation, as was the case with Jeanne of France, the first wife of Claude's father, but no one has ever furthered the cause of Queen Claude's beatification.
[8] *Letters and Papers, Foreign and Domestic, Henry VIII,* Volume 4, 1524-1530, n. 2520.

[9] Ibid., n. 2544.
Journal d'un bourgeois de Paris sous le règne de François Ier, 1515-1536, pp. 207-8.
[10] Ibid. The anonymous author of *Journal d'un bourgeois de Paris sous le règne de François Ier* asserted that the daughter buried with Claude was Madame Louise, who "was about six years old" at the time of her death. This, however, is incorrect. Madame Louise died as a two-year-old in 1517; it was Madame Charlotte who was buried with her mother in 1526.
[11] R.J. Knecht, *Francis I*, p. 192.
[12] Kathleen Wellman, *Queens and Mistresses of Renaissance France*, p. 144.
[13] *Letters and Papers, Foreign and Domestic, Henry VIII,* Volume 4, 1524-1530, n. 2079, 2091.
[14] Ibid., n. 2606.
[15] *Calendar of State Papers Relating To English Affairs in the Archives of Venice,* Volume 2, 1509-1519, n. 1230.
[16] She was a daughter of Katharine of Aragon's sister, Maria of Aragon, and thus Katharine's niece.
[17] *Letters and Papers, Foreign and Domestic, Henry VIII,* Volume 4, 1524-1530, n. 2651.
[18] Ibid., n. 2705, 2707.
[19] *Calendar of State Papers Relating To English Affairs in the Archives of Venice,* Volume 4, 1527-1533, n. 105.
[20] *Letters and Papers, Foreign and Domestic, Henry VIII,* Volume 4, 1524-1530, n. 2981.
[21] Sarah Gristwood, *Blood Sisters*, p. 49.
[22] *Letters and Papers, Foreign and Domestic, Henry VIII,* Volume 4, 1524-1530, n. 2988.
[23] Ibid., n. 3982.
[24] Margaret married Louise's younger brother, Philibert of Savoy.
[25] H. Noel Williams, *Henri II: His Court and Times,* pp. 52-55.
[26] *Calendar of State Papers, Spain,* Volume 4 Part 1, *Henry VIII,* 1529-1530, n. 368.

CHAPTER 11
LOVE AND LOSS

Early in 1531, preparations were made for Eleanor's coronation. Although Francis I lavished gifts upon her and spared no expense to enhance her appearance, the Queen soon discovered that her husband had no romantic feelings for her. The King, in the thralls of love with Anne de Pisseleu, was already showing signs of tiring of Eleanor. The Queen was crowned at St Denis on 5 March 1531 and made her official entry into the city of Paris on the sixteenth day of that month. She wore a mantle of purple velvet decorated with bands of gold, a pearl-embroidered bodice and an overdress trimmed with ermine.[1] By all accounts, Eleanor, who was "clad richly and pompously with regard to her habit, pearls, and jewels, which sparkled all over her", cut a striking figure. Sebastiano Giustiniani, one of the Venetian ambassadors to France, reported:

"She was accompanied by the Dauphin and the Duke of Orléans, who, on the right and left, assisted her to support the mantle; and the Cardinals de Grammont and Triulzi, who went from the church to meet her at her palace, held up her arms; the three Duchesses of Vendôme, Lorraine, and Nemours, bearing her train, which was very long indeed. Her Majesty was followed by the most Serene 'Madame', the King's mother, by her daughter the Queen of Navarre [Margaret], by the sister of the King of Navarre, and by the two daughters of his most Christian Majesty, with other ladies, eleven in all, all wearing coronets, as they were all of the blood-royal; and having been conducted to a richly decorated stage prepared in front of the altar, she sat in the middle on a small platform on which was her chair and throne; so that she was seen sitting absolutely alone in her majesty, though the Dauphin and the Duke of Orléans stood immediately behind her the whole time with their hands on the chair. The ceremony of the coronation was performed by giving Her Majesty the honours and insignia usually given to Queens, after which the Mass was sung, the Cardinal de Vendôme officiating with much solemnity and the instruments and music being endless. Four Cardinals were present, besides a great plenty of the chief Bishops of the kingdom, and seven ambassadors resident at the Court, as also many Princes and Barons, so that the greatest part of the chief personages of France attended this ceremony, at which the Lord Steward acted as master of the ceremonies".[2]

The King showed the utmost disrespect towards his wife when he failed to appear at her coronation; even when Kings were absent from the coronations of their wives, they were usually observing the whole ceremony from behind a specially erected screen, but Giustiniani reported that Francis I was absent "nor is he known to have been at St Denis on that day".³ Then, on the day when Eleanor entered Paris, Francis rode to a house where his mistress, Anne de Pisseleu, lived and set her before him in an open window, "devising with her two long hours in the sight and face of all people, which was not a little marvelled at of the beholders".⁴

The English ambassador, Francis Bryan, sent a detailed description of the relations between Francis and Eleanor to Henry VIII. They were not a happy couple because "being both in one house, they lie not together once in four nights" and the French King "speaks very seldom unto her openly". He also spent hours on end in his mother's chambers and rushed to his mistress whenever he pleased.⁵ Two years later the King's sister told the Duke of Norfolk that no man could be less satisfied with his wife than her brother, who failed to have sexual relations with his wife for seven months. When the stunned duke asked why, Margaret replied that it was "because he does not find her pleasing to his appetite". Eleanor, Margaret continued unabashed, "is very hot in bed and desired to be too much embraced", causing Francis to shun her company.⁶ Perhaps one of the reasons for Francis's distaste was Eleanor's appearance. Brantôme wrote that he heard rumours that "when she was dressed, she seemed a very beautiful princess of rich and beautiful height, but when she was undressed, the height of her body appeared so long one would have believed that she

Love and loss

was a giant, but so short were her legs and thighs, she made one think of a dwarf".[7] Whatever she looked like, the new Queen of France found life at court difficult. Her relationship with Francis turned sour, she had to compete for his affection with his mother and mistress and even his erudite sister, who seemed kind and approachable, favoured Anne de Pisseleu, with whom she shared similar interests in literature and religion. Margaret, it seemed, preferred the company of her mother and Francis's mistress to that of Eleanor's.

Margaret's life had changed significantly since her return from Spain. In 1527, she married Henri d'Albret, Count of Béarn and titular King of Navarre. Now referred to as Queen of Navarre in diplomatic correspondence, Margaret was becoming a force to be reckoned with. Her life also changed on a personal level. Her second marriage was a love match, and Margaret soon started hoping that she was pregnant. For many years during her first marriage, Margaret believed she was barren and bemoaned her "sterility", but as soon as she became pregnant for the first time at the age of thirty-six, it dawned on her that it must have been her first husband who was unable to sire children. When the first signs of pregnancy appeared in February 1528, Margaret was cautious not to rush with the news to her mother because she was afraid that this might have been a false alarm, similar to the one which occurred during the winter of 1527. Louise of Savoy, it seemed, came to terms with the fact that her daughter would have no children, but Margaret never stopped dreaming that one day she would be able to share happy news with Louise.

When, in December 1527, Margaret thought that she was with child because her menstruation was "eight days overdue", she wrote to Anne de Montmorency, Great Master of France, that "I do not dare to announce it, for fear that it may be nothing", asking him to urge Francis to cover for her and tell Louise of Savoy that she would not come to see her because she caught a cold, adding poignantly that if she was indeed pregnant, she hoped to announce it to Louise personally and "laugh with her over it myself".[8] This had been a false alarm, but by May 1528, Margaret was sure that she was expecting a child. In a letter to Cardinal Wolsey dated 16 May 1528, she revealed that she was four months pregnant and added that she and her husband prayed for a son who would "inherit their affection for the King and Wolsey".[9]

Like every woman in the sixteenth century, Margaret feared the day of her delivery; by the end of her pregnancy, she took to bed and started worrying about "the suffering that I fear to undergo, as much as I desire it".[10] She also wanted Francis to be present at her side during labour and believed she would have a daughter. She gave birth to a girl, Jeanne d'Albret, on 16 November 1528, after a long and arduous labour. Two years later, she gave birth to the longed-for son, Jean, who died at the age of six months, plunging Margaret into lifelong mourning; she would wear black until the end of her life. The death of her son was only the first event that shattered Margaret's newfound happiness. On 22 September 1531, she lost her mother, Louise of Savoy. Their relationship was not always easy; in one of her personal letters to Guillaume Briçonnet, Bishop of Meaux, Margaret revealed that when she was younger, her mother had "beaten and berated" her to the point that Margaret started doubting whether Louise truly loved her.[11]

Growing up in the shadow of Louise's adoration of Francis I, Margaret seemed to question the strength of her mother's feelings for her, yet the historical evidence clearly points out that Louise of Savoy was fiercely proud of both of her children, and it was Margaret who provided her mother with comfort when she needed it. It was also Margaret who was by Louise's side during her last hours, as Francis I failed to show up at his mother's deathbed, allegedly because he was fleeing from pestilence in the nearby area. Many years later, Margaret described her mother's last hours in the poem entitled *Les Prisons*. The poem contains a heartbreaking scene in which Louise realizes that her beloved son will not come to her:

"When the reading ceased for a bit, she moaned loudly, for her poor body was wracked by pain from kidney stones, and worse still, she had the painful news to bear that in the time left to her she would not have the King her son with her. When she heard that, she cried out, and weeping bitterly, she said: 'Oh, my child! I will not see you! You will fail me at the last! I must leave this earthly place without kissing you for the last time!'"[12]

Yet even in this moment, Louise excused Francis, believing that his absence was for the best because she would not be able to cope with parting from him. It was Margaret who provided succour at this final moment, and Louise was able to recognize it. Taking Margaret by the hand, the dying mother told her that her heart was "full of the strong love for you and for my son" and asked Margaret to leave her presence because "when I look at you, I cannot keep myself from feeling pleasure". The reason for this was the conviction that if one wanted to die a good death, all earthly ties should be renounced.[13] Louise of Savoy slipped quietly away on 22 September 1531, leaving both of her children bereft. In *Les Prisons*, Margaret paid tribute to her mother's virtues and devotion to her family, and especially to her children and grandchildren.

Louise was laid to rest on 17 October 1531 in the Basilica of St Denis. In England, Henry VIII paid tribute to Francis I's mother on 27 October, the eve of the Feast of St Simon. Dressed in royal blue for mourning, the King was followed by twenty-four lords in long black robes. The imperial ambassador Chapuys noted that "there was a general commemoration in the churches" in London, "as at the death of the Emperor Maximilian and of Louis XII".[14]

Two months later, on 28 December 1531, Giovanni Antonio Vernier, Venetian ambassador to France, approached Margaret to console her on the death of her mother. Margaret, always the astute politician, told him that Venice "has in truth incurred a great loss, for Madame greatly loved and honoured the Republic, and to the last desired its welfare and peace". Vernier responded with flattery and observed that Margaret had now taken her mother's place at court:

"Replied that the Doge thanked God that 'Madame' had left her own image in her daughter, both with regard to every virtue, wisdom and integrity, and also by reason of the affection which the Queen of Navarre bore His Excellency, whose late love, and the observance of the State towards Madame, will now be transferred to her Majesty alone. Considered this compliment necessary, as the Queen of Navarre is now in great repute at the French Court; and they apparently communicate everything to her, as they did to her late most Serene mother, after whose death, indeed, when she purposed retiring with her consort to Navarre, King Francis insisted on her remaining and following the Court; so that great honour and respect are paid her."[15]

Vernier was right. Margaret was now the most important woman at court. Her sister-in-law might have been a crowned Queen of France, but Eleanor had no real power. It was Margaret who now became her mother's worthy successor as a skilled stateswoman.

NOTES

[1] Janet Cox Rearick, *Power-Dressing at the Courts of Cosimo de' Medici and François I: The "Moda alla Spagnola" of Spanish Consorts Eléonore d'Autriche and Eleonora di Toledo*, p. 43.
[2] *Calendar of State Papers Relating To English Affairs in the Archives of Venice,* Volume 5, 1534-1554, n. 1006.
[3] Ibid.
[4] R.J. Knecht, *Francis I*, p. 237.
[5] Ibid.
[6] *Letters and Papers, Foreign and Domestic, Henry VIII,* Volume 6, 1533, n. 692.
[7] Kathleen Wellman, *Queens and Mistresses of Renaissance France,* p. 165.
[8] Patricia F. Cholakian and Rouben C. Cholakian, *Marguerite de Navarre: Mother of the Renaissance*, p. 141.
[9] *Letters and Papers, Foreign and Domestic, Henry VIII,* Volume 4, 1524-1530, n. 4267.
[10] Patricia F. Cholakian and Rouben C. Cholakian, *Marguerite de Navarre: Mother of the Renaissance*, p. 144.
[11] Ibid., p. 36.
[12] Ibid., pp. 164-168.
[13] Ibid.
[14] *Letters and Papers, Foreign and Domestic, Henry VIII,* Volume 5, 1531-1532, n. 488, 512.
[15] *Calendar of State Papers Relating To English Affairs in the Archives of Venice,* Volume 5, 1534-1554, n. 1024.

CHAPTER 12
"MORE FRENCH THAN A FRENCHWOMAN BORN"

Although Henry VIII was the proud father of Princess Mary, he soon realised that with each passing year it became less and less probable that Katharine of Aragon would bear him a living son. In 1519, there came a blow for the Queen when she learned that her husband's mistress, Elizabeth Blount, was with child. The mother-to-be enjoyed all the care and attention she could desire until, on 15 June 1519, she gave birth to Henry VIII's illegitimate son. The boy, subsequently acknowledged by the King, received the name Henry Fitzroy, the surname being Norman-French for "son of the King". Henry VIII became much attached to the boy, whose birth proved conclusively to him that it must be his wife, not he, who was at fault for the lack of male heirs.

In 1527, when Henry decided to discard Katharine of Aragon, Cardinal Wolsey dreamed of pairing his sovereign with Madame Renée, the younger daughter of Louis XII and sister of the late Queen Claude of France. As far as Wolsey was concerned, the King wanted to annul his marriage to Katharine of Aragon because he saw in Scripture that God had forbidden their union. Indeed, the King strenuously maintained that the source of his doubts was the book of Leviticus, where a marriage to one's brother's widow was strongly condemned: "And if a man shall take his brother's wife, it is an unclean thing: he hath uncovered his brother's nakedness; they shall be childless". Henry cleverly substituted the word "childless" for "sonless", because after eighteen years of marriage, he and Katharine had no surviving sons. What the cardinal was unaware of was the fact that his sovereign was propelled to act against his wife because he was in love with one of her maids of honour.

At some point in 1526, the King fell passionately in love with Anne Boleyn, his former mistress's sister. The young woman was not like any other he had met. She was a sallow-skinned, slender brunette with an oval face and high cheekbones, whose luminous black eyes were quite striking. But she stood out at court not only because of her rather exotic dark features. She had a Continental gloss about her that most other Englishwomen lacked.

At twelve, Anne was sent by her ambitious father, courtier and diplomat Thomas Boleyn, to the court of Archduchess Margaret of Savoy. Anne did well there, and the archduchess wrote to Thomas that she found his daughter, the "little Boleyn", as he often called Anne, "so bright and pleasant for her young age that I am more beholden to you for sending

"More French than a Frenchwoman born"

her to me than you are to me".[1] Over a year later, Anne was recalled from her post as the archduchess's demoiselle to attend Henry VIII's sister, Mary Tudor, the French Queen, at her coronation in November 1514. This was the beginning of Anne's association with Henry VIII's sister.

At eighteen, Mary was a young lady "not understanding the language perfectly" and had to use translators during her entry to Paris.[2] She obviously valued Anne's command of the French language and requested Thomas Boleyn personally to recall his daughter from the Netherlands.[3] After Mary Tudor returned to England, the fifteen-year-old Anne was "kept back by Claude, who succeeded as Queen". Anne was said to have learned the language quickly. She also "wisely listened to maids of honour, trying hard to use all her wits to imitate them well".[4]

Little is known about Anne's time at the French court, but she must have been a visible presence there because in January 1522, when the threat of the Anglo-French war loomed large, the French King noticed that "Monseigneur Boleyn's daughter" was to be recalled to England and took it as a sign of worsening relations with Henry VIII.[5] Five years later, the French ambassadors instantly recognized Anne as Queen Claude's former maid when she danced with Henry VIII during the banquet celebrating the ratification of the Treaty of Westminster.[6]

By that time, Anne reigned supreme over Henry VIII's heart, waiting for the day when he would make her his wife, although at first the King was interested only in a sexual relationship with Anne. When he started pursuing her, Henry VIII believed that he would share the same sort of relationship with Anne as he had with her elder sister, Mary Boleyn. Mary, who also served in France as Mary Tudor's maid of honour, gained a notorious reputation while at the French court, or at least this is what historians believe was implied by Francis I, who recalled in 1536 that Anne's sister was "a great whore and infamous above all others".[7] Some scholars doubt whether Francis I ever spoke in such manner about Mary Boleyn, but in 1585 hostile Catholic reports circulated in Europe claiming that it was Anne Boleyn who was known in France for her "shameless behaviour" and was called "an English mare" or a "royal mule" upon becoming "acquainted with the King of France", strongly suggesting that she was his mistress.[8] Many historians assume that the abovementioned report was actually referring to Mary Boleyn, who may have been Francis I's mistress—a view that still circulates today.[9] Thomas Boleyn later refused to support Mary financially, but whether it was because of her alleged misbehaviour at the French court or her affair with Henry VIII remains unclear.

As to Anne Boleyn, no breath of scandal touched her name at the time of her sojourn in France, and later on Henry

VIII never accused her of promiscuity prior to their relationship. Instead of agreeing to become Henry VIII's mistress like her sister, Anne refused to countenance his overtures and shunned court. The King was intrigued and soon started penning passionate love letters to the young woman who had rejected him. Anne stood firm and informed the King that she would not become his mistress. Henry persevered through Anne's refusal and, taking the example of Francis I, offered for Anne to become his maîtresse-en-titre, his official royal mistress:

"But if you please to do the office of a true loyal mistress and friend, and to give up yourself body and heart to me, who will be, and have been, your most loyal servant, (if your rigour does not forbid me) I promise you that not only the name shall be given you, but also that I will take you for my only mistress, casting off all others besides you out of my thoughts and affections, and serve you only."[10]

Although Henry VIII never had an official mistress, always preferring to conduct his affairs in private, Anne Boleyn knew very well what this position entailed. She was an eye-witness to how Francis I paraded his mistresses at court and how he eventually discarded one after another to pursue new amours. She may well have been wary of becoming royal mistress after Henry VIII seduced and later abandoned her own sister. Later rumours claimed that Mary Boleyn's son, born during her marriage to William Carey and suggestively named Henry after the King, was a royal bastard. If that was indeed so and her nephew was the King's child, Anne had yet another reason to shudder at the thought of becoming the King's lover. One contemporary later observed that Anne learned "from the example of her own sister, how soon you [Henry VIII] got tired of your mistresses; and she resolved to surpass her sister in retaining you as her lover".[11] Anne, as intelligent and cunning as she was, was probably aware that sooner or later Henry VIII's sexual desire would wane, and he would tire of her as he did with all the other women in his life, so she decided to adhere to higher moral values and bluntly informed the King that she had "already given my maidenhead into my husband's hands".[12]

For centuries, historians and authors ascribed Anne's reluctance to becoming Henry's mistress to her cold ambition, but it seems more likely that she did what was expected of a lady who was a product of upbringing at the French court. She spent almost seven years serving as Queen Claude's maid of honour, and, although Claude's husband was a notorious womaniser, no one who knew her at the time spoke unfavourably about Anne's early youth.

Both English and French courts emphasized that virtue was highly prized. Anne was certainly acquainted with Anne of Beaujeu's *Lessons for My Daughter*, a medieval best-seller and a manual for girls. Anne of Beaujeu advised her daughter and the successive generation of young girls to "devote yourself completely to acquiring virtue". She also advised that a young woman should guard her chastity and "avoid all private meetings" with men because women were often judged and gossiped about even if such meetings were innocent.[13] Anne Boleyn took these and other tips to heart and refused the King's advances, but it seems highly unlikely that she was hoping that Henry VIII would marry her. This, as recently pointed out by historian George W. Bernard, was not a realistic expectation.[14] Nevertheless, Henry VIII was stunned by Anne's refusal and decided to seek annulment of his marriage to Katharine of Aragon. He and Anne Boleyn were engaged on 1 January 1527, and on 17 May of that year, Henry VIII's "secret matter", as the annulment proceeding came to be known in its early stages, commenced.[15]

When Cardinal Wolsey, Henry VIII's chief advisor and chancellor, learned about his sovereign's plans, he started thinking about a possible bride for his master. Over a year later, Wolsey had even alleged in a conversation with the French ambassador that he was responsible for the search of Henry VIII's divorce in order to break the imperial alliance and bring about the union between England and France.[16] This was clearly not the case as evidenced during the Blackfriars Trial of 1529, when Wolsey requested the King "to declare before all this audience, whether I have been the chief and first mover of this matter unto your majesty, or no: for I am greatly suspected herein".[17] Henry admitted that Wolsey was at first against such proceedings, and it was the question posed by the Bishop of Tarbes, one of the French ambassadors, in the spring of 1527 that prompted him to question the validity of his marriage to Katharine of Aragon and therefore their daughter's legitimacy. Henry adamantly claimed that over the course of betrothal negotiations for Mary and Francis I's son, the bishop enquired whether Mary was legitimate because Henry "begat her on his brother's wife, which is directly against God's law and his precept".[18]

Wolsey, anti-imperial and strongly pro-French in his political sympathies, decided that Henry VIII should marry a French bride after his divorce from Katharine of Aragon. Gossip among the foreign ambassadors had it "that the Chancellor, by advocating this divorce, is anxious to bring about the marriage of Henry with Madame Renée".[19] "I think his idea was, if this divorce took place", the French ambassador later wrote, "that he would fall back upon Madame Renée".[20] Indeed, such rumours circulated around the time of Wolsey's embassy to France. Shortly before he was sent there in the summer of 1527, Wolsey met up with the Hungarian ambassador, Jerome Lasco, who had recently returned from the French court, and talked to him about the current political situation. Lasco was instructed by his master, John Zápolya, to enter the negotiations "with the French King upon alliance and marriage with Dame Renée, having ample instructions to conclude the same". Lasco didn't open the negotiations because he was disappointed when he set his eyes on Renée, whom he deemed "not meet to bring forth fruit, as it appeared by the lineation of her body".[21] Renée, just like her late sister, Claude, inherited a limp and deformed hip from their mother, and her ability to produce children was questioned. The Venetian ambassador who saw her observed that "Madam Renée is not beautiful", although "still, she will make up for this with her other good qualities".[22] Brantôme later wrote that although "she did not have an external appearance of grandeur, her body being weakened, there was so much majesty in her royal face and speech that she showed plainly enough she was daughter of a king and of France".[23]

In the end, Wolsey never talked with Henry VIII about the intended marriage to Renée because he, like Jerome Lasco, realized that Henry needed, above all, a noblewoman with an unquestioned ability to bear him sons, and Renée appeared unable to bear children. But the wild rumours swirled at both courts. According to Wolsey's gentleman usher, George Cavendish, "a certain book" was printed and shipped off to England. This "book", a derogatory pamphlet, proclaimed that Wolsey went to France in order to arrange two marriages: one between Princess Mary and Francis I's second son, the Duke of Orléans, and "one between the King our sovereign lord and Madame Renée".[24] It was only after Wolsey returned to England in September 1527 that he realized that Henry VIII already had a bride in mind.

Whenever Wolsey was back from diplomatic missions or had a matter of great importance to communicate to Henry VIII, he would be invited to retire to the King's Privy Chamber to discuss business with him there. Not this time. When the Cardinal arrived at Richmond Palace on 30 September 1527, he sent a messenger to the King asking when and where they should meet. Wolsey did not realize that Anne Boleyn was closeted with Henry VIII in his Privy Chamber. "Where else is the Cardinal to come?" she snapped at Wolsey's messenger. "Tell him that he may come here, where the King is." Henry confirmed the message, and Wolsey entered the room "extremely annoyed at a circumstance which boded no good to him".[25]

Seeing Anne Boleyn at the King's side must have been a huge shock for Wolsey. In the past, he deemed this "foolish girl" unworthy of becoming the wife of Henry Percy, an heir of the grand northern magnate the Earl of Northumberland, so how could he accept her as Henry VIII's future Queen? Wolsey was now in a quandary. His grand scheme of a French marriage was shattered to pieces, and the candidate for a new Queen hated him as much as Katharine of Aragon ever did. Foreign dignitaries commented that no one considered Anne Boleyn English in her ways, but "more French than a Frenchwoman born". Her perfect knowledge of the language, her use of French mannerisms and immaculate elegance singled her out from the crowd. She made friends at the French court too. Many years later, Madame Renée would recall in a conversation with the English ambassador that "there was an old acquaintance" between herself and Anne, who "was one of my sister Queen Claude's maids of honour".[26]

Wolsey now quaked in his shoes because Anne was a friend and supporter of the French policy, and she was no friend of his; he now became expendable. After his downfall, largely engineered by Anne and her faction, the imperial ambassador Eustace Chapuys observed that the King of France had lost nothing by Wolsey's downfall because he now had Anne as the greatest supporter of the French policy at Henry VIII's court. A natural Francophile, Anne was inclined to seek an alliance with Francis I rather than the one with Katharine of Aragon's nephew, Charles V. Anne had enjoyed greater favour than Wolsey ever did, and, Chapuys remarked, King Francis was not obliged to pay her an annual pension of 25,000 crowns as he did to the cardinal, "but pays her only in flattery and in promises of forwarding the divorce at Rome."[27]

In the meantime, Anne's old acquaintance Renée married Ercole d'Este, Duke of Ferrara, on 28 June 1528. The Venetian ambassador, overawed with the spectacle, described the event and Renée's appearance in great detail:

"Madame Renée has been married in regal attire in the fashion of the Queens of France, with a mantle of purple velvet lined with ermine over a robe embroidered with gold, of which mantle the sister of the King of Navarre carried the train. She wore on her head the crown of a Queen, and an infinity of jewels, and a pectoral adorned with so many emeralds and diamonds that they were worth a kingdom; and she was led to and from the church by the hand by the Most Christian King".[28]

The duke was pleased with the match because Renée was a King's daughter, but he was somewhat disappointed with her appearance. "As far as I can gather", wrote one of the Ferrarese agents to the duke's father, "my Lord would have been content if Madame Renée had been more beautiful". If not beautiful, Renée was accomplished and knew how to make a grand entrance. When she arrived to her new duchy of Ferrara in Italy, she wore the same clothes as during her wedding. The crown perched on her head "has given rise to much comment, as she is not a Queen, albeit she is daughter of a King".[29]

Three years after her grand wedding, Renée proved her critics wrong when she gave birth to a healthy daughter, Anne, named after her mother, followed by Alfonso, Lucrezia, Eleanor and Luigi, all of whom survived into adulthood and outlived their mother. Brantôme, aware that this was a great accomplishment considering Renée's bodily restrictions, paid her the ultimate compliment when he wrote that "like her sister Claude, she was fortunate in her issue, for she bore to her husband the finest that was, I believe, in Italy, although she herself was much weakened in body".[30]

While Renée had successfully entered into her childbearing years, her former friend Anne Boleyn complained that she was losing her time and youth "for no purpose at all".[31] The imperial ambassador, with a streak of malicious glee, reported that Anne, who was nearing her thirtieth birthday, bitterly complained that she had been "waiting long and might in the meanwhile have contracted some advantageous marriage, out of which I might have had issue, which is the greatest consolation in this world".[32] She had reason to complain because by 1531 Henry VIII's divorce case had reached a stalemate, and both he and Anne started losing hope. While Henry was eager to wait for the pope's final verdict on his marriage to Katharine of Aragon, Anne started devising other solutions. She leaned towards the evangelical religious views and managed to show Henry her own copy of William Tyndale's *The Obedience of a Christian Man*. In this book, labelled as heretical and banned in England, Tyndale argued that popes had no authority over kings, a controversial view that was eminently suitable in Henry VIII's situation. Apart from that, Tyndale also argued that the Bible should be available to every man in his own tongue, an argument that Anne Boleyn and her brother, George, had enthusiastically adopted and worked hard to carry into life. But Henry's mind was not there, or at least not yet. Deeply attached to Catholic principles, Henry VIII believed that the pope would eventually rule in his favour. For that, Henry thought, the pope needed a little extra push from none other than his Most Christian Majesty, Francis I.

Francis was now the only ally who could help Henry solve his matrimonial problems, and the King decided to renew the Anglo-French alliance. In 1532, Henry decided to repeat the Field of the Cloth of Gold, only this time he would not take his wife with him. Instead, Henry VIII ruled, Anne Boleyn would go and be presented to the French nobility as his future wife. For her part, Anne hoped that Calais—where the two monarchs were to meet—would be the stage of her great triumph.

NOTES

[1] Eric Ives, *The Life and Death of Anne Boleyn*, p. 19.
[2] Mary Anne Everett Green, *Lives of the Princesses of England*, Volume 5, p. 48.

Pierre Gringore, Cynthia Jane Brown, *Les Entrées Royales à Paris de Marie d'Angleterre (1514) et Claude de France*, p. 143.

[3] Thomas Boleyn wrote to the Archduchess Margaret that "to this request I could not, nor did I know how to refuse" because Mary Tudor had been betrothed to Margaret's nephew, Charles of Castile, since 1508. The regent was disappointed to see the alliance with England broken, especially because she nurtured a dislike towards the French for discarding her as a bride of Charles VIII when she was a child.

[4] Susan Walters Schmid, *Anne Boleyn, Lancelot de Carle, and the Uses of Documentary Evidence*, p. 112.

[5] *Letters and Papers, Foreign and Domestic, Henry VIII*, Volume 3, 1519–1523, n. 1994.

[6] John Lingard, *The History of England*, Volume IV, p. 486.

[7] Francis I's comment touching on Mary Boleyn's reputation was uttered in 1536, prompting many historians to question what period of time he was actually referring to. There are various theories: that Mary was the French King's mistress in 1514 (Josephine Wilkinson, *Mary Boleyn*); that he was referring to Henry VIII's affair with Mary and her possible presence at the Field of the Cloth of Gold in 1520 (Leanda de Lisle, *Tudor: The Family Story*); or that Francis I formed his final conclusion about Mary Boleyn's character while she accompanied her sister to Calais in 1532 (Retha M. Warnicke, *Wicked Women of Tudor England*).

[8] Nicholas Sander, *The Rise and Growth of the Anglican Schism*, pp. 25, 26.

[9] Historian Philippa Jones suggested that "since these comments are obviously not applicable to Anne... it has been assumed that they must apply to Mary when, in truth, they were written to discredit Anne and are largely based on vulgar invention..." (*The Other Tudors*, p. 106)

[10] Eric Ives, *The Life and Death of Anne Boleyn*, p. 85.

[11] Reginald Pole, *Defence of the Unity of the Church*, p. 185.

[12] BL, Sloane MS 2495, f. 3, quoted in Eric Ives, *The Life and Death of Anne Boleyn*, p. 84.

[13] Sharon L. Jansen, *Anne of France: Lessons for My Daughter*, p. 40.

[14] George W. Bernard, *Did Anne Boleyn Crave the Crown?*, BBC History Magazine, June 2015.

[15] I follow Dr David Starkey's dating of Henry VIII's engagement to Anne Boleyn (Starkey, *Six Wives: The Queens of Henry VIII*, p. 282).

[16] *Letters and Papers, Foreign and Domestic, Henry VIII*, Volume 4, 1524-1530, n. 4865.

[17] Edward Hall, *Hall's Chronicle*, pp. 754-756.

Charles Dodd, *Dodd's Church History of England*, p. 186, 190.

[18] Ibid., p. 187.

[19] Jean Marie Vincent, *The Life of Henry the Eighth: And History of the Schism of England*, p. 159.

[20] *Letters and Papers, Foreign and Domestic, Henry VIII*, Volume 4, 1524-1530, n. 4649.

[21] *State Papers Published Under the Authority of His Majesty's Commission King Henry the Eighth: Parts 1 and 2*, Volume 1, p. 203.

[22] Edmund Garratt Gardner, *The King of Court Poets*, p. 192.

[23] Pierre de Bourdeille, seigneur de Brantôme, *The Book of the Ladies*, p. 220.

[24] George Cavendish, *The Life of Cardinal Wolsey*, p. 118.

[25] *Calendar of State Papers, Spain*, Volume 3 Part 2, 1527-1529, n. 224.

[26] *Calendar of State Papers Foreign, Elizabeth I*, Volume 2, 1559-1560, n. 3.

[27] *Calendar of State Papers, Spain*, Volume 4 Part 2, 1531-1533, n. 995.

[28] Marino Sanuto, *I Diarii di Marino Sanuto*, Volume 48, p. 233.

[29] Edmund Garratt Gardner, *The King of Court Poets*, p. 202.

[30] Pierre de Bourdeille, seigneur de Brantôme, *The Book of the Ladies*, p. 220.

[31] Eric Ives, *The Life and Death of Anne Boleyn*, p. 128.

[32] Ibid.

CHAPTER 13
"DEVIL IN A WOMAN'S DRESS"

In 1532, Anne Boleyn was at the apogee of her power and influence. On 23 June, the mutual peace treaty between England and France was signed, and on 1 September, Anne was made Marchioness of Pembroke, a peeress in her own right with a substantial annual income of £1,000 per year.[1] She feted the French ambassador, Gilles de la Pommeraye, in her newly acquired and splendidly decorated house at Hanworth and invited him on a hunting expedition, where she presented him with a coat, a hat and a greyhound. Shooting at deer with crossbows—a sport that Anne particularly enjoyed—they talked about current politics and the upcoming interview with Francis I. Anne made sure the ambassador knew that she played the key role in convincing Henry VIII to cultivate his alliance with France. De la Pommeraye quickly sensed Anne's true intent:

"The greatest pleasure that the King of France can do to this King [Henry VIII] and Madame Anne, is to ask the King to bring Madame Anne with him to Calais, so that they may not be there without ladies, but then the King must bring the Queen of Navarre with him to Boulogne".[2]

The imperial ambassador Chapuys heard similar reports. The King desired Francis I's sister, Margaret, now Queen of Navarre, to be present during the meeting to greet Anne and show to all the world that Anne was accepted as the future Queen of England. This was not to be, however. Henry was angry because Margaret was "indisposed and unable to attend"; she would not greet the King of England's mistress, as Anne was perceived by the French nobility.[3]

Henry could hardly blame Francis for not bringing Margaret with him because his own sister also refused to accompany Anne Boleyn. In April 1532, Mary Tudor Brandon publicly referred to her former maid of honour using "opprobrious language", causing a stir at court.[4] There was no love lost between the two women. Mary was not only loath to acknowledge Anne as the King's future wife, but also refused to bow to her former servant. She was raised on old values; servants had to know their place, and Anne had blatantly turned the social order upside down. Anne was the one who was paraded at court as if she were already Queen, occupying the consort's throne while Katharine of Aragon was exiled, and taking precedence over all other noblewomen, including Mary herself. As a crowned Queen of France, Mary was adamant in not tolerating all this and chose a domestic life with her children rather than attending court, where she once shone along Katharine of Aragon and Princess Mary, taking part in banquets, masks and tournaments. Mary blamed Anne for sowing discord in the royal family, and when the King's sweetheart attacked Mary's husband, Charles Brandon, all hopes of reconciliation disappeared.

Charles Brandon was among a small group of intimates who dared to speak openly with Henry VIII. He had once told the King that there was an intimate relationship between Anne Boleyn and an unidentified member of the court in the past.[5] Whatever this relationship's nature, it appears that Henry knew about it from Anne, but Brandon was nevertheless briefly banished, although he quickly returned to the King's good graces. Anne wasn't as forgiving as Henry and accused Brandon of having a "criminal intercourse with his own daughter".[6] Whereas Brandon was able to put his grievances aside, or so he pretended, his wife defied Anne Boleyn until her death in June 1533.

Despite the fact that the sisters of Henry VIII and Francis I refused to entertain her in Calais, Anne made the necessary preparations for the journey. The King ordered "rich and most expensive dresses and ornaments" for her and commanded Katharine of Aragon to yield her royal jewels. At first, the Queen refused to countenance the outrageous prospect of giving up her jewellery "for such a wicked purpose as that of ornamenting a person who is the scandal of Christendom", but when she received a formal order signed by Henry VIII, she agreed out of wifely obedience. Soon, Anne was parading in the Queen's rings, necklaces and bracelets, setting the tongues wagging: even the French King had never presented his mistresses with valuables belonging to his wives.[7]

Amidst all the intense preparations, Anne chose to ignore the fact that it was agreed that there would be no ladies in Calais to greet her on French soil. The imperial ambassador Chapuys thought that after this decision was made, the meeting between Henry VIII and Francis I would be an all-male assembly. He was thus surprised when he learned that Anne was busy sending invitations to her favourite ladies to attend her in Calais.[8] Anne confessed to one of her closest friends that she wished that all of her dreams would come true there. Some took it as a sign that Anne was talking about marriage to Henry, and indeed Katharine of Aragon feared that her husband might make her his wife while in France. As it soon became apparent, Anne was not talking about marriage because "even if the King wished to marry her now, she would never consent to it, for she wants the ceremony to take place here, in England, at the usual place appointed for the marriage and coronation of Queens".[9]

She was talking about the consummation of her relationship with the King.

Anne's enemies believed that most of her elaborate preparations had proved in vain, for no suitable royal lady in France was willing to receive her. Henry VIII made it clear that Queen Eleanor's presence was out of the question, as she was the emperor's sister and Katharine of Aragon's niece. He must have been aware that Katharine sought Eleanor's help on at least one occasion and that Charles V ordered his sister to speak with Francis I in Katharine's favour when the English King sent scholars to collect opinions on the matter of his annulment from the French universities.[10] Henry vented his frustrations, saying that seeing Eleanor dressed in Spanish fashions would be like seeing "Devil in a woman's dress".[11]

Even if she wanted to be in Calais to obey her husband, Eleanor was in no way fit to travel because in the end of September 1532 she miscarried a child, and Francis hastened to her side, spending several days in her company before leaving for Paris and then for Boulogne and Calais.[12] In the end, there were no women on the French side. Francis suggested that one of the leading noblewomen of his court, Françoise of Alençon, Duchess of Vendôme, should come, but this idea was quickly discarded when it became apparent that the insolent duchess planned to bring with her companions of bad reputation to insult Anne Boleyn. Anne seemed to be undeterred and took thirty noblewomen of her own, among them seven of her family relations. By ten o'clock on the crisp morning of 11 October 1532, Anne Boleyn and Henry VIII arrived on board the *Swallow* from Dover. Acknowledging Anne's presence, the French King sent her pears and grapes through Anne de Montmorency, the Great Master of France. On 21 October, Henry rode off to spend four days with Francis in Boulogne, leaving Anne behind in Calais, lodged comfortably in the Exchequer. On Friday, 25 October, the two monarchs came to Calais, where it was the English King's turn to entertain.

The French King, paying compliment to her yet again, sent Anne a jewel worth a staggering amount of £3,500. Two days later, she thanked him in person when, making a spectacular entry with seven other ladies, she performed her bewitching dance. All masked and "gorgeously apparelled" in costumes of "strange fashion", each of the ladies singled out French gentlemen to dance with. Anne, naturally, claimed King Francis. After a couple of dances, Henry VIII approached the dancers, taking the visors off all the masked ladies. Dancing continued while Francis led Anne to a window embrasure, where they talked for about an hour until the banquet was over. On Tuesday, Francis left for Paris. Anne and Henry lingered in Calais, prevented from crossing the Channel by unfavourable, stormy weather. They left on 12 November 1532.[13]

Both Henry VIII and Anne Boleyn believed that Calais was an unqualified success, but it later became apparent that Francis I entertained a different opinion, telling the pope over a year later that he tried to dissuade Henry from marrying Anne or at least tried to convince him to wait for some time until a set of more favourable circumstances would emerge.[14] But Henry could not wait and secretly married the already pregnant Anne on 25 January 1533, hoping that the pope would eventually sanction his new marriage.

Two months later, in March 1533, Henry appointed Anne's brother as ambassador to the French court. George Boleyn was to announce to Francis I that his master, according to the French King's advice given in Calais, as well as because he wished to have male issue, married Anne and intended to crown her. George was to emphasize that Henry expected that Francis's "deeds will correspond with his promises" and that the French King would intercede with the pope on Henry's behalf.[15]

The marriage in itself did not mean that Henry broke with the Catholic Church; he now wanted his ambassadors in Rome to convince Pope Clement VII that the divorce should be tried in England, not in Rome. When this plan turned to ashes after the pope allied himself with Charles V, Katharine of Aragon's nephew, Henry began efforts to strengthen his own authority and annul his first marriage. On 23 May 1533, the new Archbishop of Canterbury, Thomas Cranmer, declared Henry's first marriage null and void, arguing that his marriage to Anne Boleyn was valid because the King had been free to remarry all along.[16] Katharine of Aragon was given a new title: Princess Dowager of Wales, but it changed nothing in her perception of her royal dignity.

On 1 June 1533, Anne Boleyn was crowned, and although she looked splendid in her overdress and mantle of cloth of tissue furred with ermines, people refused to exclaim the customary "God save the Queen" as she passed. The French ambassador Jean de Dinteville, who accompanied her through the crowded streets of London, was abused with insults; people called him a "French dog" and a "whoreson knave".[17] Anne's Frenchness now became a disadvantage in the eyes of the English subjects, who feared that their King would be excommunicated and their country invaded by Charles V's forces.

On 7 September 1533, Anne Boleyn gave birth to a daughter, Elizabeth, dashing Henry VIII's hopes for a son. Later that autumn, Francis I met with the pope in Marseilles and, according to the stipulations of the Franco-Papal alliance, married his son Henri to Clement's niece, the fifteen-year-old Catherine de Medici. Henry felt betrayed because Francis had promised him in Calais that he would not marry his son to the pope's niece unless and until Clement VII granted Henry his longed-for divorce. Francis argued that "he had promised the Pope for a long time to make this marriage", but Henry was outraged and during a parting audience with the French ambassador Dinteville accused Francis of double-dealing.[18]

Anne Boleyn, on the other hand, believed that the Anglo-French relations could be mended and spoke in favour of the French.[19] When the new French ambassador arrived in December 1533, it was Anne who made sure that Jean du Bellay felt welcome. She made him a very gracious reception and kissed him on the cheek when he presented her a letter from Francis.[20] Anne had high hopes for the French alliance and saw herself as a nourisher of peace between the two nations. The crowning achievement of her ambitions was to see her infant daughter Elizabeth matched to Francis I's youngest son, Charles.

Although Elizabeth was not the longed-for male heir, Anne was nevertheless a proud mother who took a keen interest in her daughter's upbringing. When she was three months old, Elizabeth was placed in her own establishment, where an array of governesses, wet nurses and rockers tended to her every need. As Queen, Anne was not expected to raise her daughter, but she was a constant presence in Elizabeth's life. Whenever the child came to visit her parents in the royal palaces, Anne sat on a throne under a canopy of estate while

Elizabeth was placed on a richly embroidered cushion next to her so that everyone might look upon this new Princess of England.[21]

In the spring of 1534, Anne made sure that the three French ambassadors paid visit to her daughter and reported to Francis I that she was a healthy and lively child. Castillion, Morette and La Pommeraye witnessed Elizabeth presented to them "in very rich apparel, in state and triumph as a Princess, and afterwards they saw her quite naked".[22] This show had its own purpose because by March 1534, Henry VIII had completed his break from Rome and passed the new Act of Succession, designating his daughter by Anne Boleyn and any subsequent sons they might have as heirs to the throne. Now, Queen Anne had to succeed where her predecessor had failed and deliver a male heir.

NOTES

[1] This was an enormous sum of money. Anne earned more than speakers of the House of Commons, who usually received £100 per year.
[2] *Letters and Papers, Foreign and Domestic, Henry VIII*, Volume 5, 1531-1532, n. 1187.
[3] *Calendar of State Papers, Spain*, Volume 4 Part 2, 1531-1533, n. 1003.
[4] *Calendar of State Papers, Venice*, Volume 4, 1527-1533, n. 761.
[5] *Calendar of State Papers, Spain*, Volume 4 Part 1, Henry VIII, 1529-1530, n. 302. Historians identify this gentleman as Thomas Wyatt.
[6] Ibid., Volume 4 Part 2, 1531-1533, n. 765.

[7] *Calendar of State Papers, Spain,* Volume 4 Part 2, 1531-1533, n. 1003, 1047.
[8] Ibid., n. 986.
[9] Ibid., n. 824.
[10] Ibid., Volume 4 Part 2, 1531-1533, n. 450.
Letters and Papers, Foreign and Domestic, Henry VIII, Volume 4, 1524-1530, n. 6535.
[11] *Letters and Papers, Foreign and Domestic,* Henry VIII, Volume 5, 1531–1532, n. 1187.
[12] *Calendar of State Papers, Spain,* Volume 4 Part 2, 1531-1533, n. 998.
[13] Eric Ives, *The Life and Death of Anne Boleyn*, pp. 159-160.
[14] *Letters and Papers, Foreign and Domestic, Henry VIII,* Volume 6, 1533, n. 1331.
Letters and Papers, Foreign and Domestic, Henry VIII, Volume 13 Part 2, August-December 1538, n. 804.
[15] Ibid., n. 230.
[16] Catherine Fletcher, *Our Man in Rome*, p. 190, 191.
[17] *Letters and Papers, Foreign and Domestic, Henry VIII,* Volume 6, 1533, n. 585.
[18] Ibid., n. 1386.
[19] Paul Friedmann, *Anne Boleyn*, Volume 1, pp. 258-259.
[20] *Calendar of State Papers, Spain,* Volume 4 Part 2, 1531-1533, n. 1165.
[21] *Chronicle of King Henry VIII (The Spanish Chronicle),* p. 42.
[22] *Letters and Papers, Foreign and Domestic, Henry VIII,* Volume 7, 1534, n. 469.

CHAPTER 14
"RUINED AND LOST"

In 1534, Henry VIII decided to postpone another intended meeting with Francis I; the two Kings were to meet in Calais for a third time, but they never did. Henry instructed his ambassador, Anne Boleyn's younger brother, George, to use Margaret, Queen of Navarre, as an intermediary. The ambassador was to tell the French King's sister that it was Anne who wished to defer the interview because she was unable to leave England on account of her advanced pregnancy and desired to have Henry at her side when her child was born. The ambassador was also to tell Margaret that there was nothing Anne regretted more than the fact that she and the Queen of Navarre did not meet in Calais in 1532.[1]

Henry VIII decided to use this woman-to-woman approach because apparently some sort of a relationship between Anne Boleyn and the French King's sister had developed during Anne's sojourn in France. The sixteenth-century biographer William Camden claimed that Anne served as Margaret's maid of honour after Queen Claude's death in 1524, but this served Camden's agenda of portraying Anne as the patroness of the reformed Church because Margaret, he emphasized, "was a prime favourer of the Protestant religion then springing up in France".[2] Camden was clearly mistaken because Anne came back to England two years before Queen Claude's death.

It is certain, however, that she would have seen Margaret on a daily basis at court and, just as she had formed an acquaintance with Madame Renée, Claude's sister, she had a chance to develop a relationship with the French King's sister. Just what sort of a relationship it was is hard to define due to the paucity of evidence. When the intended meeting between Henry VIII and Francis I was cancelled altogether, Anne confessed to one of Margaret's messengers that her greatest wish, next to having a son, was to see Margaret again.[3]

Margaret clearly supported Anne's elevation to queenship. When Anne's uncle, the Duke of Norfolk, was sent to France as a special envoy in June 1533, he was under the impression that Margaret was Henry VIII's and Anne Boleyn's "good and sure friend" and as affectionate as if she were their sister.[4] On Anne's accession, the French King's sister sent congratulations and "very humble recommendations" to the new Queen of England.[5] Another piece of evidence supporting the friendly relationship between Anne and Margaret is the book Francis I and Margaret sent to Anne and Henry. It was comprised of a lengthy poem presumably authored by Clément Marot and included Anne Boleyn's device and her coat of arms.

The poem touchingly addressed Anne with a prophecy that Christ would give her a son, "the living image of the King his father", whom they both would see grow into manhood.[6] The longed-for son never came, but some seven years after Anne Boleyn's death, her daughter, Elizabeth, translated Margaret's poem, *Mirror of a Sinful Soul*, from French into English; it's believed that Anne owned a copy of this poem, published in 1531, and her daughter was well aware of the connection between the Queen of Navarre and her own mother.[7]

Anne was an avid collector of French theological books and owned a copy of the French translation of the Bible by the humanist Jacques Lefèvre d'Étaples, printed in Antwerp in 1534. It is also believed that while in France, Anne received a music book from Margaret.[8] It is clear that the French King's sister was Anne's role model when it came to religion and patronage. Margaret was the first source of information about reform for Anne Boleyn, and Anne's later religious views neatly correspond with those of Margaret's. Just like Margaret, Anne sought correction of the major abuses within the Church. Both women believed in making the Bible available to everyone in vernacular and thus encouraged its translation. Anne and Margaret were recognized as loyal promoters of the reformed religion and people often turned to them for help. Anne Boleyn helped at least two French religious refugees during her tenure as Queen. Her chaplain, William Latymer, described how she sheltered a certain "Mistress Marye", a French gentlewoman who sought refuge in England:

"As for an example, a gentlewoman of France named Mrs Marye[9] fled out of France into England for religion. Whom immediately after her arrival the Queen Her Majesty sent for, and understanding the certainty of the matter, entertained her so lovingly and honourably as she confessed that her trouble had purchased her liberty, and that she gained more by her banishment than she could have hoped for at home amongst her dear friends and natural countrymen of France".[10]

There was also Nicolas Bourbon, a French poet and Protestant who was maintained at Anne's expense in Dr William Butts's house. He hailed from Champagne and had Margaret of Navarre as his patroness before he decided to flee to England in 1535, when the religious persecution in France became so fierce that even the French King's sister had no power to help him. Bourbon returned to France shortly after Anne's death, but he never forgot her hospitality. In his collection of verses entitled *Nugae* (*Trifles*), he included laudatory poems addressed to Anne Boleyn, William Butts and other members of the evangelical circle at Henry VIII's court, including Thomas Cranmer and Thomas Cromwell, but it was Anne who was the most prominent in these verses.

However, neither the similarities between Margaret of Navarre and Anne Boleyn nor Anne's efforts on behalf of the French religious refugees were enough to restore the good relations between England and France. By 1534, England became isolated on the international political stage. Henry VIII's break from Rome naturally meant that any alliance between him and Charles V was impossible as long as Henry kept his first wife, Charles's aunt, Katharine of Aragon, away from court. While Charles V would only ally with Henry if he took Katharine back as wife, Henry was eager to seek the recognition of his marriage with Anne Boleyn and thus decided to ally with Francis I.

In the autumn of 1534, a mission from the French King headed by the Admiral of France, Philippe de Chabot, seigneur de Brion, came to England. Its main goal was to negotiate the marriage between one of Francis I's sons to Princess Elizabeth, or so Henry VIII believed. The admiral's treatment of Anne Boleyn was cold, and he went to see her only after the King asked if he wished to visit her. Then the admiral proposed a marriage between the French Dauphin and Henry VIII's daughter by Katharine of Aragon, Mary, who had been recently excluded from succession and proclaimed a bastard. Both Henry and Anne were shocked at this proposal, and the King later complained to the admiral that "Francis could not have spoken seriously of that affair, but merely by way of a joke".

"Ruined and lost"

The fact that Francis desired to marry his eldest son and heir to Katharine of Aragon's daughter meant that he, as most of the Catholic rulers in Europe, believed that Mary was legitimate and Elizabeth was not. Anne was not only "exceedingly annoyed" at this, but she soon became fearful that the King might abandon her.[11]

She had great reason to worry because the son who would consolidate her position as Queen was not yet born. Just as Katharine of Aragon before her, Anne gave birth to a healthy daughter but struggled to deliver a male heir. The pregnancy that served as an excuse for annulling the French interview ended in mysterious circumstances during the summer progress of 1534. Whatever happened that fateful summer was kept secret, but various stories leaked, and soon rumours started swirling in the English countryside that Anne "had one child by the King, which was dead-born, and she prayed she might never have other."[12]

When the French admiral's secretary, Palmedes Gontier, arrived to England in February 1535, he recorded Anne Boleyn's insecurities in the following letter:

"She said the Admiral must think of applying some remedy, and act towards the King so that she may not be ruined and lost, for she sees herself very near that and in more grief and trouble than before her marriage. She charged him to beg the Admiral to consider her affairs, of which she could not speak as fully as she wished, on account of her fears, and the eyes which were looking at her, her husband's and the lords' present. She said she could not write, nor see him again, nor stay longer. She then left him, the King going to the next room, where the dance was beginning, without the said Lady going thither."[13]

Despite this, Henry VIII was still committed to Anne. In stipulations of the newly proposed treaty with France, he emphasized that Francis should acknowledge Henry's marriage to her as lawful and their offspring as legitimate.[14] In May 1535, the previously cancelled conference between England and France was held in Calais. This time it was an all-male assembly, but Henry VIII and Francis I did not appear in person, instead being represented by their selected ambassadors. Henry was represented by George Boleyn and Thomas Howard while Francis had chosen Admiral de Brion. There was no understanding reached during the meeting.

When the English envoys returned home, Anne Boleyn received firsthand information about the negotiations from her brother, George, who had a long discussion with her before reporting to the King himself. Both Anne and Henry desired that Francis I's son Charles, Duke of Angoulême, should marry their daughter Elizabeth and come to live and be educated at the English court prior to the marriage, yet Francis strongly opposed this idea, saying that he would not send his son to be a hostage in England. Francis's indignation with Henry deepened when the English envoys were heard saying that Henry VIII alleged that Francis promised him to send his son to England, yet the French King recalled no such promise.[15]

It was around that time when Francis told the papal nuncio that Henry VIII was "the hardest friend to bear in the world; at one time unstable, and at another time obstinate and proud, so that it was almost impossible to bear with him". He complained that Henry treated him like his subject—indeed, the English King demanded that Francis adopt the same anti-papal policy in France—and was afraid that he could "do no good with him" yet was prepared to put up with him because it was "no time to lose friends".[16] However, the French admiral broke off the negotiations "on account of his refusal to allow the Duke of Angoulême to go to England until the girl [Elizabeth] was old enough to be married and because he would not declare in any way against the Church, or in favour of the King's second wife".[17] He was also "sick of his mission . . . on account of the haggling and carping of the English".[18] Disappointed and angry, Anne Boleyn was soon publicly uttering unfavourable comments about Francis I and the French nation as a whole. When the new French ambassador, Antoine de Castelnau, arrived in England in June 1535, Anne snubbed him when she deliberately failed to invite him for a splendid banquet she held at her palace of Hanworth.[19]

By 1536, Henry VIII and Anne Boleyn had great reason to rejoice because Anne was pregnant again, and her rival, Katharine of Aragon, died on 7 January 1536. Henry VIII was heard saying that he could now reconcile with Charles V because Katharine, who was the reason for the discord between them, was gone. He also instructed his ambassadors in France to be more aloof in dealings with Francis I.[20] Anne's pregnancy gave Henry hope of finally having a male heir, but by February 1536 Anne had miscarried a son, and Henry was so disappointed that he started entertaining doubts as to the validity of his marriage to her. "I see that God will not give me male children", he uttered to Anne when he visited her after the miscarriage.[21]

Anne's influence began to wane, and Henry found a new mistress in the person of the submissive Jane Seymour, one of Anne's maids of honour. Anne knew that her only chance of getting Henry's favour back was to give him a son and accept his political choices. In the spring of 1536, she reverted to anti-French policy when she was heard uttering unfavourable remarks about Francis I and willingly agreed to accept the alliance with Charles V.[22] She must have been aware that Francis was spreading unfavourable reports about her in his country. In March 1536, for instance, he revealed to the papal nuncio that Anne—"that woman", as he coldly referred to her—was not really with child but pretended to have miscarried a son.[23]

Anne now gravitated towards the imperial alliance, but Charles V was willing to accept Henry VIII as an ally only if he restored his daughter Mary to the succession. This meant that the elder Mary would take precedence over her younger half sister, who, in Charles's eyes, was merely a bastard. Henry was not about to allow the emperor to interfere in his family matters and scolded his ambassador in the presence of the whole court. This development frightened Thomas Cromwell, the King's right-hand man, who now believed that Anne Boleyn was an obstacle to their foreign policy and had to be removed from power. Cromwell reasoned that with Anne gone, Henry would be able to put the controversy of his divorce and subsequent remarriage behind him and start afresh.

On 2 May 1536, Queen Anne was taken by barge to the Tower of London and accused of multiple counts of adultery, incest with her brother, George, and plotting Henry VIII's death; all this constituted treason. There was no truth to these allegations. The four men accused of being Anne's paramours—Henry Norris, Francis Weston, William Brereton and musician Mark Smeaton—were courtiers who had daily access to her chambers and were often seen in her company. Anne's recent quarrel with Henry Norris was taken out of context and twisted in its meaning; Weston told the Queen that Norris was frequenting her chambers because he fancied her and not Anne's cousin and Norris's fiancée, Mary Shelton. Anne scolded Norris for his tardiness in marrying her pretty cousin, accusing him for looking for "a dead man's shoes, for if aught came to the King but good, you would look to have me."[24] This was a dangerous thing to say, for it was treason to predict the King's death. Anne realized her foolish mistake the next day when she sent her chaplain to Norris so that he could swear that she was a good woman and there was no malicious intent in what she said, but it was too late. Rumours spread like wildfire within the claustrophobic confines of the court, setting hostile tongues wagging.

Cromwell seized this opportunity and decided to strike against the Queen, accusing her of "incontinent living" and intimidating her ladies-in-waiting into confessing the names of other gallants who frequented Anne's chambers.[25] Crucial evidence, however, came from Anne herself. While pacing her royal apartments in the Tower, she was nervously talking to her four female attendants, recalling her conversations with Henry Norris, Francis Weston and Mark Smeaton; these women were ordered to spy on the distraught Queen and inform Cromwell of everything she said. When Anne finally learned of the charges laid against her, she protested her innocence and said that no one could bring witnesses against her misconduct because she was not guilty.

Indeed, the bewildered imperial ambassador Eustace Chapuys recorded that no witnesses were brought against Anne or her brother during their separate trials, as was custom when the accused denied their guilt. Thomas Cromwell's letter to the English ambassadors at the French court—hungry for details and anxiously urging him to provide more information—reveals that evidence so painstakingly collected against the Queen was flimsy because "the very confessions . . . were so abominable that a great part of them were never given in evidence but clearly kept secret".[26] Chapuys, a skilled lawyer himself, was shocked that Anne and her alleged lovers "were sentenced on mere presumption or on very slight grounds, without legal proof or valid confession".[27] Only Mark Smeaton confessed to have had three sexual encounters with Anne, but he may have been tortured; historical sources are not unanimous on this issue. Thomas Cromwell later told Chapuys that the King ordered him to get rid of his Queen. Henry VIII's "peculiar remorse for the wrong he had done Anne Boleyn by putting her to death on a false accusation" expressed on his deathbed and recorded by the contemporary Franciscan French monk André Thevet, who resided in England at that time, confirm his words.[28]

The four men co-accused with Anne Boleyn were executed on 17 May 1536. Anne faced death two days later. She addressed the crowds with the following words:

"Good Christian people, I have not come here to preach a sermon; I have come here to die. For according to the law and by the law, I am judged to die, and therefore I will speak nothing against it. I am come hither to accuse no man, nor to speak of that whereof I am accused and condemned to die, but I pray God save the King and send him long to reign over you, for a gentler nor a more merciful prince was there never, and to me he was ever a good, a gentle, and sovereign lord. And if any person will meddle of my cause, I require them to judge the best. And thus I take my leave of the world and of you all, and I heartily desire you all to pray for me."[29]

When she knelt on a wooden scaffold draped in black cloth and covered with straw, one of her ladies-in-waiting stepped forward and bandaged her eyes. Anne prayed fervently, constantly turning her head back as if afraid the swordsman of French-held Calais, ordered especially for her execution, would slice through her neck without warning. "Oh, Lord, have mercy on me, to God I commend my soul, Jesus receive my soul", she kept repeating in prayer. The stroke was clean and swift; the French executioner charged £23 for the job well done.

Shortly after Anne's execution, Lancelot de Carle, a secretary to the French ambassador, Antoine de Castelnau, penned a poem about her life and tragic death. De Carle was clearly very well informed because many of his assertions were confirmed by other contemporary sources. It is Lancelot de Carle who gives Anne a voice that reaches us across the centuries; he tells us about her eloquent trial speeches, where Anne said, among other things:

"I do not say that I always borne towards the King the humility which I owed him, considering his kindness and the great honour he showed me and the great respect he always paid me; I admit, too, that often I have taken it into my head to be jealous of him . . . But may God be my witness if I have done him any other wrong".[30]

This and other bold assertions uttered by Anne and her co-accused reached the Continent thanks to Lancelot de Carle, and soon many people abroad started believing that they were all unjustly condemned to die. When Henry VIII learned that "the French book, written in form of a tragedy" authored by "one [de] Carle, attendant upon the French ambassador" was being disseminated in France, he immediately ordered a copy for himself from his ambassador. Henry was not pleased with what he read, perhaps because most of it was true, but mostly because it was written in England under his very own royal nose.[31] Yet Henry could do nothing about the fact that Anne

Boleyn's life and death was slowly turning into a legend. Two years after her execution, Étienne Dolet—another Frenchman—wrote an epitaph for "the Queen of Utopia" falsely accused of adultery by a tyrant of a husband.[32]

Historians could never satisfactorily explain why Henry VIII turned against Anne Boleyn and signed her death warrant. It has been recently proposed that he became a suspicious tyrant because of a personality change following a serious jousting accident. The accident occurred at a tournament at Greenwich Palace on 24 January 1536, when the forty-four-year-old King, in full armour, was thrown from his horse, itself armoured, which then fell on top of him. Dr Ortiz, the emperor's ambassador in Rome, recorded that in France Francis I was heard saying that Henry was unconscious for two hours, but no eyewitness mentioned this fact—not even the usually well-informed imperial ambassador Chapuys.[33] Henry survived, but the accident ended his jousting career and aggravated serious leg problems that plagued him for the rest of his life. It is also believed that the accident may well have caused a brain injury that profoundly affected the King's personality because from 1536 onwards, Henry VIII became more suspicious, more tyrannical and more paranoid than ever before.[34]

It is interesting to compare Henry VIII's jousting accident to two similar accidents suffered by Francis I. In 1516, the French King had a fall from his horse that rendered him speechless for an hour. Seven years later, he was thrown from his horse and knocked unconscious for two days. His life was in danger, and many believed that he would never recover, being paralysed on one side; "as touching his own person, either in wit or activity for the war, he is not like to do any great feat".[35] Contrary to such grim predictions, Francis recovered and suffered no greater physical consequences. There was also no personality change recorded. If Henry VIII's fatal accident in 1536 did not change his personality, it certainly convinced him that he desperately needed a male heir. Beheading Anne Boleyn was one of the steps towards achieving that goal.

NOTES

[1] *Letters and Papers, Foreign and Domestic, Henry VIII*, Volume 7, 1534, n. 958.
[2] William Camden, *The History of the Princess Elizabeth Late Queen of England*, p. 3.
[3] *Letters and Papers, Foreign and Domestic, Henry VIII*, Volume 9, August-December 1535, n. 378.
[4] *Letters and Papers, Foreign and Domestic, Henry VIII*, Volume 6, 1533, n. 692.
[5] Pierre Jourda, *Correspondance de Marguerite d'Angouleme*, p. 127.
[6] Eric Ives, *The Life and Death of Anne Boleyn*, p. 273.
[7] Susan Snyder, *Guilty Sisters*, p. 443.
[8] Lisa Urkevich, *Anne Boleyn's French Motet Book, a Childhood Gift*, pp. 95-119.
[9] There is no record of a Frenchwoman named Marye or Marie being in Anne Boleyn's service, but her household is poorly documented.

[10] *William Latymer's Cronickille of Anne Bulleyne,* Volume 39 of Camden Fourth Series, p. 56.
[11] *Calendar of State Papers, Spain,* Volume 5 Part 1, 1534-1535, n. 112, 118.
[12] *Letters and Papers, Foreign and Domestic, Henry VIII,* Volume 8, January-July 1535, n. 196.
[13] Ibid., n. 174.
[14] Ibid., n. 340.
[15] Ibid., n. 846.
[16] Ibid., n. 837.
[17] Ibid., n. 909.
[18] Ibid., n. 847.
[19] Ibid., n. 826, 876.
[20] *Letters and Papers, Foreign and Domestic, Henry VIII,* Volume 10, January-June 1536, n. 359, 760.
[21] Ibid., n. 351.
[22] Ibid., n. 699.
[23] Ibid., n. 450.
[24] Eric Ives, *The Life and Death of Anne Boleyn,* p. 335.
[25] Roger B. Merriman, *Life and Letters of Thomas Cromwell,* Volume 2, p. 12.
[26] Ibid., p. 21.
[27] *Calendar of State Papers, Spain,* Volume 5 Part 2, 1536-1538, n. 55.
[28] Agnes Strickland, *Lives of the Queens of England,* Volume 2, p. 271.
[29] Raphael Holinshed, *Holinshed's Chronicles of England, Scotland and Ireland,* Volume 3, p. 797.
[30] Eric Ives, *The Life and Death of Anne Boleyn,* p. 341.
[31] *Letters and Papers, Foreign and Domestic, Henry VIII,* Volume 12 Part 2, June-December 1537, n. 78.
[32] Paul Friedmann, *Anne Boleyn: A Chapter of English History (1527-1536),* Volume 2, p. 300.
[33] *Letters and Papers, Foreign and Domestic, Henry VIII,* Volume 10, January-June 1536, n. 427.
[34] Read more in Suzannah Lipscomb's *1536: The Year That Changed Henry VIII,* Lion Hudson, 2009.
[35] *Letters and Papers, Foreign and Domestic, Henry VIII,* Volume 3, 1519-1523, n. 2833, 2846.

CHAPTER 15
"IT IS NOT THE CUSTOM IN FRANCE"

The day after Anne Boleyn's execution, the French ambassador rushed to Henry VIII's private chambers to propose a new marriage treaty. Francis I desired Henry VIII to marry his own daughter, the sixteen-year-old Madame Madeleine. The match was vigorously approved by the pope, who saw it as the most effectual way of convincing the English King to return to the Catholic Church.[1] Henry protested. He would not marry Madame Madeleine because she was "too young for him", and besides, he already had "too much experience of French bringing up and manners", alluding to the late Anne Boleyn.[2] He also added that he preferred to marry an Englishwoman because he could punish her if she misbehaved.

Indeed, Henry already had a bride in mind. On 30 May 1536, only eleven days after Anne Boleyn's beheading, the King married Jane Seymour. Henry VIII's new wife was pro-imperial in her political sympathies and decided to ban the seductive low-cut French gowns so popular during her predecessor's reign to make a loud statement that she was not like Anne Boleyn.

Over the next two years, the two Kings could share their grief over losses of their loved ones. In the summer of 1536, they both lost their sons. Henry VIII's illegitimate son, Henry Fitzroy, died on 23 July amidst rumours of poisoning. It was generally believed that he was administered poison by Anne Boleyn and her brother because he "pined inwardly in his body long before he died".[3] It is more likely that tuberculosis killed him. On 10 August, Francis I's son, Dauphin Francis, also died after taking a sip of cold water during a vigorous tennis match. Suspicions arose that someone poisoned the eighteen-year-old heir to the throne, and the blame fell on the man who passed the Dauphin a cup of iced water; he was executed several months later. Henry VIII wrote a letter of condolence to Francis I. He urged him "to be of good comfort" because he was "blessed with other fair issue".[4] Unlike Henry, Francis still had two younger sons who could succeed him.

This was not the end of deaths in the two royal families. When the proposed match between Henry VIII and Francis I's daughter Madeleine backfired, the French King married her off to James V, King of Scotland. Madeleine, whose health was fragile at the time, was warned that the climate in Scotland was much different than the one in France. Undeterred, the spirited teenager was heard saying: "At least I shall be Queen so long as I live". Upon her arrival to Scotland, Madeleine's health began to deteriorate, but she believed she would recover and began ordering jewellery and clothes for her impending coronation. Madeleine wrote to her father on 8 June 1537, informing him that since he sent his own physician to treat her, "all my sufferings are abated to my perfect cure".[5] Unfortunately, Madeleine fell sick again and died on 7 July 1537. She was the third daughter of Francis I to die during his lifetime.

On 12 October 1537, Henry VIII's third wife gave birth to the long-awaited male heir, Prince Edward, but she died twelve days later. She was twenty-nine years old. Jane Seymour had achieved in death the perfection that no other woman could aspire to in life and earned a place in the King's affections. Shortly after her death, Henry wrote to Francis informing him that he finally had a son, but "Divine Providence has mingled my joy with the bitterness of the death of her who brought me this happiness".[6] Despite his obvious grief, Henry was talking about a new marriage only a month after the late Queen's interment because his councillors believed the King should sire more sons. The French soon proposed three candidates: Marguerite of France, Francis I's fourteen-year-old daughter; Marie of Guise, twenty-two-year-old widowed Duchess of Longueville and mother of two small sons; and Marie of Vendôme, the twenty-three-year-old daughter of Charles, Duke of Vendôme, and Françoise d'Alençon. All of these noblewomen were related to Francis I, but Henry had his own opinions about each one. The French King's daughter was "too young", whereas

Marie of Vendôme was once promised to James V of Scotland, who, upon seeing her, decided to marry Francis I's daughter Madeleine instead. Marie was "hunchbacked and deformed", and Henry exclaimed that he would not "take the King of Scotland's leftovers".[7] It was Marie of Guise who captured the King's attention. She was strikingly tall, slender and had long auburn hair. Marie's physique appealed to Henry, who said that since "he was big in person", he had "a need of a big wife".[8]

The French ambassador Castillon reported that Henry was "so amorous of Madame de Longueville" that he could not talk about any other candidate. When the ambassador asked Henry who caused him to be more inclined to Marie of Guise more than to any other candidate, the King replied that his ambassador, John Wallop, "was so loud in her praises that nothing could exceed them".[9] Unfortunately for the English King, Marie's hand in marriage was already promised to James V of Scotland, Henry's detested nephew who had previously been married to Madame Madeleine of France. How could Francis I give Marie's hand in marriage to that "beggarly and stupid King of Scots?"[10] Henry wondered.

Henry decided to push through the French King's refusal and, despite the fact that formal articles of marriage were drawn up in January 1538, he dispatched Peter Mewtas, gentleman of the Privy Chamber, to France in order to obtain

Marie's portrait. The mission failed, and Mewtas was back in England by March, without the longed-for portrait of a woman whose description so enchanted Henry VIII. The King's hopes were further dashed when Marie of Guise married James V on 9 May 1538.

Fortunately for Henry, Marie had two charming sisters, and the French ambassador Castillon praised one of them, Louise, saying that she was "as beautiful and as graceful, clever and well fitted to please and obey him as any other". She was also a virgin. "Take her!" Castillon encouraged, "she is a maid, so you will have the advantage of being able to shape the passage to your measure". Henry laughed at this lascivious comment and tapped the ambassador on his shoulder before leaving to attend Mass.[11] Henry now decided to repeat the procedure and sent another trusted servant to obtain the lady's portrait. Philip Hoby, accompanied by Hans Holbein, went to visit Louise of Guise, who resided at Le Havre on the northwestern French coast, in the household of her mother, Antoinette de Bourbon, Duchess of Guise. The duchess reported back to her elder daughter, Marie, now Queen of Scotland, who had apparently developed an interest in Henry VIII's matrimonial affairs:

"It is but two days since the gentleman of the King of England, who was at Havre, and the painter, were here. The gentleman came to me, pretending that he was going to the Emperor, and having heard that Louise was ill would not go without seeing her, that he might report news of her to the King his master. He saw her (it was the day of her fever) and talked with her as he had done to me."[12]

When Henry VIII saw the portrait of Louise of Guise, he thought that she was "not ugly", but it seems he wasn't as thrilled as the French expected him to be.[13] Perhaps the King feared that her health was frail because Louise suffered from a mysterious fever; her mother was still worried about her on 30 September 1538, twenty-nine days after the English ambassador visited her in her sickroom. Soon the King heard that there was one more Guise girl, Renée, who was "still more beautiful" than Louise. She had apparently expressed a wish to join a religious order but was not yet professed as a nun.[14]

Throughout these negotiations, Henry VIII frequently suggested that a selection of ladies should be brought to Calais for his personal inspection, in charge of either Francis I's sister, Margaret of Navarre, or his wife, Queen Eleanor. The King of France was outraged, and when the English ambassador, Francis Bryan, proposed the interview, the King exclaimed: "It is not the custom in France to send damsels of that rank and of such noble and princely families to be passed in review as if they were hackneys for sale". Queen Eleanor, who was with the King at the time, told Bryan that "she was not the keeper of harlots and that the daughters of the royal blood of France never went out except in company with the Queen of that country". "I trust no one but myself", Henry told the bemused French ambassador, "the thing touches me too near. I wish to see them and know them some time before deciding". Castillon's reply was sharp and bawdy:

"Then perhaps Your Grace would like to mount them one after the other and keep the one you find to be the best broken in. Is that the way the Knights of the Round Table treated women in your country in times past?"[15]

The English King "laughed and blushed at the same time and recognised that the way he had taken was a little discourteous".[16] He finally revealed what troubled him. Francis I was warming up to the idea of rapprochement with Charles V, and Henry felt betrayed by his "good brother". Just as Henry was amassing his own private portrait gallery of prospective queens of England, Francis and Charles were putting the finishing touches on their new peace treaty. Henry was playing both sides, and whereas he was inclined to pick his future wife from among the French ladies, he was also hotly pursuing Charles V's niece, Christina, Duchess of Milan.

Christina's attitude towards her prospective marriage to Henry VIII may well reflect what other candidates thought about the ageing King of England. Christina, well aware of the King's reputation as a spouse, was heard saying that her council suspected that her great aunt, Katharine of Aragon, "was poisoned", that Anne Boleyn was "innocently put to death" and Jane Seymour "was lost for lack of keeping in childbed".[17] To Henry, it didn't really matter because he was so enamoured with Christina's full-length portrait, executed by Hans Holbein, that he was heard saying he would take her even if she came to him naked and penniless. Charles V ensured this would never happen, and the negotiations stalled over the question of dispensation. Christina was closely related to Henry VIII's first wife, and a papal dispensation was needed, but Henry, seeing himself as the head of the English Church, proposed that he would issue the necessary document himself. Charles would not accept this and pulled Christina out of the international marriage market. Soon it became apparent that the Franco-imperial rapprochement isolated England on the political stage of Europe, and the English began to fear a joint invasion. The only reasonable choice for the King of England now was to find an ally who would provide him military and financial aid in case he was invaded by Francis I and Charles V.

NOTES

[1] Paul Friedmann, *Anne Boleyn,* Volume 2, pp. 305-307.
[2] *Calendar of State Papers, Spain,* Volume 5 Part 2, 1536-1538, Additions and Corrections, n. 61.
[3] *Wriothesley's Chronicle,* Volume 1, pp. 53-4.
[4] *Letters and Papers, Foreign and Domestic, Henry VIII,* Volume 11, July-December 1536, n. 317.
[5] Rosalind K. Marshall, *Scottish Queens,* pp. 107, 108.

[6] *Letters and Papers, Foreign and Domestic, Henry VIII,* Volume 12 Part 2, June-December 1537, n. 972.
[7] Edmond Bapst, *Les Mariages de Jacques V*, p. 241.
[8] *Letters and Papers, Foreign and Domestic, Henry VIII,* Volume 12 Part 2, June-December 1537, n. 1285.
[9] Ibid.
[10] *Letters and Papers, Foreign and Domestic, Henry VIII,* Volume 13 Part 1, January-July 1538, n. 56.
[11] Ibid., n. 994.
[12] *Letters and Papers, Foreign and Domestic, Henry VIII,* Volume 13 Part 2, August-December 1538, n. 262.
[13] Ibid., n. 1451.
[14] *Letters and Papers, Foreign and Domestic, Henry VIII,* Volume 13 Part 1, January-July 1538, n. 1217.
[15] *Letters and Papers, Foreign and Domestic, Henry VIII,* Volume 13 Part 2, August-December 1538, n. 77.
[16] Ibid.
[17] *Letters and Papers, Foreign and Domestic, Henry VIII,* Volume 14 Part 2, August-December 1539, n. 400.

CHAPTER 16
"ANNOYED AND HUMILIATED"

Just as Henry VIII was going through portraits of various European noblewomen he was interested in marrying, Queen Eleanor was doing her best to reconcile her warring brother and husband. Hostilities between Francis I and Charles V resumed when the French invaded Savoy and Piedmont in 1536. Charles countered with an invasion of Provence while France attacked the Netherlands. By 1538, neither side was able to claim victory.

In June 1538, the pope negotiated a truce between the two monarchs in Nice, and Francis and Charles met face-to-face on 14 July in Aigues-Mortes. Having Charles's sister as his wife, Francis I was well aware that he had a great helper in achieving peace. In the past, Francis had "made her arbiter of his differences with the Emperor" and the foreign ambassadors proclaimed Eleanor "the principal soul" who "through her great talent, prudence and generosity, brought about this change in the politics of France".[1]

During the meeting in Aigues-Mortes, Eleanor played a prominent role, arriving with "an infinite number of ladies", including the Dauphin's wife, Catherine de Medici, Francis I's daughter, Marguerite of France, and Margaret of Navarre's daughter, Jeanne d'Albret. To Eleanor, this was the moment she revelled in because, for the first time since becoming Queen of France, she managed to foster peace between her brother and husband. The reunion with Charles V was especially important to Eleanor, who yearned to see her beloved brother.

On 10 June 1538, the siblings saw each other for the first time in eight years. Charles ordered the open ground in front of his palace to be carefully swept and awnings of linen cloth to be prepared to ward off the sunrays. Because Eleanor was travelling by barge, a large wooden pier was hastily erected near the palace to enable the embarkation. Always the gentleman, Charles ordered his galleys to receive Eleanor at sea and escort her to his palace:

"They went as far as Nice when, perceiving that the French galleys were coming out of port, all hoisted their flags and displayed the imperial standard in sign of friendship, the French galleys on their side returning the compliment. When the galley of the King of France came near ours, she lowered her standard and saluted that of the Emperor, on board of which Prince Doria was doing the same. After which the galleys of both fleets, 48 in number, that is, 30 Imperial and 18 French, fired their guns, and rowed into port at Villafranca all together in beautiful order, the galley of the King of France and that of

Prince Doria being first. Arrived at the port, all the galleys, Imperial and French, again fired their guns. It was a fine sight indeed, that of so many flashes and reports, which ultimately produced such a smoke on sea and land, and so thick a cloud, as to obscure heaven and earth."

Finally, the emperor's person emerged amidst smoke and the heavy scent of gunpowder. He stood on a wooden pier, waiting for the disembarkation of the French ladies, "whom he received one by one with great glee, embracing and kissing every one of them on the lips as they landed". When the barge with Eleanor and her female relatives approached, Charles could not wait any longer. He advanced a few steps, stretching his hand to his sister, and when she finally stepped off the barge onto the pier, he "embraced and kissed her most affectionately, his countenance beaming with joy". It was as if the world around them melted away in the reassuring warmth of that moment. The brother and sister remained in each other's arms for some time until large, pressing crowds gathered around them, and the makeshift pier suddenly collapsed:

"The Emperor fell in also, but seized hold of his sister, the Queen of France, who fell sideways, whilst he himself was up to his knees in water. At this juncture, sailors and men came and helped them out, the Emperor leading the Queen by the hand, and laughing heartily at the ridiculous figure presented by the ladies, frightened and wet as they were. The Archbishop of Santiago, the Marquis of Saluzzo, the Duke of Najera, and several other noblemen and gentlemen, took a cold bath. The Emperor lost his cap, without which, however, after giving his arm to the Queen, he walked back to his palace, followed by the princesses and other ladies of their suite, all escorted by many cavaliers. Nor was the walk a very easy one, owing to the crowds of people pressing on, anxious to inquire what had happened. There was at first some confusion and noise, especially among the French; but when the cause of the mishap was ascertained, and it was found that nobody had been hurt by the fall, the alarm ceased and everything was quiet. Then the Emperor, the Queen, the ladies and gentlemen went up to the palace, where orders were issued for dry dresses for the former, and clothes for the latter. You should have seen the gentlemen sending home for long breeches for the ladies!"[2]

The teary reunion with her brother brought back happy memories for Eleanor, who was raised with Charles and the rest of their siblings at the cultured court of their paternal aunt, Margaret of Savoy. But these memories seemed distant now, and Charles could see a worried expression on his sister's face as she glanced behind to see whether her husband was paying attention to the blond beauty bearing the long train of her gown.

The Queen's trainbearer, Anne de Pisseleu, Duchess of Étampes, had displaced Françoise de Foix as Francis I's official mistress in 1526 and reigned supreme over the court. In 1534, the King arranged her marriage to Jean de Brosse, to whom he gave the county of Étampes, which he made into a duchy to elevate Anne to the rank and status appropriate for a royal mistress. This thirty-year-old woman was one of the youngest of twenty-three children born to Guillaume de Pisseleu, seigneur de Heilly, a minor courtier with no great income. Equipped only with her beauty and remarkable intelligence—she was said to have been "the most beautiful of learned ladies and the most learned of the beautiful"—she started her career as Louise of Savoy's maid of honour. After Louise's death, she transferred to the combined household of Francis I's daughters, Madeleine and Marguerite, soon joined by another lady to serve, Catherine de Medici. Madame d'Etampes, as she was widely known at court, secured lucrative appointments for her relatives and friends and wielded an influence such as no royal mistress had exerted ever before.

Queen Eleanor usually kept her feelings to herself, but when she met her brother for the first time in eight years, she unburdened herself. Amidst general rejoicing, Eleanor confessed to Charles how matters really stood between her husband and Madame d'Etampes. "She said how much humiliated and annoyed she was" by Francis's extramarital affair but begged her brother "to go and pay his court to the said lady in so signal a manner that all should see and notice it".

It must have been humiliating for Eleanor to implore Charles to pay respects to the woman whose sole presence diminished her own position at court, but it shows that Eleanor was far more intelligent and politically savvy than she is given credit for. Madame d'Etampes wielded an extraordinary influence over Francis I, who could refuse her nothing. One word from the formidable duchess could make or unmake any alliance, and Eleanor knew it. Ignoring the King's favourite could have had disastrous effects for the newly created alliance, and Charles V did as he was told and, "with cap in hand went forward and embraced and kissed the lady most affectionately, waiting upon her all the time the collation lasted and saying many sweet things to her, as for instance that he wished very much to become the object of her affections, and to surpass even King Francis in his devotion and attentions."[3] Madame d'Etampes saw it as her unqualified success; Queen Eleanor saw it as a necessary evil.

By 1539, the relationship between Francis I and Charles V was more cordial than ever before, and when the emperor asked for a safe conduct through France on his way to Flanders, he was received with great festivities. Henry VIII, excommunicated by the pope in December 1538 after three years of suspension, now feared that the Franco-imperial alliance would aim at deposing him. The English King started mustering his forces for war when the French and imperial ambassadors were simultaneously recalled from his court.

He also turned his attentions to the little Protestant duchy of Cleves, where Duke William had two single sisters to marry into the European noble houses. One of them, the twenty-four-year-old Anne, had been proposed as a candidate for Henry VIII's bride in 1538, but the King was more interested in other potential brides at the time. Now he had no other option but to send his ambassadors and report back about Anne of Cleves's "beauty and qualities". Luckily for Henry VIII, Anne was described in glowing terms as young and beautiful. His ambassador even compared her to the beautiful Duchess of Milan, who had instantly caught Henry's eye when he saw her portrait, stating that Anne excelled Christina "as the golden sun excelled the silver moon".[4] Henry VIII's imagination now ran wild with visions of Anne of Cleves's beauty, although she had no characteristics that Henry valued in a woman. She was neither a card-player nor could sing, dance or perform on any musical instrument. She also spoke no other language but her native German. The King chose to ignore all this and signed the treaty with William, Duke of Cleves. Anne was to become his fourth wife, but the King was to be brutally disappointed.

Their first meeting was a disaster. The impatient Henry decided to seek Anne out before their officially scheduled meeting and burst into her chambers disguised as a royal messenger, surrounded by six of his fellow courtiers. Dressing up played an important part of courtly gallantry, and Henry, reared up on chivalrous tales about the Knights of the Round Table, decided to surprise his future wife. She stood by the window, watching a bear baiting—in which a bear was chained to a post and set on by dogs—when the hooded Henry approached her and suddenly embraced and kissed her, presenting gift from the King. Anne was supposed to recognise him instantly by the virtue of his kingly office and appearance, but she failed to do so and "regarded him little", paying more attention to the bloody spectacle unfolding just outside her window than to the ruddy giant of a man who stood in front of her.

Henry was no longer the athletic young prince who ascended the throne so many years ago. He was now a bald, limping and grossly overweight shadow of a man he used to be and looked nothing like a King without his golden crown and rich attire. Seeing the lack of interest in his person on Anne's part, the King left her and returned dressed in a splendid cloak of purple velvet.[5] This time everyone bowed when he entered, and Anne, speechless at the sight, fell on her knees in stony silence. Although they talked awhile, neither of them could forget the awkward first impressions that were now etched in their hearts and minds.

The King was so disappointed that he decided not to present Anne with the bejewelled furs he had brought for her. Instead, he sent Anthony Browne of the Privy Chamber the next morning with presents and "cold message". "I see nothing in this woman as men report of her", Henry told Browne as they made their way back from Rochester to Greenwich.[6] Just what bothered Henry about Anne of Cleves's appearance after their disastrous first meeting remains unknown. Her portrait by Hans Holbein shows a fairly attractive young woman with a dreamy half smile, olive skin, hazel eyes and hands clasped at her tiny waist. Holbein's portrait was said to have been a faithful depiction of Anne, but her manner apparently was not at all what Henry VIII had expected.

When the King asked John Russell, Lord Admiral, who saw Anne in Rochester, whether "he thought the woman so fair and of such beauty as report had been made of her", the admiral replied that she was not "fair" but of a "brown complexion".[7] Considering that Henry was so disgusted with Anne's appearance, the admiral's comment seems unrevealing. All he could say about this woman who was to become the next Queen of England was that her complexion was not pale, but this was hardly a surprise considering that Holbein's portrait clearly showed that Anne of Cleves's skin was not snowy white, and Henry had been able to fall in love with olive-skinned women in the past.

True, when dressed in the unflattering fashions of her native duchy of Cleves, Anne looked older than she truly was, as the newly arrived French ambassador Charles de Marillac observed with a streak of malicious glee, but she quickly grasped that if she wanted to look fresh and attractive, she should wear the fashionable French clothes so popular at Henry VIII's court. This did not help, however, and when the wedding day approached, Henry exclaimed that "if it were not to satisfy the world, and my realm, I would not do that I must do this day for no earthly thing". The King was forced to put his royal "neck in the yoke", and he did not like it one bit. The only person who truly recognized why the King was so disappointed with Anne of Cleves was Anthony Browne's wife, who served in the new Queen's Privy Chamber. The perceptive Lady Browne confessed that "she saw in the Queen such fashion and manner of bringing up so gross that in her judgment the King should never heartily love her".[8]

And what about Anne of Cleves? Shortly before the wedding took place, she was asked to appear before the Privy Council and swear that her previous engagement to the Duke of Lorraine was not binding and that she was free to marry Henry VIII. She did so, but she must have sensed that something was amiss because she was late for the wedding ceremony. Whatever she knew or thought she knew, the wedding went on as planned. The bride wore her "fair, yellow and long" hair loose, as unmarried women did during that period. A rich "gold coronet of gemstones and pearls" set with branches of the herb rosemary adorned her head. Her gown of cloth of silver was adorned with "great Oriental pearls" and jewels. The King, to whom she curtsied three times, after the custom of her country, cut a striking figure in his black fur-trimmed gown of cloth of gold beneath a cloak of crimson satin strewn with diamonds.

Mass in the royal chapel was followed by banquets and dances, but the King was in no mood for entertainment.[9] And then the wedding night came. When the heavy oak doors closed behind the nuptial chamber and Anne of Cleves was left alone with Henry VIII, the real drama unfolded. Although Anne was spared the humiliating bedding ceremony witnessed by the entire court, a humiliation of another kind awaited her. The King attempted to consummate the match, but as soon as his hand started travelling up and down his new wife's body, he "felt her belly and breasts" and judged that "she was no maid". Having "neither will nor courage to proceed any further in other matters", Henry bid Anne good night and fell asleep. The next day, when Thomas Cromwell—architect of the Cleves marriage—asked the King how he liked his new bride, Henry retorted: "Surely, you know, I liked her before not well, but now I like her much worse".[10] Despite the discouraging failure in the marital bed, Henry kept visiting Anne's bedchamber each night,

"Annoyed and humiliated"

but he started preparing the grounds for an annulment behind the scenes.

In late February 1540, Henry VIII decided to renew his strained relationship with Francis I. Thomas Howard, Duke of Norfolk, was sent as a special emissary to the French court and warned Francis against trusting Charles V. Norfolk was also instructed to renew contact with Francis's sister, Margaret of Navarre. It wasn't difficult since Margaret knew Norfolk well and remembered their long and fruitful audiences of 1533. On 17 February 1540, Norfolk had an audience with Margaret and praised her as "the most frank and wise woman he ever spake with".[11] She briefed him about the political situation at court, revealing that she was no friend of the Constable Anne de Montmorency and advised him "to try and win Madame d'Etampes".[12]

By April, Norfolk was replaced by Sir John Wallop, who was specifically instructed to curry favour with the King's sister and mistress. Acknowledging Madame d'Etampes's influence and trying to win her approval, Henry VIII even sent her richly caparisoned palfreys, but it was Margaret of Navarre whose opinion counted the most for him.[13] Henry deeply admired Francis's sister and built a close diplomatic relationship with her over the years. Margaret once mused that she and Henry should have married when they had the chance because they shared similar political and religious views:

"I must needs love that Prince, for sundry causes; I should have been once his father's wife, and I should have been his wife, and he and I both of one opinion in religion, for neither of us loved the Pope; and I think he would be glad to see both our destructions, for the which purpose he practised with the Emperor, that is to say, with hypocrisy. For the Emperor is Hypocrisy and the Pope is Devil..."[14]

From as early as 1503, there had been offers for Margaret's marriage with Henry VIII's father, Henry VII, or even with Henry himself, who was then Prince of Wales. Margaret, who from an early age displayed a strong character and independent spirit, was never interested in marrying the old and decrepit Henry VII and retorted that she would prefer to marry without the need of crossing the sea. Now, almost thirty-eight years later, she and her brother took an active interest in Henry VIII's marriage to Anne of Cleves. Always eager to weaken Charles V's hold on the German estates, Francis I decided to ally himself with the new Queen of England's brother, William, Duke of Cleves, and arranged his marriage to Margaret of Navarre's daughter, Jeanne d'Albret.

When in July 1540 Francis learned that Henry annulled his marriage to Anne of Cleves, he sighed: "Oh, Jesus, he is leaving her!"[15] To Francis, Henry's decision to repudiate his wife made no sense at all. "It was more to be marvelled at than any other", the French King declared to Sir John Wallop and expressed his wish to learn more about Henry's motives.[16] He kept repeating that he desired to learn about the process of annulment that took place in England and asked Wallop if it was Anne's alleged pre-contract with the Duke of Lorraine that nullified her marriage to the King. What Francis did not know was that Henry annulled his marriage simply because he found Anne of Cleves unattractive. He claimed that the tall and thin Anne failed to "excite and provoke any lust in him" and used non-consummation as grounds for annulment.[17] In other words, Henry claimed that with Anne he was impotent, but he believed that he was able to have intercourse with other women. The King was already thinking about another wife, and, as in times past, he had a particular lady in mind.

NOTES

[1] *Calendar of State Papers, Spain,* Volume 5 Part 1, 1534-1535, n. 81.
[2] *Calendar of State Papers, Spain,* Volume 5 Part 2, 1536-1538, n. 206.
[3] Ibid.
[4] *Letters and Papers, Foreign and Domestic, Henry VIII,* Volume 14 Part 1, January-July 1539, n. 552.
[5] *Wriothesley's Chronicle*, Volume 1, pp. 109-110.
[6] *Letters and Papers, Foreign and Domestic, Henry VIII,* Volume 15, 1540, n.7.
[7] Ibid., n. 6.

[8] Ibid.
[9] *Hall's Chronicle*, pp. 836-837.
[10] *Letters and Papers, Foreign and Domestic, Henry VIII*, Volume 15, 1540, n. 823.
[11] Ibid., n. 223.
[12] Ibid.
[13] Ibid., n. 459.
[14] *Letters and Papers, Foreign and Domestic, Henry VIII*, Volume 17, 1542, n. 128.
[15] *Letters and Papers, Foreign and Domestic, Henry VIII*, Volume 15, 1540, n. 870.
[16] Ibid., n. 890.
[17] John Strype, *Ecclesiastical Memorials*, Volume 1, p. 461.

CHAPTER 17
"LIGHTNESS OF A WOMAN"

On 28 July 1540, Henry VIII married for the fifth time. His new bride was Katherine Howard, the nineteen-year-old niece of Thomas Howard, and Anne Boleyn's first cousin. Raised in the household of her step-grandmother Agnes Howard, Dowager Duchess of Norfolk, Katherine received an education fit for a girl who aspired to become a maid of honour to Henry VIII's wife and joined Anne of Cleves's household in early 1540. She was an attractive young lady whose sparkling personality—she loved to sing, dance and play cards—reminded Henry VIII of his lost youth.

By now, the years of misuse of his body and the dangerous fall he suffered when jousting in 1536 were beginning to show on his ever-expanding frame. Henry's swollen legs and large bulk did not permit him to indulge as frequently in the physical pursuits such as hunting or jousting, so he whiled away his days at his desk or in bed, poring through paperwork and books. He was still able to ride, but long hours in the saddle were now only a distant memory. Henry's legs, covered with fistulas and ulcers, were a source of constant pain, and many believed that "the King's leg will kill him". In 1538, for instance, one of the fistulas closed up, and the King remained speechless for almost two weeks, "black in the face and in great danger". The royal physicians lanced the fistula with a red-hot poker, allowing drainage of the 'humours' and saving the King's life. From that point on, the fistulas were kept open for the King's safety, producing a putrid stench that could be identified three rooms away, often announcing Henry's arrival.[1]

If Katherine Howard felt any distaste for her much older, sickly husband, she cloaked it with a display of wifely obedience. There was "no other will but his", a motto she adopted upon becoming Queen and wore embroidered in gold thread around her sleeves.[2] The King, enamoured with Katherine, believed that he had acquired a "jewel of womanhood" and spared no expense to enhance her appearance. "The King had no wife who made him spend so much money in dresses and jewels as she did", observers remarked.[3]

The royal family in France was curious as to what this new, young Queen of England looked like and whether she was fertile. In October 1540, Sir John Wallop reported that Margaret of Navarre requested "Your Majesty's picture with the Queen, my lord Prince, and the ladies Mary and Elizabeth". She also asked "whether Her Grace was with child yet".[4] Whether Henry VIII was able to father a child on his bride remains speculative considering the state of his health, but he was certainly sending signals that he and Katherine shared an intense sexual relationship; he often caressed her in public, leading Charles de Marillac to remark that he was "so amorous of her that he knows not how to make sufficient demonstrations of his affection, and caresses her more than he did the others".[5]

Katherine was attractive, short and plump and possessed that sort of vivacious wit and charm that Henry VIII valued in a woman. Influenced by his young bride, the King made an attempt to lose weight. He adopted a new rule of life, rising even in winter between five and six, hearing Mass at seven, and riding about on horseback till ten, by which he found himself to be restored to health, or so he naively believed. The idyll was not to last for very long. In early 1541, the King fell ill when one of his troublesome fistulas closed in again. He suffered from fever and was bedridden for several days. The illness and unbearable pain served as a reminder of his mortality, and Katherine Howard was to experience the King's changing moods for the first time since their wedding.

Shrovetide that year was a particularly sombre affair, with no music and traditional pastimes at court. Shrovetide, which started on Shrove Sunday, the seventh Sunday before Easter, marked the beginning of Lent and was the last opportunity to have fun and eat meat before the court plunged into a series of religious observances and a diet consisting mostly of fish. The King took Katherine and a small band of servants to Hampton Court, where they lived like a "private family" according to the French ambassador, who had never seen anything like this before.[6]

All pleasures and rowdiness were abandoned when Lent started, and Henry VIII refused to see his young Queen for a period of ten days. Various rumours swirled at court as to why the King, previously so enamoured, was now avoiding Katherine Howard's company. Some surmised that she must have been with child, others that the King avoided her on account of his illness. The imperial ambassador Chapuys thought that the reason behind the King's decision was more sinister. "There was much talk of a divorce", he wrote to Charles V.[7] He heard that Katherine was "sad and thoughtful" because she heard the rumours that Henry VIII intended to repudiate her and take back Anne of Cleves. The King did little to dispel her worries. "She was wrong to believe such things of him or attach faith to reports of the kind", he said, adding somewhat sinisterly that "even if he had to marry again, he would never retake Madame de Cleves".[8]

Henry was certainly telling the truth. He had no intention of marrying Anne of Cleves, who became a member of the royal family as Henry's "beloved sister" after the annulment. She was now one of the most high-profile ladies in England, with a steady income of £3,000 per year and several royal residences where she lived depending on the season. But there was no place for her at court since, as the former Queen, her high rank made it impossible for her to serve as Katherine Howard's lady-in-waiting. The King was eager to show that this time around he treated his former wife with respect, and he often visited her, sent her valuable presents and entertained her at court. This honourable treatment gave birth to rumours that the King regretted his decision to repudiate Anne of Cleves, but he was still in love with Katherine Howard, even if he sometimes failed to show her his devotion.

Upon returning from the northern progress in the autumn of 1541, Henry VIII ordered that on 2 November, All Souls' Day, there should be special prayers offered for "the good life he led and trusted to lead" with Katherine Howard.[9] Unbeknown to Henry, this "good life" with Katherine was about to end in one of the biggest scandals of the King's reign. While the King was on progress, Thomas Cranmer, Archbishop of Canterbury, received confidential information from one John Lascelles about the Queen's scandalous past. His sister, Mary Hall, shared a dormitory with Katherine while they were both living in the Dowager Duchess of Norfolk's household and was aware that the young Queen was "light both in living and in conditions". There was a young man named Francis Dereham who used to sneak into the maidens' chamber and spend a "hundred nights" making love to the teenaged Katherine Howard. There was "such puffing and blowing between them" that one of the maidens who shared a bed with Katherine decided to leave. There was also Henry Manox, a music master, who "used to feel secret and other parts of her body".[10]

The King refused to believe in these sensational claims but ordered an investigation to clear his wife's name from slander. Henry Manox, the lewd music teacher, confessed that he touched Katherine's "secret parts" but never had carnal knowledge of her. Francis Dereham, on the other hand, admitted that he had known Katherine carnally "many times". He claimed, much to the councillors' horror, that he and Katherine had been betrothed. This effectively meant that their relationship had not been sinful in the eyes of the Church and even that Katherine's marriage to Henry VIII was invalid because she entered into a pre-contract with Dereham. Confronted with these confessions, Katherine threw herself on the King's mercy, blaming "the subtle persuasions of young men" for her misdemeanours:

"First at the flattering and fair persuasions of Manox, being but a young girl, suffered him at sundry times to handle and touch the secret parts of my body which neither became me with honesty to permit nor him to require. Also Francis

Dereham by many persuasions procured me to his vicious purpose and obtained first to lye upon my bed with his doublet and hose and after within the bed and finally he lay with me naked and used me in such sort as a man doth his wife many and sundry times, but how often I know not, and our company ended almost a year before the King's Majesty was married to my Lady Anne of Cleves and continued not past a quarter of a year or little above."[11]

During her interrogation, Katherine wept, sobbed and was consumed by "vehement rage". The Archbishop of Canterbury found her in "such lamentation and heaviness, as I never saw no creature".[12] He believed that if Katherine admitted that there was a pre-contract between herself and Dereham, she might be saved from the executioner's axe, but the young Queen insisted that there never was any pre-contract. True, Dereham called her his "wife" and she called him her "husband", they exchanged gifts, kissed and made "good cheer" in the maidens' chamber, but she never promised to marry him. Furthermore, she claimed "that all that Dereham did unto her was of his importune enforcement, and, in a manner, violence, rather than of her free consent and will".[13] In other words, Katherine implied that she was sexually abused. But was she really?

Other girls who shared a dormitory with Katherine were of a very different opinion. Katherine Tilney, the girl who shared a bed with Katherine Howard on many occasions, confessed that the Dowager Duchess of Norfolk knew very well that there was "love" between Katherine and Dereham, but that she was displeased about it. She had once "found Dereham embracing Mistress Katherine Howard in his arms and kissing her"; there they were, kissing and touching, with no struggle involved.[14] The angry Dowager slapped Katherine and Dereham for their secret affair because Katherine was too fine a match to be wasted on such a nobody as Francis Dereham. Also, when the Dowager Duchess herself was informed that Katherine and Dereham were interrogated, she suspected that it was because they shared a steamy relationship under her roof.[15] Dereham himself was said to have confessed to a sexual relationship with Katherine because there were at least three girls who knew about their nightly sessions of "puffing and blowing", and there was no point in denying anything.

The councillors who interrogated Dereham feared that Katherine Howard employed him as her usher and secretary because she wanted to continue their secret affair. Dereham was outraged, and to clear himself of all suspicion, he declared that "Culpeper had succeeded him in the Queen's affections".[16] Thomas Culpeper was distantly related to Katherine's mother, and the two met for the first time soon after Katherine's arrival at court. Their relationship was apparently serious since rumours circulated at the time that they would be soon engaged. They renewed their contact when Katherine became Queen. As gentleman of the Privy Chamber, Culpeper was very close to the King, who favoured his young servant, and he saw the royal couple on a daily basis.

In November 1541, Culpeper's quarters were searched for evidence of his involvement with the Queen while he was rigorously interrogated in the Tower. A letter from Katherine was found. In it, she wrote achingly that "it makes my heart die to think what fortune I have that I cannot be always in your company". Both Culpeper and Katherine revealed that they had many secret meetings, but they never made love. It was Jane Boleyn, Lady Rochford, who encouraged them to meet in private, they both unanimously claimed. Lady Rochford, widow of George Boleyn, had another story to tell. She believed that "Culpeper has known the Queen carnally".[17]

Despite Henry VIII's initial belief in Katherine Howard's innocence, the evidence against her was simply too damning to ignore. Francis Dereham and Thomas Culpeper were executed on 10 December 1541. Katherine Howard and her lady-in-waiting, Lady Rochford, followed them to the scaffold on 13 February 1542. The young Queen's guilt was never properly established, and she was "condemned on great suspicion of adultery" rather than for adultery itself.[18]

The people of England were shocked, but some whispered that "the whole thing seemed a judgment of God, for the Lady of Cleves was really the King's wife".[19] Anne of Cleves rejoiced when she heard about Katherine Howard's execution, or at least this is what the imperial ambassador heard and reported. She hoped that, with so many people singing her praises, and with such powerful allies abroad, the King would finally take her back as his wife.

Upon learning of Katherine Howard's misconduct, King Francis I wrote to Charles de Marillac that he was "sorry for Henry's grief" and promised to send a gentleman "to condole with him". Later, he told Henry VIII's ambassador that he was "sorry to hear of his good brother's trouble, caused by the naughty demeanour of her lately reputed for Queen", and reminded the King that "his honour did not rest in the lightness of a woman".[20] Francis hoped that Henry would marry Anne of Cleves, whose brother was now allied to Francis against Charles V.

In early 1542, a book entitled *Remonstrance of Anne of Cleves* was published in France. It was a sensational work of someone who clearly wanted to see Anne reinstated to her former glory. Henry VIII was furious and ordered his ambassador in France to urge Francis I to suppress the book. When the ambassador broached the subject of this slanderous publication with the French King, Francis pretended he knew nothing of the book and thought that the Duke of Cleves, Anne's brother, probably had no idea about it either. At the same time, Francis revealed his true feelings about Henry's reconciliation with Anne: "the lady Anne is yet of age to bear children, and albeit the wind hath been contrary, it may fortune to turn".[21]

Francis's sister, Margaret of Navarre, felt genuinely sorry for Anne and decided to reach out to Henry VIII's discarded bride. She was interested in Anne's position when Katherine Howard became Queen, fearing, perhaps, that Henry would treat Anne the same way he treated his first wife, Katharine of Aragon. When she learned that Anne of Cleves received a large annuity and her own establishment, Margaret praised the King's "good and honourable treatment of my lady Anne". Now, she employed the French ambassador Marillac to send Anne her friendly advice and a portrait. Marillac thought that Margaret's portrait would bring Anne joy because "she has long desired it", which proves that the two women kept in touch either through letters or through the French ambassador's agents.[22] Anne, in turn, promised to deliver a painting of herself to Marillac. Her hopes for the reconciliation with Henry VIII were to be dashed, however. She would never become his wife again.

Staying in England turned out to be a blessing in disguise for Anne. Although she complained that she would "rather lose everything in this world and return to her mother than remain longer in England", she never found enough courage to return to her native duchy of Cleves.[23] She feared that her brother would "slay" her if she returned because she brought shame upon herself when Henry VIII had repudiated her, but it later became apparent that William of Cleves blamed Henry rather than Anne for their annulment.[24] By 1542, when her native duchy was "ravaged and desolated with fire and plunder by the Imperial forces", Anne may have felt that she made the right choice after all.[25]

NOTES

[1] Chalmers, C.R. and E.J. Chaloner, "500 Years Later: Henry VIII, Leg Ulcers and the Course of History", *Journal of the Royal Society of Medicine*, 102 (2009), pp. 513-517.
[2] *Letters and Papers, Foreign and Domestic, Henry VIII*, Volume 16, 1540-1541, n. 12.
[3] *Chronicle of King Henry VIII (The Spanish Chronicle)*, p. 77.
[4] *Letters and Papers, Foreign and Domestic, Henry VIII*, Volume 16, 1540-1541, n. 204, 240.
[5] Ibid., n. 12.
[6] Ibid., n. 589.
[7] Ibid., n. 1328.
[8] *Calendar of State Papers, Spain*, Volume 6 Part 1, 1538-1542, n. 163.
[9] Sir Harris Nicolas, *Proceedings and Ordinances of the Privy Council of England*, Volume, p. 352.
[10] Ibid.
[11] *Examination of Queen Katherine Howard* (Calendar of the Manuscripts of the Marquis of Bath, Volume 2, p. 10)
[12] Thomas Cranmer, *Miscellaneous Writings and Letters of Thomas Cranmer*, ed. The Parker Society, p. 408.
[13] Ibid.

[14] *Letters and Papers, Foreign and Domestic, Henry VIII,* Volume 16, 1540-1541, n. 1385.
[15] Ibid., n. 1400.
[16] Ibid., n. 1366.
[17] Ibid., n. 1339.
[18] *Letters and Papers, Foreign and Domestic, Henry VIII,* Volume 17, 1542, n. 10.
[19] *Letters and Papers, Foreign and Domestic, Henry VIII,* Volume 16, 1540-1541, n. 1441.
[20] Ibid., n. 1372, 1453.
[21] *Letters and Papers, Foreign and Domestic, Henry VIII,* Volume 17, 1542, n. 128.
[22] Ibid., n. 35.
[23] *Calendar of State Papers, Spain,* Volume 6 Part 2, 1542-1543, n. 188.
[24] Elizabeth Norton, *Anne of Cleves: Henry VIII's Discarded Bride*, p. 192.
[25] Hastings Robinson, *Original Letters Relative to the English Reformation*, p. 633.

CHAPTER 18
THE PEACE-MAKING QUEEN

On 12 July 1543, as plague began to rage in London, two dozen guests crammed into a small chapel at Hampton Court to witness Henry VIII's sixth marriage. The King was now fifty-two and weary of "taking young wives".[1] After Katherine Howard's execution, it became treason to marry the King without confessing any past indiscretions beforehand. "There are few, if any, ladies at court nowadays likely to aspire to the honour of becoming one of the King's wives", wrote the imperial ambassador Chapuys.[2]

Despite several failed marriages, Henry VIII was still in a mood to remarry, and when Katherine Parr caught his eye, he decided that she was the perfect candidate for his sixth bride. She was thirty-one, twice widowed and an experienced stepmother to her late husband's two children. She was also a tall, elegant and attractive woman with a deep interest in religion and education. The King selected her not only because she already had the experience of being married to an older man, but also because her spotless reputation carried a promise that, unlike her executed predecessor, she would be the most suitable wife to an aging monarch.

Despite the fact that he was growing older and stouter, Henry VIII still nurtured hope of invading France and defeating Francis I, his long-term rival on the international political stage. By now, the French King stood by his earlier opinion that Henry was "the strangest man in the world", and there was no love lost between the two.[3] In July 1544, just over a year after allying himself with Charles V and declaring war on France, Henry VIII crossed the Channel to direct the English siege of Boulogne, leaving Katherine Parr as Regent of England.

In a prayer composed at the time of this last Anglo-French war, Katherine prayed to God that her husband's victories should be bought "with small effusion of blood and little damage of innocents".[4] She also busied herself with diplomacy, politics, writing her own book and exchanging letters with Henry VIII, who seemed to genuinely admire and appreciate her wit. In one of his letters, Henry addressed Katherine as his "most dearly and most entirely beloved wife" and wrote in great detail about the news from the front, telling her, among other things, that "we have won (and that without any loss of men) the strongest part of the town [of Boulogne], which is the bray of the castle". The fact that the King described his military campaign in such vivid detail proves that he deemed his sixth wife to be intelligent enough to understand

and share his joy about the victory. It also proves that Katherine Parr must have been a patient listener. The first part of the abovementioned letter pertains to political, military and financial matters, but the last paragraph allows us to see what kind of relationship these two shared:

"No more to you at this time, sweetheart, both for lack of time and great occupation of business, saving we pray you to give, in our name, our hearty blessings to all our children, and recommendations to our cousin Margaret [Douglas] and the rest of the ladies and gentlewomen, and to our Council also. Written with the hand of your loving husband,

Henry R."[5]

Boulogne surrendered to Henry VIII on 14 September 1544, and the King entered the town in full military glory four days later. His victory, however, was bittersweet. The previously agreed upon Anglo-imperial military strategy required Henry VIII and Charles V to lead their respective armies towards Paris. Henry realised that it was wiser to lay siege to Boulogne and Montreuil rather than advance on the capital of France. On 18 September 1544, the very day Henry entered Boulogne, Charles V and Francis I signed a peace treaty at Crépy, ending the friendly relations between Henry and Charles.

Charles V's sister, Eleanor, was overjoyed with this turn of events. She dreamed about a firm peace treaty between her brother and husband for years, and now, yet again, she was instrumental in attaining it. She left France to meet with her brother and cement peace in the autumn of 1544, taking Francis I's younger son Charles, Duke of Orléans, with her.[6] She was also accompanied by her husband's mistress, Anne de Pisseleu, Duchess of Étampes.

By now, Eleanor had learned to accept Anne de Pisseleu's presence in her life. It was not always easy. In 1541, for instance, three of Eleanor's Spanish ladies-in-waiting were banished from court "for speaking ill of Madame d'Etampes", which means that they must have followed the Queen's example.[7] By 1544, the Queen and the royal mistress had learned how to live in harmony and were even travelling together in one litter to meet Charles V.[8] The reason Madame d'Etampes was invited in the first place was because Queen Eleanor realized that Madame's approval of the course of foreign policy was essential in bringing peace between her brother and husband to fruition.

In 1538, Eleanor herself had exhorted her brother to curry favour with Anne de Pisseleu, but when Charles V was passing through France in late 1539, he failed to make much of the French King's mistress, incurring her wrath. It was reported that after the emperor's visit, Anne de Pisseleu nurtured "angry feelings" towards him. If the emperor thought that he could get away with ignoring Francis I's mistress, he was wrong. The imperial ambassador at the French court, Jean de Saint-Mauris, reported that her heart was hardened against him "in such a way that it will be very difficult, nay, almost impossible, to appease her".[9] In 1544, both Charles V and Eleanor knew that they could gain much by inviting Francis's mistress to their meeting. This time, the emperor made much of Anne de Pisseleu, presenting her with a jewel worth 6,000 crowns, half the value of the one he gave his sister the Queen.[10]

The royal mistress was not amused, and by the end of the year, she was already opting for a peace treaty with Henry VIII. The news that "the said Madame d'Etampes is one among a few that bareth good affection to the amity with the King's Majesty" had reached Henry VIII, who ordered his Privy Council to instruct Edward Seymour and Stephen Gardiner to speak to her secretly during her meeting with the emperor. Seymour and Gardiner were specifically instructed to seek her out as though they found her by chance and tell her that Henry VIII was informed many times and by many people "of her good disposition towards His Highness, and the amity with England". For this, they should "give unto her most hearty thanks" in the King's name and determine whether her declarations were genuine.[11] Seymour and Gardiner had no opportunity to meet with Anne de Pisseleu as she departed early the next day.

Despite this, Anne de Pisseleu and Margaret of Navarre decided to make a secret overture to Henry VIII in late 1544. They informed him through their messengers that they could end war and build towards a union between France, England and the Schmalkaldic League if only Henry would accept a large settlement from Francis I for Boulogne. By 1545, Madame d'Etampes was diligently working for the Anglo-French peace, sending her secretary to England.[12] In 1545, the unexpected death of Francis I's youngest son Charles voided the Treaty of Crépy since the duke was expected to marry either Charles V's daughter or his niece. The peace between England and France was finally signed in Ardres on 7 June 1546.

To cement the peace treaty, Francis I invited Henry VIII to be the godfather of his granddaughter born on 2 April 1545. She was the daughter of Dauphin Henri, who was himself the King of England's godson. Henry VIII was also invited to name the infant girl, and he chose the name Elizabeth to honour his late mother, Elizabeth of York, who died on 11 February 1503. Sir Thomas Cheyne, who was sent to represent Henry VIII at the baptism, recalled that the King chose this name because his mother was "as good and as virtuous a woman as ever lived in this world".[13] It is interesting that after six marriages Henry VIII believed that only his mother lived up to the unattainable idea of a perfect woman. Not even his third wife and mother of his son, Edward, was worthy, in Henry's view, of becoming the namesake of Francis I's newly born granddaughter. This Elizabeth, baptised in a lavish ceremony during the summer of 1546, was to become the third wife of Charles V's son, Philip, and die in childbirth, just like her English namesake.

NOTES

[1] *Chronicle of King Henry VIII (The Spanish Chronicle)*, p. 107.
[2] *Calendar of State Papers, Spain,* Volume 6 Part 1, 1538-1542, n. 232.
[3] *Letters and Papers, Foreign and Domestic, Henry VIII,* Volume 8, January-July 1535, n. 837.
[4] Agnes Strickland, *Lives of the Queens of England* , Volume 3, p. 216.
[5] Janel Mueller, *Katherine Parr: Complete Works and Correspondence*, p. 70.
[6] From his birth until the death of his oldest brother Francis, Dauphin of France (Francis I's eldest son) in 1536, Charles was known as the Duke of Angoulême. After his brother's death, he became Duke of Orléans, a title previously held by his surviving brother Henry, who had succeeded Francis as Dauphin and would later become King of France as Henri II.
[7] *Letters and Papers, Foreign and Domestic, Henry VIII,* Volume 17, 1542, n. 128.
[8] *Letters and Papers, Foreign and Domestic, Henry VIII,* Volume 19 Part 2, August-December 1544, n. 568.
[9] *Calendar of State Papers, Spain,* Volume 6 Part 1, 1538-1542, n. 117.
[10] *Letters and Papers, Foreign and Domestic, Henry VIII,* Volume 19 Part 2, August-December 1544, n. 570.
[11] *State Papers, Henry VIII,* Volume 10, pp. 151-152.
[12] *Calendar of State Papers, Spain,* Volume 8, 1545-1546, n. 98.
[13] *State Papers, Henry VIII,* Volume 11, pp. 151-152.

CHAPTER 19
THE DAUPHINE AMONG ENEMIES

Elizabeth de Valois, Henry VIII's goddaughter, was the second child born to Dauphin Henri and his wife, Catherine de Medici. The Dauphine's position seemed cemented, but it was not always so. The orphaned niece of Pope Clement VII, born to a French mother and Italian father, was at first thought to have been a great catch, and Francis I married her to his second son Henri in 1533, incurring the displeasure of his ally Henry VIII. Two years later, the Venetian ambassador Marino Giustiniani wrote that the marriage dissatisfied the entire nation because it was generally muttered that Pope Clement deceived the King as he failed to turn over Catherine's full dowry. With Clement VII's death in 1534, Catherine de Medici's political value decreased dramatically, and Francis I was heard complaining that "the girl was given to me stark naked".

Catherine was well aware of her situation and decided to ingratiate herself with Francis I, who took an instant liking to her. She asked Francis to allow her to join his "little band of the court ladies", whom the King sought among "the most beautiful and the most noble" damsels. These ladies, many of whom were the King's mistresses, often joined Francis on hunting parties, and Catherine, who enjoyed the chase, was delighted to become a member of this elite club. Brantôme recorded that she did this more for the sake of observing the King's actions and extracting his secrets than for the sake of hunting. After this reflection, Brantôme added:

"King Francis was pleased with this request, for it showed the goodwill that she had for his company; and he granted it heartily ; so that besides loving her naturally, he now loved her more, and delighted in giving her pleasure in the hunt, at which she never left his side, but followed him at full speed. She was very good on horseback and bold; sitting with ease, and being the first to put the leg around a pommel; which was far more graceful and becoming than sitting with the feet upon a plank."[1]

Catherine needed all her prudence to avoid the courtly snares already laid out for her. The French nobles, so sensitive about lineage, scoffed that the Medici were but a family of merchants and Catherine was not worthy of being the wife of one of the King of France's sons. At that time, however, she was married to the King's second son and was not expected to play an important political role. Everything changed in 1536, when Dauphin Francis's sudden death made Henri his father's heir and the next Dauphin of France. Some people even believed that Henri and Catherine were behind Dauphin Francis's death since they gained so much by it. Although it was never proved that the Dauphin was poisoned, the man who passed him the ice-cold water during a tennis match, Sebastiano de Montecuculli, was tortured and later executed in Lyon.

The whole court was stunned by the Dauphin's sudden death, and Francis I faced the prospect of being succeeded on the throne by Henri, whom he never particularly liked. The new Dauphin's childhood had been scarred by four years of imprisonment in Spain, where he was not always treated as a royal child. When he returned to his father's court in 1531, he was not the same vivacious boy anymore. Forced to relearn his native language, he became shy and withdrawn. He enjoyed military exercises more than he did the life at court. He was "so well built that one would think that he was made of muscle, indefatigable in exercises of arms or hunting", remarked one ambassador. Francis I, irritated by his son's behaviour, once callously remarked that "he did not care for dreamy, sullen, sleepy children", instead pouring all his love and attention on the youngest, Charles.[2] The coldness of Francis's treatment of Henri was clear to all, and the Venetian ambassador once observed that the King did not love Henri much.[3]

There was, however, someone who loved Henri and embarked on a task of moulding him into what he subsequently became. Born in or around 1500, Diane de Poitiers was the widow of Louis de Brézé, the Grand Seneschal of Normandy.

She had been Queen Claude's lady-in-waiting and a longtime member of the royal court. She was nineteen years older than Dauphin Henri, but this seemed not to have been an obstacle for the awkward youth to fall in love with her. Henri, who lost his mother at the age of five and was starved of his father's affection, found not only a perfect companion and a tender caretaker in the person of Diane de Poitiers, but also a passionate mistress. The Venetian ambassador reported that "this woman had undertaken to indoctrinate, to correct, and to counsel Monsieur the Dauphin and to push him to all the actions worthy of him".[4]

Even when Diane became Henri's mistress, some observers believed there was nothing lascivious about their relationship because they shared a bond similar to the one between mother and son. The one person who knew exactly what kind of relationship her husband shared with Diane de Poitiers was Catherine de Medici. The young Dauphine could not possibly compete with the older and more beautiful Diane, herself being described as stout and not particularly attractive, but she soon found an unexpected ally in her husband's mistress.

Critics of Catherine de Medici's marriage advised Francis I to annul his son's union on account of Catherine's barrenness. Ten years had passed, and she was still struggling to get pregnant. In 1537, Henri had a brief romance with an

Italian woman named Philippa Duci, whose daughter he acknowledged as his and subsequently legitimised, naming her Diane, after his much loved mistress. The birth of Diane de France proved to Henri that it was Catherine, not he, who was to blame for their childlessness. His view was consistent with sixteenth-century sexism, according to which it was a woman who was to blame for any reproductive troubles.

Rumours about the annulment started swirling at court and abroad. Francis I was once heard saying to his wife, Eleanor, that he would consider another marriage for Dauphin Henri "in the event of anything happening to his present wife, the Dauphine, who is much subject to catarrhs, and is continually in bad health".[5] It is clear that he considered repudiating Catherine since it was necessary to continue the line of succession, and most people at court felt sorry "that such a marriage did ever take place, owing chiefly to her having no children yet".[6] Catherine was well aware of her predicament and decided to act. According to the Venetian ambassador:

"She went to the King and told him she had heard it was His Majesty's intention to give his son another wife, and as it had not yet pleased God to bestow on her the grace of having children, it was proper that, as soon as His Majesty found it disagreeable to wait longer, he should provide for the succession to so great a throne; that, for her part, considering the great obligations she was under to His Majesty, who had deigned to accept her as a daughter-in-law, she was much more disposed to endure this affliction than to oppose his will, and was determined either to enter a convent or remain in his service and his favour. This communication she made to Francis I with many tears and much emotion. The noble and indulgent heart of the King was so greatly moved by it that he replied; 'Daughter, do not fear that, since God has willed you to be my daughter-in-law, I would have it otherwise; perhaps it will yet please Him to grant to you and to me, the grace we desire more than anything else in the world".[7]

Catherine's best safeguard was to become pregnant, and she decided to do everything she could to finally see her belly grow. She surrounded herself with the most skilled doctors but also listened to the advice of astrologers and magicians. The prescribed medicines she drank every day ranged from mild herbal potions to smelly concoctions made of urine of pregnant animals and the powdered sexual organs of boars, stags and cats. She also drank potions made of a mixture of animal milk and blood, with additions of unicorn's horn and vinegar.[8] The Venetian ambassador Dandolo remarked that although Catherine swallowed "all possible medicines that might aid conception", she was, in his opinion, "more at risk of increasing her difficulty than finding the solution".[9] If we are to believe Brantôme, Catherine also ordered her carpenter to drill a hole in the floor of her bedroom, placed directly above Diane de

Poitiers's private suite, so she could observe her husband in bed with his mistress for her own education.

At this point, when Catherine was desperate to conceive, her husband's mistress stepped in to help the couple. It was in Diane de Poitiers's best interest to help Catherine, who failed to inspire lust in Dauphin Henri, because she was afraid that if Catherine was repudiated, the new wife of her lover would not be as patient with the royal mistress or, worse, could inspire warm feelings in the Dauphin. Henri's lack of any kind of interest in Catherine suited Diane, who reigned supreme over his heart and in his bed, but who now decided it was of paramount importance to her own position to exhort Henri to visit his wife's bedchamber. Diane gave the young couple a series of instructions. One of them suggested that Catherine and Henri should make love "à levrette", a levrette being a small greyhound bitch.

Diane urged Henri to sleep with Catherine and employed the help of one of the best physicians at the French court, Jean Fernel. Fernel examined Catherine and Henri and discovered that both of them suffered from certain malformations. The Dauphin was diagnosed with a condition known today as hypospadias, a congenital malformation of the penis, while Catherine suffered from tortuosity of the vaginal canal.[10] Henri's condition was commented upon by Brantôme who had reliable informants within royal circles. The seventeenth-century author Jean-Louis Guez de Balzac concluded that the cause of Catherine de Medici's failure to conceive lay in her husband's penile malformation, a statement that prompted some modern historians to echo his sentiments and suggest the fault lay more with Henri than with Catherine.[11]

It remains unknown what kind of remedy Fernel advised for Henri's condition. Some scholars over the centuries suggested that he underwent a penile operation, but this seems highly unlikely since this is not mentioned in contemporary accounts. Considering Diane de Poitiers's earlier suggestion, it is more likely that the royal physician counselled a particular position to be used by Henri during intercourse.[12]

Finally, on 19 January 1544, Catherine de Medici went into labour and gave birth to a long-awaited son, who was named Francis to honour the King. After a decade of childlessness spent worrying about her position, Catherine could breathe a sigh of relief. Francis I and his sister, Margaret of Navarre, were ecstatic. Margaret had been entrusted with the education of Catherine de Medici and grew to love her as much as Francis I did. She remained Catherine's solid supporter through the fertility crisis, and when the Dauphine shared her worries with Margaret, the King's sister wrote her a reassuring letter:

"My brother will never allow this repudiation, as evil tongues pretend. But God will give a royal line to Madame la Dauphine when she has reached the age at which women of the House of the Medici are wont to have children. The King and I will rejoice with you then, in spite of these wretched backbiters."[13]

Margaret's confidence stemmed also from her own personal experience. She, who for many years bemoaned her "sterility", became a first-time mother at the age of thirty-six. Her confidence was well placed, and when she heard that Catherine gave birth to a son, ensuring survival of the Valois line into the third generation, she expressed her happiness in a touching letter addressed to Francis I.

"This is the most beautiful, the most longed for, and the most needed day that you and your kingdom have ever seen", she wrote to her brother. She was so "overwhelmed by joy" that she could hardly see through eyes full of tears as she rose from her sickbed to compose this congratulatory letter to her beloved brother. The poem she attached to the letter was a testament to Margaret's feelings and teemed with visions of happiness and joy. The infant Francis was the one who "bestows youth on his grandfather" and heralds the coming of a new age. As for Margaret herself, she was thrilled to hear that the boy had the family's "big nose", a trait she was always proud of.[14]

As to the triumphant mother, Catherine de Medici would go on to provide her husband with a brood of ten royal children, seven of whom would survive to adulthood. She triumphed over all those who had the audacity to call her a "merchant's daughter" and ensured that Henri would never replace her with another wife.

NOTES

[1] Pierre de Bourdeille, seigneur de Brantôme, *The Book of the Ladies*, pp. 29-30, p. 53.
[2] Williams, H. Noel, *Henri II: His Court and Times*, p. 85.
[3] Kathleen Wellman, *Queens and Mistresses of Renaissance France*, p. 197.
[4] Ibid., p. 199.
[5] *Calendar of State Papers, Spain,* Volume 6 Part 1, 1538-1542, n. 78.
[6] Ibid.
[7] Imbert de Saint-Amand, *Women of the Valois Court*, p. 178.
[8] Jennifer Grodetsky, Ronald Rabinowitz, Jeanne O'Brien. *The "infertility" of Catherine de Medici and its influence on 16th century France.*
[9] Princess Michael of Kent, *The Serpent and the Moon*, p. 196.
[10] Jean Héritier, *Catherine de Medici*, p. 43.
[11] Michael G. Paulson, *Catherine de Medici: Five Portraits*, p. 5.
[12] For further discussion about whether Henri underwent an operation, see *Annals of Medical History*, ed. Francis R. Packard, Volume 2, pp. 91-92.
[13] Edith Sichel, *Catherine de Medici and the French Reformation,* pp. 38-39.
[14] Patricia Francis Cholakian, Rouben Charles Cholakian, *Marguerite de Navarre: Mother of the Renaissance*, p. 252.

CHAPTER 20
"SILLY, POOR WOMAN"

Queen Katherine Parr walked energetically through the cold, tapestried hallways of Whitehall Palace, lit only by the occasionally flickering candle carried by one of her ladies-in-waiting, who walked a few steps in front of her. Her heart was racing, and in her head, the Queen was reiterating the speech she was about to deliver to the King. Earlier that day, she received chilling news from one of the royal physicians, who came to warn her that the Catholic conservatives at court hatched a plot against her and the King had issued an order for her arrest. She was beside herself with fear, but the physician, apparently sent by Henry VIII, who was reluctant to see yet another wife perish in the Tower of London, advised her to visit the King this evening and try to clear herself from charges of heresy. She was now making her way to Henry's bedchamber, where the King spent hours on end due to his health problems.

When the heavy oak doors opened wide, Katherine approached the King, whom she found sitting in his chair and talking with several courtiers. Henry welcomed her very courteously and, out of the blue, started talking about religious issues, requiring Katherine's opinion. He knew that she would come, and he hoped that she would grasp this chance and exculpate herself from the heretical opinions she was accused of. A hush fell over the King's bedchamber, a silence so profound that Katherine could hear the beating of her heart. She trained all her attention on the giant of a man seated upon the cushioned chair, the man who held her life in his hands. Why, she asked, the King—"being so excellent in gifts and ornaments of wisdom"—did he require her judgment? Was she not but a "silly poor woman, so much inferior in all respects of nature to you"? She had no views of her own, but was ready to "refer my judgment in this, and in all other cases, to Your Majesty's wisdom, as my only anchor, supreme head and governor here on earth, next under God, to lean to".

This was a masterstroke. Katherine, the honest and opinionated woman who was devoted to the cause of the Protestant religion, was now humbling herself in front of her King and husband. But Henry decided to tease her further and show her the place he believed she should occupy as his Queen. "Not so, by St Mary", he replied, shaking his head, "you are become a doctor, Kate, to instruct us, as we take it, and not to be instructed or directed by us". She trembled but replied that the King was mistaken if he believed this. She thought it was "unseemly and preposterous for a woman to take upon her the office of an instructor or teacher to her lord and husband". She was eager to learn from her husband and "be taught by him".

"Silly, poor woman"

Having said that, Katherine staked everything on one last appeal:

"And where I have, with Your Majesty's leave, heretofore been bold to hold talk with Your Majesty, wherein sometimes in opinions there has seemed some difference, I have not done it so much to maintain opinion, as I did it rather to minister talk, not only to the end Your Majesty might with less grief pass over this painful time of your infirmity, being attentive to our talk, and hoping that Your Majesty should reap some ease by it; but also, that I, hearing Your Majesty's learned discourse, might receive myself some profit. Wherein, I assure Your Majesty, I have not missed any part of my desire in that behalf, always referring myself in all such matters to Your Majesty, as by ordinance of nature it is convenient for me to do."

The King's lips curled in a secretive smile. "And is it even so, sweetheart?" Henry asked, satisfied, "and tended your arguments to no worse end?" Katherine nodded, smiling. "Then perfect friends we are now again, as ever at any time heretofore". He extended his arms, embraced and kissed Katherine. She stayed with the King and his company for the evening and left his abode sure that she was safe.

She must have been profoundly shocked when, walking in the gardens with Henry the next day, she witnessed a dramatic scene. Unaware of the change of plan, Chancellor Thomas Wriothesley came with the guards to arrest the Queen. He was surprised to see Henry VIII immersed in pleasant conversation with Katherine Parr. Seeing Wriothesley, Henry burst into a fit of uncontrollable rage, calling the chancellor an "arrant knave, beast and fool". Katherine pretended she knew nothing about why Wriothesley came to the garden with armed men and tried to intercede with Henry on the chancellor's behalf. "Ah poor soul", the King sighed, "he has been towards you an arrant knave, and so let him go".[1] Both Katherine Parr and Thomas Wriothesley had experienced the truth behind the rumours about the King being "of a different opinion in the morning than after dinner".[2]

The King's rash and unpredictable temper originated largely in the pain emanating from his ulcerated legs. Henry, overweight and immobile, was now moved about in a sedan chair carried by four attendants. Thomas Howard, Duke of Norfolk, once told his mistress that the King "was much grown of his body and that he could not go up and down stairs and was let up and down by a device".[3] His younger son Thomas confirmed this when he said that "the King old lived and moved by engines and art rather than by nature".[4] A sight of the corpulent Henry "passing in his chair" was the norm during the last months of his life.[5]

"Silly, poor woman"

In these last critical months, the old King's attention turned to the future reign of his son, the nine-year-old Prince Edward. Now more than ever, Henry was eager to purge the court from those who would oppose his last wishes concerning the new regime. On 26 December 1546, a month before he died, Henry modified his last will, which was designated primarily as an "instrument of control from beyond the grave".[6] The King's last wish was to see a regency council established during his son's minority. This regency council was to be comprised of trusted men who would carry out the dying King's wishes. These were the men who adhered to the principles of the new Protestant religion. Men such as Stephen Gardiner, the conservative Bishop of Winchester who was responsible for plotting against Katherine Parr, and Thomas Howard, Duke of Norfolk, were removed from the list. While Gardiner was allowed to live out his days away from court, Norfolk was arrested and thrown into the Tower of London, where he awaited further news of his future. If Henry VIII believed that Norfolk betrayed him, he was wrong; the Duke remained faithful to the King, but he had a rash and impetuous son who constituted a threat to the newly forming regime, or at least this is what Henry came to believe.

Henry Howard, Earl of Surrey, was Norfolk's eldest son and heir. He was always a particular favourite of the King, who never forgot about Surrey's close relationship with his late illegitimate son, Henry Fitzroy. The two boys became friends and spent a year at the court of Francis I in the early 1530s. Fitzroy married Surrey's sister, Mary Howard, and became closely linked to the Howards. When Fitzroy died, Surrey became alienated and could never fit into the new reality. He detested "the new men at court", especially the ambitious Seymour brothers and their adherents. Unfortunately for Surrey, the Seymours, whose sister, Jane, bore Henry VIII's only legitimate son, quickly emerged as the King's favourites and the leading luminaries of the newly forming regime under Edward VI. Surrey found refuge in poetry and, disillusioned, painted a horrible picture of the dying Henry VIII, "whose glutton cheeks sloth feeds so fat as scant their eyes be seen".

Ambitious and slightly detached from reality, Surrey recklessly advised his sister that she should make efforts to talk often to the King, who might "take such a fantasy to her" so that Mary could become a royal mistress and "bear as great a stroke about him as Madame d'Etampes doth about the French King".[7] Mary Howard was horrified and vowed that she would rather "cut her own throat" than stoop so low, but Surrey's words reached the ear of Henry VIII, who was very much offended.[8] He had been married to two Howard brides already, and both of them had been executed for presumed adultery; now yet another Howard tried to plant his female relative in the King's affections. Surrey, who had a chance to observe Francis I and his relationship with Anne de Pisseleu, was dangerously implying that Henry could have been as easily manipulated through a woman as Francis I had been. Indeed, the French King's dependency on his mistress was already widely commented on in court circles, and he was generally perceived as a weak ruler who was bounced into action by Anne de Pisseleu, who effectively ruled at court and dictated the course of foreign policy. Whenever she wished to achieve her ends, she would come to Francis's chambers "with the sad, displeased expression she adopts on these occasions, without vouchsafing the cause of her anger".[9]

Yet Henry VIII was no Francis I, and he would never allow any woman to meddle into the matters of politics and religion, as clearly pointed out by his recent displeasure over Katherine Parr's radical views. He not only hated to be taught by a woman in his "old days", but had firmly adhered to such views during his entire life. When his much-loved third wife, Jane Seymour, fell on her knees in front of the King interceding on the behalf of the dissolved monasteries, she was ordered to get up and warned "not to meddle with his affairs", or else she would end up like "the late Queen [Anne Boleyn]".[10] The sole fact that Henry linked Anne Boleyn's execution to meddling in state affairs rather than to her alleged adultery and plot to assassinate him proves that the King had a mind of his own and strongly disliked the idea of being governed by a woman.

The old King returned to London in November 1546. On the tenth day of that month, the French ambassador Odet de Selve reported that Henry "took preparative medicine for certain baths which he usually has at this season".[11] From early December onwards, the King's health began to deteriorate, forcing him to cancel several audiences with foreign diplomats. The Spanish ambassador Van der Delft reported that on 5 December 1546 the King pulled him aside and excused for the cancelled audience, confessing that "he had suffered from a sharp attack of fever, which had lasted in its burning stage for thirty hours, but that he was now quite restored". The perceptive ambassador was not fooled and recorded that Henry's "colour does not bear out the latter statement, and he looks to me greatly fallen away".[12] Around 10 December, the King cancelled his audience with the French ambassador, allegedly due to "such a cold that he could not speak", but de Selve was sceptical since he saw the King hunting daily.[13] But it was not the hunting Henry was used to in his younger days, when his restless energy meant that he had to ride several horses during each escapade. Now, he was usually observing from a hilltop or hunting at Great Standing, a three-storey building without walls used to either shoot at game or watch the bloody spectacle unfold.

Due to his deteriorating health, Henry VIII spent the Christmas season of 1546 alone in Whitehall Palace, propped against his embroidered cushions in a bed of estate. Queen Katherine Parr, together with her stepdaughters, Mary and Elizabeth, spent the festive season in Greenwich. The puzzled imperial ambassador noticed that Katherine had never before left the King on a solemn occasion like this. "I do not know what to think or suspect", he wrote to Charles V.[14]

The King was seen publicly for the last time on 17 January 1547, when he had two brief audiences with the French and Spanish ambassadors. His condition started to rapidly deteriorate, and ten days later he received Communion from one of his confessors. Although Henry's death was obviously imminent, his own physicians were afraid to tell him he was dying because they could be arrested for treason under the Treason Act by predicting the death of a King.

Sir Anthony Denny, one of Henry VIII's closest advisors and a personal friend, decided to tell his sovereign lord that he was on his deathbed and should prepare his soul to depart this world. He approached him and said that in "man's judgment you are not like to live", urging him to call for a confessor. The King believed that "the mercy of God is able to pardon me all my sins, yes, though they were greater than they be". Still, Henry was not in a hurry to call for a priest. Denny asked if the King would like to see "any learned man to confer withal and open his mind unto". Henry nodded and said: "If I had any, it should be Dr Cranmer, but I will first take a little sleep. And then, as I feel myself, I will advise you upon the matter". By the time Archbishop Thomas Cranmer was summoned, the King had lost the power of speech. Cranmer urged Henry to give him some sort of a sign that he put his trust in Christ's mercy; when the archbishop held the dying King's hand in his, the King suddenly "wring it as hard as he could". Cranmer and all those who encircled the King's bed took it as a sign that Henry VIII died in the faith of Christ.[15] The King expired on 28 January 1547 at about two o'clock in the morning and passed from history straight into legend.

He left a nine-year-old successor and a wife who aspired to become regent during Edward VI's minority. Henry made sure that Katherine Parr was a wealthy matron after his death, but he assigned her no political role in the newly created regime. Katherine, who began signing her letters as "Kateryn the Quene Regente KP", lacked a party to support her and had to withdraw from the political stage. She was quite happy to do so, as she was in love with a rakish and devilishly handsome Thomas Seymour, brother of Edward, who now became the new King's Lord Protector. Thomas was Katherine's suitor before she married Henry VIII and now, when she was a rich and independent widow, she was finally ready to become a mistress of her own fortune and marry where her heart was. In one of her love letters to Thomas Seymour, she confessed:

"As truly as God is God, my mind was fully bent, the other time I was at liberty, to marry you before any man I knew. Howbeit, God withstood my will therein most vehemently for a time, and, through His grace and goodness, made that possible which seemed to me most impossible—that was, made me to renounce utterly mine own will, and to follow His will most willingly."[16]

As a royal widow, Katherine was expected to respect her late husband's memory and marry after the customary mourning period of one year. At first, she wanted to wait two years, but Thomas was proving impatient and urged her "to change the two years into two months".[17] Katherine agreed and married Thomas in the spring of 1547, causing a great scandal at court. Thomas's brother was offended, and Henry VIII's daughters could not hide their disappointment. Only Edward VI seemed oblivious to the fact that his stepmother and uncle had lied to him when trying to obtain his agreement for a wedding that had occurred before they even set out to obtain his permission.

Yet Katherine was not sorry that she followed her heart; marrying for love was her decision, and even though she did it with unseemly haste, she was finally happy. Or at least it seemed in the beginning. Thomas Seymour was as handsome as he was ambitious, and he soon decided to seduce Henry VIII's daughter Elizabeth, who came to live in Katherine Parr's household after her father's death. At fifteen, Elizabeth was developing into an attractive young woman with a tall figure, penetrating dark eyes and long red hair. Seymour often came into Elizabeth's bedchamber early in the morning, "bare legged in his slippers", playfully spanking her on her back and buttocks. Katherine Parr, oblivious to what was happening, began to participate in this behaviour; on one occasion, she held Elizabeth's hands behind her back when Thomas Seymour cut her gown "into a hundred pieces". Perhaps Katherine deluded herself that such games were innocent, but she came to her senses when she caught Thomas and Elizabeth in a tender embrace.[18] Katherine, who was pregnant at the time, sent Elizabeth away from her household to the home of Sir Anthony Denny at Cheshunt in Hertfordshire. Elizabeth would never see her stepmother again.

Katherine Parr gave birth to her longed-for daughter, Mary, on 30 August 1548, only to die on 5 September, aged about thirty-six, a victim of childbed fever. Just hours before she died, she complained to her favourite lady-in-waiting: "My lady Tyrwhitt, I am not well handled, for those that be about me careth not for me, but standeth laughing at my grief". Thomas Seymour's reaction proves that he thought Katherine was pointing an accusatory finger at him: "Why, sweetheart, I would do you no hurt". Still sharp of mind despite impending death, Katherine shook her head and complained that Seymour gave her "many shrewd taunts". Thomas crawled into Katherine's bed, trying desperately to "pacify her unquietness with gentle communication"; she died later that day.[19] The marriage she thought would bring her such happiness brought her misery and heartbreak in the end.

As to Elizabeth, the death of her stepmother left her bereft, but it was only the beginning of her problems. Thomas Seymour made plans to marry her, kidnap the King and overthrow his hated brother, but his plans failed, and he was executed on 20 March 1549. Edward VI died of pulmonary tuberculosis four years later, and Katharine of Aragon's Catholic daughter, the thirty-seven-year-old Mary Tudor, succeeded him. Mary made much of her Spanish descent and married Charles V's son Philip, but she failed to produce an heir and, after two phantom pregnancies, died of ovarian cancer on 17 November 1558. Elizabeth, now twenty-five, succeeded her. Growing up in the shadow of her mother's memory, she was always treated as "that woman's daughter". Mary Tudor dreaded the idea of nominating Elizabeth as her heiress "because of her heretical opinions, illegitimacy and characteristics in which she resembled her mother; and as her mother had caused great trouble in the kingdom, the Queen feared that Elizabeth might do the same, and particularly that she would imitate her mother in being a French partisan".[20]

Nevertheless, Elizabeth did become Queen of England, but, unlike Mary, she never tried to legitimise her parents' marriage; she was still believed to have been a bastard, born out of wedlock, by the majority of European rulers. Despite this fact, she ruled successfully for forty years and never married. It may be one of the ironies of history that a daughter of the woman who was disparaged in Europe as "great whore" and executed for adultery she never committed became known as Elizabeth the Virgin Queen.

NOTES

[1] John Foxe, *The Acts and Monuments of the Church*, pp. 615-618.
[2] *Letters and Papers, Foreign and Domestic, Henry VIII*, Volume 16, 1540-1541, n. 590.
[3] Robert Hutchinson, *The Last Days of Henry VIII*, p. 149.
[4] Susan Brigden, *Henry Howard, Earl of Surrey, and the 'Conjured League'*, p. 510.
[5] *Letters and Papers, Foreign and Domestic, Henry VIII*, Volume 21 Part 2, September 1546-January 1547, n. 238.
[6] Suzannah Lipscomb, *The King is Dead*, p. 4.
[7] *Letters and Papers, Foreign and Domestic, Henry VIII*, Volume 21 Part 2, September 1546-January 1547, n. 555.
[8] Ibid.
[9] David Potter, *Politics and Faction at the Court of Francis I*, p. 137.
[10] *Letters and Papers, Foreign and Domestic, Henry VIII*, Volume 11, July-December 1536, n. 860.
[11] *Letters and Papers, Foreign and Domestic, Henry VIII*, Volume 21 Part 2, September 1546-January 1547. n. 380.
[12] *Calendar of State Papers, Spain*, Volume 8, 1545-1546, n. 370.
[13] *Letters and Papers, Foreign and Domestic, Henry VIII*, Volume 21 Part 2, September 1546-January 1547. n. 517.
[14] *Calendar of State Papers, Spain*, Volume 8, 1545-1546, n. 370.

[15] J. J. Scarisbrick, *Henry VIII*, pp. 495-496.
[16] Janel Mueller, *Katherine Parr: Complete Works and Correspondence*, p. 382.
[17] Ibid., p. 135.
[18] Read more in the new study of Thomas Seymour's relationship with Elizabeth under Katherine Parr's roof in Elizabeth Norton's *The Temptation of Elizabeth Tudor: Elizabeth I, Thomas Seymour, and the Making of a Virgin Queen* (Head of Zeus, 2015).
[19] Janel Mueller, *Katherine Parr: Complete Works and Correspondence*, pp. 177-178.
[20] *Calendar of State Papers, Spain,* Volume 11, 1553, n. 27.

CHAPTER 21
"SHE HAD NOT DESERVED SUCH TREATMENT"

When the news of Henry VIII's death reached France, Francis I's adherents reacted with an outburst of inappropriate glee. Anne de Pisseleu, who used to be pro-English, came running to Queen Eleanor's bedchamber announcing that, "We have lost our chief enemy, and the King has commanded me to come and tell you of it!" The Queen, pale and shocked, thought at first that it was her brother, Charles V, who died. As to Francis I himself, the imperial ambassador Jean de Saint-Mauris recorded that he deeply felt Henry VIII's death because "he had lost a good and true friend, and that at a season when there was little likelihood of finding another". He also added that although the French King appeared distressed, he was later that day seen "laughing and joking with the ladies who were dancing", which made him suspect that his grief was feigned.[1] The ambassador also wrote that the French in general showed "great joy" over Henry VIII's death because it meant that the war with Scotland would now cease and the new King of England, Edward VI, would be easier to deal with. Several days later, Francis I caught a cold and took to his bed, joking that perhaps Henry VIII was summoning him to join him in death.

"She had not deserved such treatment"

On 21 March 1547, a requiem Mass for Henry VIII was celebrated at Notre-Dame in Paris before a large crowd. During the oration, Henry's "magnanimity, liberality and prudence" were praised. The imperial ambassador at the French court recorded:

"This eulogy concluding, Sire, that where the late King of England had finally treated the last peace so as from then on to take his ease, God gave him this fruit, and added to this at the end an exhortation to the English in the form of an admonition that they should take care to keep their young King in good and perpetual peace with the King, who for his part desired to do the same in good faith."[2]

Around this time, Francis I became seriously alarmed when a messenger from England brought him a letter written by Henry VIII shortly before his death, reminding Francis that he too was mortal. The French King became so "amazed and distressed" that he "fell ill from that moment".[3] He was well aware that he and Henry were joined together by mutual rivalry, and they were of similar age and constitution; Francis now feared that he would follow Henry into the grave. He had every reason to suspect this because his health was rapidly deteriorating. Francis had been racked by exhausting fevers for several years, and a venereal disease was ravaging his body from within. Two years earlier, the imperial ambassador had described the King's failing health in great detail:

"The Christian King has been ill for a long time past, the commencement of his indisposition being a slow fever that he caught. This troubled him several times, and came on suddenly without any premonition, lasting on one occasion for five days. In addition to this fever it was discovered that he had a gathering under the lower parts, which distressed and weakened him so much that he could not stand, and he had to keep his bed. For the cure of this gathering, the most expert doctors and surgeons of Paris were summoned. After purging the King, they applied a cautery to the abscess, in order to open and destroy it. This treatment was continued until the abscess broke: but instead of discharging in one place only, as they expected, it broke out in three, in very dangerous positions: and there is at present no assurance that he will live. He has even fallen into extreme fainting and exhaustion, but he has always retained consciousness and still does so. The malady proceeds from a similar illness to that from which the King was suffering when the Emperor passed through France on his way from Spain. As the abscesses did not discharge properly, the physicians have applied three fresh cauterizes, and this has caused three issues, whence infected matter flows in great abundance. In order the better to recover from his malady, the King has commenced a course of Chinese wood, which his physicians say he must continue for 20 days. All the medical men are of opinion the malady proceeds from 'the French sickness' and for the eradication of this, the Chinese wood [sandalwood] will aid greatly, unless, as is feared, the bladder is ulcerated".[4]

By 1547, these symptoms had worsened and the King was slowly wasting away. His abscess kept troubling him, prompting the imperial ambassador to say that "if the game lasts much longer, he may cease playing altogether".[5] But, like Henry VIII, Francis remained active almost until the end. When he was young and restless, he joked that "when old and sick, he would be carried to the chase and that perhaps when he was dead, he would wish to go in his coffin".[6] He was right; Francis could not think about lying in bed waiting for death to come. "He still takes his pastime of hunting, being carried in a litter", the imperial ambassador remarked on one occasion.[7]

In the early spring of 1547—as if in an attempt to cheat death—Francis travelled through his favourite forests, trying to conjure up the ghost of his youth. Towards the end of March 1547, he arrived at the Chateau de Rambouillet, where fever forced him to take to his bed. Soon he discovered he was on his deathbed and summoned his son and heir Henri. He gave him several lessons and admonitions concerning kingship and made pressing recommendations touching his daughter, wife and mistress.

First, he urged Henri "to take care of his sister and have her married fittingly to her rank". Madame Marguerite, named after the King's own sister, was now twenty-four years old and still unmarried; she was very much attached to Francis, who doted on her since she was his only surviving daughter. Then the King spoke "long and impressively" in favour of his wife, Queen Eleanor. Consumed with guilt over her treatment, he begged Henri to "regard and protect her well, knowing how ill he (Francis) had treated her, though she had not deserved such treatment, having always been to him a good and obedient wife."[8] Last but not least, the King begged Henri to treat his mistress, Anne de Pisseleu, with respect but also warned him "not to submit to the will of others, as I have to her".[9] Overcome with grief, Henri asked Francis for his blessing and then "fell in a swoon upon the King's bed; and the King held him in a half-embrace and was unable release him".[10]

Francis I died on 31 March 1547 at Chateau de Rambouillet "of a fever which had afflicted him for thirty days".[11] His body was opened after his death, revealing an aposteme in his stomach, wasted kidneys and decayed entrails.[12] For centuries, it was widely believed that Francis I died of syphilis, but in 1856, Auguste Cullerier argued that the symptoms described by the King's contemporaries were not characteristic of syphilis, and he firmly adhered to the view that in the sixteenth century any venereal disease would have been labelled as syphilis.[13] There is no doubt that Francis I suffered from a sexually transmitted disease because he was cured with mercury, and his contemporaries often mentioned his "French disease", but today it is believed that the King died of a urinary infection, which may have had a venereal origin without being syphilitic.[14]

News of Francis I's death reached his widow, Queen Eleanor, at the convent of Poissy near Paris. She was not even informed about her husband's illness, so when the new King, Henri II, wrote her a letter informing her of Francis's death on 2 April 1547, she was surprised. The new King excused himself by saying that he failed to inform her of his father's illness because he hoped he would recover and "offered to Her Majesty all the duty that a son could pay to a mother". He sent his wife, Catherine de Medici, and sister, Madame Marguerite, to visit the widowed Queen at Poissy and offer their condolences. When Madame Marguerite saw her stepmother, pale and stiff in her black mourning gown, she had "two fainting fits".[15] Eleanor's feelings concerning Francis's death were not recorded, but her brother, Charles V, remarked that "she had not great reason to mourn the passing of the King in light of the little regard he had for her and the bad treatment she received".[16]

The only person who sincerely mourned Francis was his sister, Margaret of Navarre, who had retired from court three years earlier. She was also not informed about Francis's death and learned about it several weeks later from one of the nuns in a convent she was staying in. The news was devastating to Margaret, and she decided to write a poem entitled *Other Thoughts a Month After the King's Death*, lamenting that her "body is separated from the one to whom it was united from the time of our childhood". She continued:

"I have nothing left but my sad voice with which I go forth lamenting the cruel absence. Alas, the one I lived for, the one I was so glad to see, I have lost his happy presence".[17]

Margaret, whose health had been in decline since 1544, was now urging "Death, who conquered the Brother" to "come now in your great goodness and pierce the Sister with your lance . . . I send you my challenge".[18] She never recovered from her loss and lived away from court in quiet seclusion, spending her last years on rounds of religious observances and writing mournful verses and poetry. She died on 21 December 1549 at the age of fifty-seven. She left a living legacy in the person of her only daughter, Jeanne d'Albret, who would one day become the mother of King Henri IV.

As for Queen Eleanor, she left France in November 1548. Although Henri II promised her to be like a good son to her and treat her as if she were his own mother, he failed to show up for a formal farewell, even though Eleanor tried to arrange it before her final departure.[19] In 1551, her dowry was confiscated by Henri and given to Orazio Farnese; she got it back five years later. In January 1555, Eleanor and her sister, Mary of Hungary, sat at Charles V's right hand during his abdication ceremony, watching as their beloved brother, "feeble and suffering from illness", ceded power to his son and heir, Prince Philip.[20] In 1557, she made efforts to persuade her daughter, Infanta Maria of Portugal, to come live with her in Spain, but Maria refused the offer because Prince Philip, whom she wished to marry, chose Mary Tudor as his bride. Eleanor tried to reason with her daughter, but Infanta Maria never budged and remained in Portugal.

A meeting between mother and daughter was arranged in Badajoz in 1558, and Eleanor repeated her request, but Maria refused yet again. She felt abandoned by Eleanor, who had been forced to leave Portugal in 1521. In 1539 and then again in 1541, Eleanor had a chance to bring her daughter to France, but she wanted Maria to live at Charles V's court rather than to become Francis I's pawn on the international marriage market, although there is no doubt that she always desired "to have her nearer her person".[21] The truth behind Maria's refusal was that after so many years of separation, she felt no emotional bond with her mother and had carved out a good life for herself at the Portuguese court. In 1523, she became a ward of Eleanor's sister, Catherine, who married Manuel the Fortunate's successor, King John III. As Duchess of Viseu, Maria established her own literary salon at court and became a patron of poets and scholars.[22]

Eleanor fell sick on her way back from Badajoz and took to her bed in Talavera la Real. She died of asthma on 25 February 1558. When Charles V learned of her death, he was devastated. Although Eleanor's personal happiness was never more important than his political choices, Charles V's spirit was broken when Eleanor died. He said:

"She was a good Christian. We have always loved each other. She was my elder by fifteen months; and before that period has passed, I shall probably be with her".[23]

He died an old and sick man seven months later.

NOTES

[1] Appendix: Miscellaneous 1547 in *Calendar of State Papers, Spain*, Volume 9, 1547-1549, n. 3.
[2] David Potter, *Henry VIII and Francis I: The Final Conflict*, 1540-47, p. 475.
[3] *Calendar of State Papers, Spain*, Volume 9, 1547-1549, n. 5.
[4] *Calendar of State Papers, Spain*, Volume 8, 1545-1546, n. 115.
[5] Ibid., n. 187.
[6] Williams, H. Noel, *Henri II: His Court and Times*, p. 171.
[7] *Calendar of State Papers, Spain*, Volume 8, 1545-1546, n. 194.
[8] *Calendar of State Papers, Spain*, Volume 9, 1547-1549, n. 5.
[9] Williams, H. Noel, *Henri II: His Court and Times*, op. cit.
[10] Ibid.
[11] *Calendar of State Papers, Spain*, Volume 9, 1547-1549, n. 4.

[12] Ibid.
[13] Auguste Cullerier, *De quelle maladie est mort François Ier*, p.7.
[14] R. J. Knecht, *Francis I*, p. 419.
[15] *Calendar of State Papers, Spain,* Volume 9, 1547-1549, n. 4.
[16] Kathleen Wellman, *Queens and Mistresses of Renaissance France*, p. 169.
[17] Patricia Francis Cholakian, Rouben Charles Cholakian, *Marguerite de Navarre: Mother of the Renaissance*, p. 271.
[18] Ibid.
[19] *Compte rendu des séances de la Commission Royale d'Histoire*, Volume 12, pp. 176-178.
[20] *Calendar of State Papers, Venice,* Volume 6, 1555-1558, n. 353.
[21] *Calendar of State Papers, Spain,* Volume 6 Part 1, 1538-1542, n. 78.
[22] Kevin M. Stevens, *Documenting the Early Modern Book World*, p.102.
[23] William Hickling Prescott, *History of the Reign of Philip the Second, King of Spain*, Volume 1, p. 295.

CHAPTER 22
"THE KING IS DEAD, LONG LIVE THE NEW MISTRESS!"

Francis's son, Henri II, commissioned a splendid tomb for his father. Designed by Philibert de L'Orme, the tomb was modelled on the Roman triumphal arch and was adorned with five statues resting at the top. These statues depict Francis and his first wife, Claude, piously kneeling at their prayer stalls, flanked by three of their deceased children: Madame Charlotte, Dauphin Francis and Charles, Duke of Angoulême. Plans to install the statues of Madame Louise and Louise of Savoy never came to fruition. Below, Francis and Claude are depicted as gisants (recumbent statues) lying on a bier as nude corpses. On 20 October 1793, the resting place of Francis I and his family was disturbed when the royal tombs at St Denis were desecrated over the course of the French Revolution. Francis I's tomb was opened and revealed six leaden coffins buried within. These belonged to Francis, Claude, their abovementioned three children and the King's mother, Louise of Savoy. The following description was included in the official account:

"All these bodies were in a state of complete putrefaction, and sent fort an insupportable smell. A black liquid ran through the coffins in transporting them to the cemetery. The body of Francis I was of an extraordinary length, and very strongly built: one of his thigh bones, measured upon the spot, was twenty inches long".[1]

Upon extracting them from their original place of burial, the bodies were then transported to the nearby cemetery, where they were dumped in a mass grave.

Henri II's accession was followed by the palace revolution. Its main victim was Anne de Pisseleu, Duchess of Étampes, who had made many enemies over the years of her ascendancy. One of her formidable enemies was Diane de Poitiers, the new King's long-term mistress and confidante. During the last years of Francis I's reign, a feminine duel raged between the two royal favourites and their parties. The court, divided into two hostile camps, became a hotbed of intrigue, with Diane and Anne engaged in a war of calumnies and slanderous epigrams. The poets employed by the younger Anne de Pisseleu disparaged Diane de Poitiers's appearance, calling her a wrinkled old hag with "ruined complexion" and "false teeth".[2] In retaliation, Diane attacked Anne de Pisseleu's fidelity because it was widely known that she and Francis I had lived in an open relationship.

Anne was only some eight years younger than Diane, but she knew the only way she could harm Henri's mistress was through an attack on her appearance, of which Diane took an especial care. She rarely used cosmetics, which in the sixteenth century did women more harm than good, and devoted herself to physical exercise, which included horseback riding, regular river swims and hunting. She also drank potions made of liquid gold and spring water to preserve her good looks.[3]

Francis I's death laid Anne de Pisseleu open to the machinations of her enemies. She was so unpopular that the imperial ambassador Saint-Mauris believed she would have been stoned to death if she appeared in the streets of Paris alone. She was evicted from her luxurious royal apartments in a matter of days after the old King's death, forced to return the jewels she received from Francis and despoiled of part of her lands.[4] These were now given to Diane de Poitiers, who received the title of Duchess of Valentinois and became the most important woman at court after the new Queen, prompting a cry: "The King is dead, long live the new mistress" in recognition of Diane displacing Anne de Pisseleu in the office of the titular royal mistress.[5]

Diane de Poitiers valued her honour above anything else and did not allow her position as royal mistress to be used for casting slander against her person. She was never insolent towards Henri's wife, Catherine de Medici, and often took it upon herself to speak well of the Queen when having private conversations with Henri. As for Catherine, she later admitted that it was hard for her to live in this ménage à trois because "never did a woman who loved her husband succeed in loving his whore".[6] Catherine loved Henri, but he seemed to be oblivious to the pain he was inflicting on her.

The royal palaces were adorned with the device adopted by Henri and Diane—a letter *H* crossed with two crescent moons, a symbol of the ancient huntress Diana, with whom Diane de Poitiers liked to link herself—which could also be interpreted to depict back-to-back *C*s, standing for Catherine de Medici's name. Some confused observers remarked that although *H* was clearly visible at first glance, "one can see there also two *D*s, which are the double initial of the Duchess of Valentinois".[7] Device aside, Henri often treated Catherine as if he were punishing her for being his wife. During their formal entry to the city of Lyons, it was Diane who was celebrated for her beauty and wisdom, whereas the Queen entered next day after dark amid wild speculations that Henri arranged her late arrival "so that her ugliness should pass unnoticed".[8] Observers remarked that Catharine de Medici's tolerance of Diane de Poitiers was remarkable, and it was later said that:

"[Catherine] seemed to bear with perfect ease the King's passion for the Duchess of Valentinois, nor did she express the least jealousy of it; but she was so skillful a dissembler, that it was hard to judge of her real sentiments, and policy obliged her to keep the duchess about her person, that she might draw the King to her at the same time."[9]

Henri II allowed Diane to exercise a large influence over the politics, and early in his reign, the imperial ambassador Saint-Mauris remarked that the King was spending a third of each day in the company of his mistress. Saint-Mauris invented a nickname for Diane and called her "Silvius" in his numerous despatches to avoid detection; Henri himself was described as a shy and withdrawn person, "born to be governed rather than to govern".[10] Saint-Mauris left many detailed descriptions about the King's relationship with his mistress:

"The worst thing is that the said King allows himself to be led, and approves everything which Silvius and his nobles advise, of which the people here complain, fearing that the King will remain always in that net. After dinner, he visits the said Silvius. When he has given her an account of all the business he has transacted in the morning and up to that moment, whether with the Ambassadors or other persons of importance, he seats himself upon her lap, a lute in his hand, upon which he plays, and inquires often of the Duke of Aumale if the said Silvius 'has not preserved her beauty,' touching from time to time her bosom and regarding her attentively, like a man that is ensnared by love".[11]

Diane de Poitiers enjoyed even more influence than her predecessor, Anne de Pisseleu:

"The King has many natural good qualities, and one might hope much from him, if he were not so stupid as to allow himself to be led as he does. The Chancellor is in despair about it, saying that 'the women of today are worse than those of former times, and that they spoil everything.' It is said that not a soul dares to remonstrate with the King, lest he should offend Silvius, fearing that the said King will reveal it to her, since he loves her so intensely."[12]

Catherine de Medici had to share limelight with Diane de Poitiers for several years and accept that even her own children's upbringing was supervised by her, but she started carving out her own personal and political identity shortly after Henri II's unexpected death. Henri II sustained a fatal injury while jousting; the wooden lance of his opponent pierced his headgear, shattered it into fragments and penetrated his right orbit and temple. The best courtly physicians tried to save the King's life by performing an operation, but there was nothing they could do to save him. He died after ten days of agony, on 10 July 1559.

Aware of his impending death, Henri wanted to see his mistress one last time, but Diane de Poitiers was ordered to leave court and not disturb the King in his "pious meditations". She withdrew, probably to her chateau of Anet, where she soon received a delegation ordering her to return "sundry rings and jewels" she had received over the past twelve years. "Why, is the King dead then?" she asked. "No, Madame", was the answer, "but he can only linger a little longer". To this, Diane replied:

"As long as there is one breath of life left in his body, I would have my enemies to know I fear them not a whit, and that I will never obey them, so long as he shall be alive. My courage is still invincible. But when he is dead, I care not to live on after him, and all the vexations you could inflict on me would be but kindness compared with the bitterness of my loss. So, whether my King be quick [alive] or dead, I fear not mine enemies at all."[13]

Henri II's death marked the beginning of a new chapter in both Catherine de Medici's and Diane de Poitiers's lives. The Queen now had all the power to take revenge upon Diane, but she showed extraordinary leniency in punishing her husband's mistress. The only step she took against Diane was to urge her son to demand the return of royal jewels. The Venetian ambassador Giovanni Michieli recorded that the new King, fifteen-year-old Francis II, "has sent to inform Madame de Valentinois that because of her evil influence with the King, his father, she merited a severe punishment; but that in his royal clemency, he did not wish to disquiet her further. Nevertheless, she must restore all the jewels which the King, his father, had given her".[14] Diane promptly returned everything before retiring to her splendid chateau of Anet, where she died seven years later, aged sixty-five but, as Brantôme, who saw her six months before her death, put it, "as fair of face, as fresh looking and lovable as at thirty".[15]

As for Catherine de Medici, after a lifetime of sharing public attention with her husband's sophisticated mistress, she emerged as the ultimate golden age lady and shaped the Valois court over the next thirty years. But this, Dear Reader, is a story for another book.

NOTES

[1] *The History of Paris,* Volume 3, p. 415.
[2] Kathleen Wellman, *Queens and Mistresses of Renaissance France,* p. 201.
[3] Brantôme, *Lives of Fair and Gallant Ladies*, p. 320.
[4] In 1553, Diane was given the duchy of Étampes which formerly belonged to the disgraced Anne de Pisseleu.
[5] Kathleen Wellman, *Queens and Mistresses of Renaissance France,* p. 201.
[6] Ibid., p. 208.
[7] Ibid., p. 201.
[8] Ibid., p. 208.
[9] Madame de la Fayette, *The Princess of Cleves*, p. 5.

[10] Hugh Noel Williams, *The Brood of False Lorraine: The History of the Ducs de Guise (1496-1588)*, Volume 1, p. 72.
[11] Ibid., p. 75.
[12] Ibid.
[13] Pierre de Bourdeille, seigneur de Brantôme, *Lives of Fair and Gallant Ladies*, Volume 2, p. 73.
[14] Hugh Noel Williams, *The Brood of False Lorraine: The History of the Ducs de Guise (1496-1588)*, pp. 202-203.
[15] Pierre de Bourdeille, seigneur de Brantôme, *Lives of Fair and Gallant Ladies*, Volume 1, p. 319.

PICTURE SECTION

King Francis I as a young man. Wikimedia Commons.

Golden Age Ladies

Statues of Louis XII and Anne of Brittany in the Basilica of St Denis. Photo by the author.

Sketch of Mary Tudor, Henry VIII's younger sister, from *Album d'Aix*. A little acidic comment was inscribed on this sketch by Francis I: "More dirty than queenly" or, alternatively, "More fool than queen".

Picture section

Posthumous image of Queen Claude surrounded by her daughters: Louise, Charlotte, Marguerite and Madeleine. Francis I's second wife, Eleanor of Portugal, dressed in widow's weeds, stands in the background. Image from Catherine de Medici's prayer book. Wikimedia Commons.

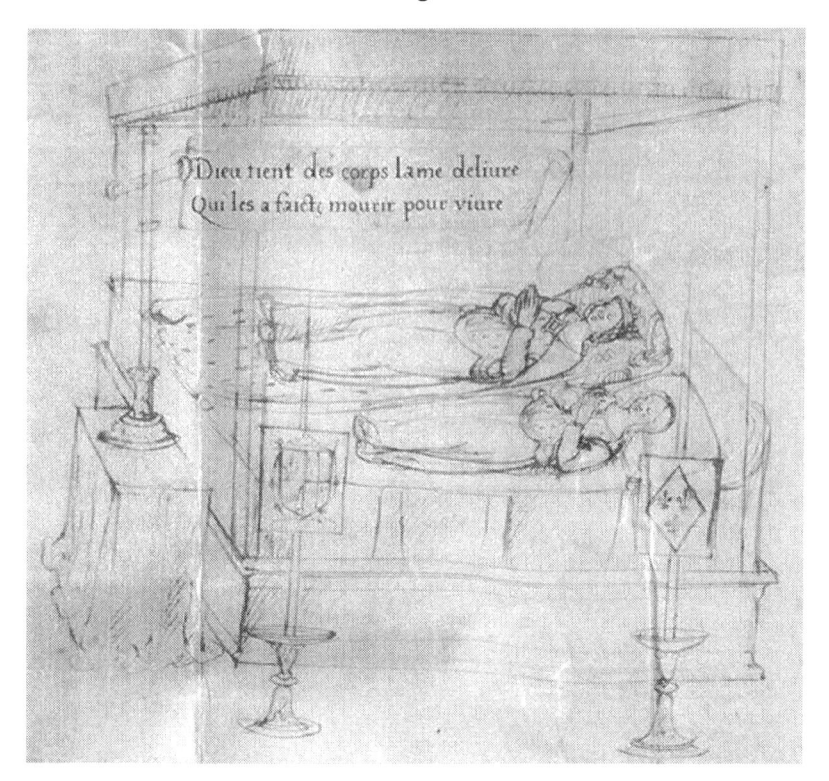

Wax effigies of Queen Claude and her eight-year-old daughter, Madame Charlotte, lying in state in Blois. The Queen died on 26 July 1524, and her daughter followed her to the grave on 18 September that same year. *Manuscrit des funérailles de Claude de France et Charlotte sa fille*, Blois-Agglopolys, Bibliothèque Abbé Grégoire, Fonds patrimonial, ms. 245.

Louise of Savoy, Francis I's imperious mother. Wikimedia Commons.

Madame Charlotte, the second daughter of Francis and Claude. She died of measles on 18 September 1524, aged only eight. Wikimedia Commons.

Margaret of Angoulême, Queen of Navarre, c. 1527. This is the only extant portrait depicting Margaret in colourful, rich clothing. Four years later, she started wearing black for mourning after the death of her six-month-old son, Jean. Wikimedia Commons.

Queen Eleanor of France, second wife of Francis I, in her late twenties. Wikimedia Commons.

Queen Eleanor as "the white queen", wearing typical French mourning garb, 1547. Her marriage to Francis I was notoriously unhappy. Charles V, Eleanor's brother, remarked that "she had not great reason to mourn the passing of the King in light of the little regard he had for her and the bad treatment she received". Wikimedia Commons.

Henry VIII in 1509, the year of his accession. He was almost eighteen years old. Wikimedia Commons.

Henry VIII in 1536, by Hans Holbein. Gone is the athletic young man of his early reign; by 1536 he became corpulent and grew a beard, a symbol of virility. The leg injury he suffered that year during a celebratory joust marked the beginning of serious health problems. Wikimedia Commons.

Picture section

Katharine of Aragon, Henry VIII's first wife, daughter of Ferdinand of Aragon and Isabella of Castile. Wikimedia Commons.

Anne Boleyn immortalised in a medal from 1534. It was cast in lead when Anne, Henry VIII's second wife, was believed to be pregnant. It is the only undisputed likeness of the controversial Queen from her lifetime. Wikimedia Commons.

Jane Seymour, Henry VIII's third wife. She gave birth to the King's longed-for male heir but died twelve days later, a victim of childbed fever. Wikimedia Commons.

Anne of Cleves, Henry VIII's discarded fourth wife. Wikimedia Commons.

Picture section

Miniature of an unknown woman. According to historian David Starkey, this is Katherine Howard, Henry VIII's fifth wife. This conclusion was reached upon the fact that the sitter is wearing a royal necklace similar to the one worn by Katherine Parr in her full-length painting (see next portrait). Wikimedia Commons.

Golden Age Ladies

Katherine Parr, Henry VIII's last wife. Wikimedia Commons.

Picture section

Anne de Pisseleu by Corneille de Lyon. She was Francis I's second officially appointed royal mistress. Wikimedia Commons.

Catherine de Medici as a young girl, by Jean Clouet. Wikimedia Commons.

Diane de Poitiers, Henri II's long-term mistress. Wikimedia Commons.

The tomb of Francis I and Queen Claude in the Basilica of St Denis. Photo by the author.

Golden Age Ladies

These statues depict Francis I and Queen Claude piously kneeling at their prayer stalls, accompanied by three of their deceased children: Madame Charlotte, Dauphin Francis and Charles, Duke of Angoulême. Photo by the author.

Queen Claude depicted as a nude corpse on a bier in the Basilica of St Denis. Photo by the author.

SELECT BIBLIOGRAPHY

In the bibliography below, I have included only those works which I have found useful while working on this book.

French court

Manuscript sources:

Manuscrit des funérailles de Claude de France et Charlotte sa fille, Blois-Agglopolys, Bibliothèque Abbé Grégoire, Fonds patrimonial, ms. 245.

Primary sources:

Barillon. *Journal de Jean Barrillon, secrétaire du Chancelier Duprat, 1515-1521*, ed. P. de Vaissière. Two Volumes, 1897-9.

Brantôme, P. de Bourdeille, abbé de. *The Book of the Ladies (Illustrious Dames)*, tr. Katharine Prescott Wormeley. Hardy, Pratt & Company, 1899.
Lives of Fair and Gallant Ladies. Two Volumes. The Alexandrian Society, Inc. London and New York, 1922.

Briçonnet, G., and Marguerite d'Angoulême. *Correspondance (1521-1524)*, ed. C. Martineau and M. Veissière, Two Volumes. Librairie Droz, 1975.

Castiglione, B. *The Book of the Courtier*, tr. L. Eckstein Opdycke. Charles Scribner's Sons, 1901.

Catalogue des actes de François Ier, 10 Volumes. 1887-1910.

De Beatis, A. *The Travel Journal of Antonio De Beatis: Germany, Switzerland, the Low Countries, France and Italy, 1517-1518*, tr. J.R. Hale and J.M.A. Lindon, ed. J.R. Hale, London, 1979.

Florange. *Mémoires du maréchal de Florange, dit le Jeune Adventureaux*, ed. R. Goubaux and P. A. Lemoisne, Two Volumes. Librairie Renouard. Paris, 1913-24.

Génin, F. *Lettres de Marguerite d'Angoulême, Soeur de François 1er, Reine de Navarre*. Paris, 1841.

Gringore, P. *Les Entrées Royales à Paris de Marie d'Angleterre (1514) et Claude de France (1517)*, ed. C.J. Brown. Librairie Droz, 2005.

Jansen, S. *Anne of France: Lessons for My Daughter*.Cambridge: D.S. Brewer, 2004.

Jourda, P. *Correspondance de Marguerite d'Angouleme*. Slatkine Reprint, 1973.

Journal de Louise de Savoie, in *Nouvelle collection de mémoires pour servir à l'histoire de France*, 1st ser. vol. 4, 83-93, ed. J. F. Michaud and J.J.F. Poujoulat. Paris, 1851.

Journal d'un bourgeois de Paris sous le règne de François Ier, 1515-1536, ed. V.L. Bourrilly, 1910.

Le Glay, A.J.C. *Négociations diplomatiques entre la France et l'Autriche*, Two Volumes, Paris, 1845.

Secondary sources:

Ambrière, F. *Le favori de François Ier, Gouffier de Bonnivet, Admiral de France; chronique des années 1489-1525*, Hachette, 1936.

Anderson, M.A. *St. Anne in Renaissance Music: Devotion and Politics*. Cambridge University Press, 2014.

Bapst, E. *Les Mariages de Jacques V*. Librairie Plon, 1889.

Select Bibliography

Benoit Rouard, E.A. *François Ier chez Mme De Boisy: Notice d'un recueil de crayons ou portraits aux crayons de couleur enrichi par le roi François Ier de vers et de devises inédites appartenant à la Bibliothèque Méjanes d'Aix*. A. Aubry, 1863.

Bertière, S. *Les Reines de France au Temps des Valois*, Two Volumes. Le Livre de Poche, 1996.

Brown, Elizabeth A.R. "The Ceremonial of Royal Succession in Capetian France: The Double Funeral of Louis X". Traditio, Volume 34 (1978), pp. 227-271.

Brown, C.J. *The Cultural and Political Legacy of Anne de Bretagne: Negotiating Convention in Books and Documents.* D.S. Brewer Gallica, 2010.

The Queen's Library: Image-Making at the Court of Anne of Brittany, 1477-1514. University of Pennsylvania Press, 2011.

Cholakian, P.F., and Cholakian, R.C. *Marguerite de Navarre: Mother of the Renaissance.* Columbia University Press, 2006.

Cox Rearick, J. "Power-Dressing at the Courts of Cosimo de' Medici and François I: The "Moda alla Spagnola" of Spanish Consorts Eléonore d'Autriche and Eleonora di Toledo". *Artibus et Historiae,* Vol. 30, No. 60 (2009), pp. 39-69.

Croizat, Y.C. "'Living Dolls': François Ier Dresses His Women". *Renaissance Quarterly,* Vol. 60, No. 1 (Spring 2007), pp. 94-130.

Cullerier, A. *De quelle maladie est mort François Ier: Extrait de la Gazette hebdomadaire de médecine et de chirurgie.* Victor Masson, 1856.

De Boom, G. *Éléonore d'Autriche: Reine de Portugal et de France.* Bruxelles, 1995.

Dickman Orth, M. "Francis Du Moulin and the Journal of Louise of Savoy". *The Sixteenth Century Journal,* Vol. 13, No. 1 (Spring, 1982), pp. 55-66.

Freeman, J. F. "Louise of Savoy: A Case of Maternal Opportunism". *The Sixteenth Century Journal,* Vol. 3, No. 2 (Oct., 1972), pp. 77-98.

Héritier, J. *Catherine de Medici.* St Martin's Press, 1963.

Hourihane, C. *The Grove Encyclopaedia of Medieval Art and Architecture.* Volume 2. OUP USA, 2012.

Knecht, R.J. *Francis I.* Cambridge University Press, 1984.

Kolk, Caroline zum. "The Household of the Queen of France in the Sixteenth Century", *The Court Historian* 14, 1 (June 2009), pp. 3-22.

Lacroix, P. *Louis XII et Anne de Bretagne.* Hurtrel, 1802.

Matarasso, P.M. *Queen's Mate: Three Women of Power in France on the Eve of the Renaissance.* Ashgate, 2001.

Maulde-La Clavière, R. *Louise de Savoie et François Ier: Trente ans de Jeunesse (1485-1515).* Perrin et Cie, 1895.

Michael of Kent, P. *The Serpent and the Moon: Two Rivals for the Love of a Renaissance King.* Simon and Schuster, 2005.

Moulton Mayer, D. *The Great Regent: Louise of Savoy 1476-1531.* Wiedenfeld and Nicolson. 1966.

Noel Williams, H. *Henri II: His Court and Times.* Charles Scribner's Sons, 1910.

The Pearl of Princesses: The Life of Marguerite d'Angoulême, Queen of Navarre. Eveleigh Nash Company, 1916.

Paulson, M. G. *Catherine de Medici: Five Portraits.* P. Lang, 2002.

Pigaillem, H. *Claude de France, Première Épouse de François Ier.* Pygmalion, 2006.

Potter, D. *Henry VIII and Francis I: The Final Conflict, 1540-47.* Brill, 2011.

Select Bibliography

"Politics and faction at the court of Francis I: the duchesse d'Etampes, Montmorency and the Dauphin Henri". *French History,* July 2007, pp. 127-146.

Richardson, W.C. *Mary Tudor: The White Queen.* Owen, 1970.

Sadlack, E.A. *The French Queen's Letters: Mary Tudor Brandon and the Politics of Marriage in Sixteenth-Century Europe.* Palgrave Macmillan, 2011.

Sichel, E.H. *Catherine de Medici and the French Reformation.* Archibald Constable & CO, 1995.

Walker Freer, M. *The Life of Marguerite D'Angoulême: Queen of Navarre, Duchesse D'Alençon and de Berry, Sister of Francis I, King of France.* Two Volumes. Hurst and Blackett, 1854.

Wellman, K. *Queens and Mistresses of Renaissance France.* Yale University Press, 2013.

Whittaker, G.B. *The History of Paris from the Earliest Period to the Present Day: Containing a description of its antiquities, public buildings, civil, religious, scientific, and commercial institutions.* Paris: A. and W. Galignani, 1827.

English court

Primary sources:

Calendar of State Papers, Spain. Ed. Brewer, J.S. & Gairdner. J. Institute of Historical Research (1862-1932).

Camden, W. *The History of the Most Renowned and Victorious Princess Elizabeth Late Queen of England.* Flesher, 1688.

Cavendish, G. *The Life and Death of Cardinal Wolsey.* S.W. Singer, Harding and Leppard, ed. 1827.

Cranmer, T. *Miscellaneous Writings and Letters of Thomas Cranmer.* Ed. J.E. Cox for The Parker Society. University Press, 1846.

Ellis, H. *Original Letters Illustrative of English History,* Volume 2. (2nd series). Harding and Lepard, 1827.

Everett Wood, A. *Letters of Royal and Illustrious Ladies of Great Britain.* Three Volumes. London, H. Colburn, 1846.

Examination of Queen Katherine Howard in Calendar of the manuscripts of the Marquis of Bath, preserved at Longleat, Wiltshire. Volume 2. John Falconer, 1907.

Foxe, J. *The Actes and Monuments of the Church.* Ed. Hobart Seymour. M. Robert Carter & Brothers, 1855.

Giustiniani, S. *Four Years at the Court of Henry VIII.* Two Volumes. London, Smith, Elder, 1854, tr. Rawdon Brown.

Hall, E. *Hall's Chronicle.* J. Johnson, 1809.

Harris, N. *Proceedings and Ordinances of the Privy Council of England.* Volume 7. G. Eyre and A. Spottiswoode, 1837.

Latymer, W. "William Latymer's Cronickille of Anne Bulleyne". Ed. Maria Dowling, *Camden Miscellany,* xxx. Camden Soc. 4th ser. 39. 1990.

Letters and Papers, Foreign and Domestic, of the Reign of Henry VIII. 28 Volumes. Ed. Brewer, J.S. & Gairdner. J. Institute of Historical Research (1862-1932).

Mueller, J. *Katherine Parr: Complete Works and Correspondence.* University of Chicago Press, 2011.

Sharp Hume, M.A. *Chronicle of King Henry VIII of England.* George Bell and Sons, 1889.

Pole, R. *Pole's Defense of the Unity of the Church.* Newman Press, 1965.

Sander, N. *Rise and Growth of the Anglican Schism.* Burns and Oates, 1877.

Wriothesley, C. *A Chronicle of England During the Reigns of the Tudors, from A.D. 1485 to 1559.* Camden Society, 1875.

Secondary sources:

Arnold, J. *Queen Elizabeth's Wardrobe Unlock'd.* Maney Publishing, 1988.

Benger, E. *Memoirs of the Life of Anne Bolyn, Queen of Henry VIII.* Volume 2. Longman, Hurst, Rees, Orme, and Brown, 1821.

Bernard, G.W. "Did Anne Boleyn crave the crown?" *BBC History Magazine,* June 2015.

Brigden, S. "Henry Howard, Earl of Surrey, and the 'Conjured League'". *The Historical Journal*, Vol. 37, No. 3 (Sep., 1994), pp. 507-537.

Chalmers, C.R. and Chaloner, E.J. "500 years later: Henry VIII, leg ulcers and the course of history". *Journal of the Royal Society of Medicine,* 2009 Dec 1; 102(12): pp. 514–517.

De Lisle, L. *Tudor: A Family Story.* Vintage Digital, 2013. Kindle edition.

Evans, V.S. *Ladies-in-Waiting: Women Who Served at the Tudor Court.* CreateSpace Independent Publishing Platform, 2014.

Everett Green, M.A. *Lives of the Princesses of England, from the Norman Conquest.* Volume 4. Longman, Brown, Green, Longman & Roberts, 1857.

Fletcher, C. *Our Man in Rome: Henry VIII and his Italian Ambassador.* Random House, 2012.

Friedmann, P. *Anne Boleyn: A Chapter of English History, 1527-1536*. Two Volumes. Macmillan and Co., 1884.

Gledhill Russell, J. *The Field of Cloth of Gold: Men and Manners in 1520*. Barnes & Noble, 1969.

Gristwood, S. *Blood Sisters: The Women Behind the Wars of the Roses*. Harper Press, 2012.

Hutchinson, R. *The Last Days of Henry VIII: Conspiracy, Treason and Heresy at the Court of the Dying Tyrant*. Phoenix, 2006.

Ives, E. W. *The Life and Death of Anne Boleyn: The Most Happy*. Blackwell Publishing, 2010.

Jones, P. *The Other Tudors Henry VIII's Mistresses and Bastards*. Metro Books, 2010.

Levine, M. "A 'Letter' on the Elizabethan Succession Question, 1566". *Huntington Library Quarterly*, Volume 19, No. 1 (Nov., 1955), pp. 13-38.

Lingard, J. *The history of England, from the first invasion by the Romans to the accession of William and Mary in 1688*. Volume 4. C. Dolman, 1849.

Lipscomb, S. *1536: The Year that Changed Henry VIII*. Lion Hudson, 2009.
The King is Dead. Head of Zeus, 2015.

Marshall, R.K. *Scottish Queens, 1034-1714*. Tuckwell, 2003.

Merriman, R.B. *Life and Letters of Thomas Cromwell*. Two Volumes. Clarendon Press, 1902.

Norton, E. *The Temptation of Elizabeth Tudor: Elizabeth I, Thomas Seymour, and the Making of a Virgin Queen*. Head of Zeus, 2015.

Scarisbrick, J.J. *Henry VIII*. Yale University Press, 2011.

Select Bibliography

Snyder, S. "Guilty Sisters: Marguerite de Navarre, Elizabeth of England, and the Miroir de l'âme Pécheresse". *Renaissance Quarterly*, Vol. 50, No. 2 (Summer, 1997), pp. 443-458.

Starkey, D. *Six Wives: The Queens of Henry VIII*. Vintage, 2004.

Strickland, A. *Lives of the Queens of England, from the Norman conquest*. Volume 2. London, 1864.

Urkevich, L. "Anne Boleyn, a music book, and the northern Renaissance courts: Music Manuscript 1070 of the Royal College of Music, London." PhD dissertation, University of Maryland, 1997.

"Anne Boleyn's French Motet Book, a Childhood Gift. The Question of the Original Owner of MS1070 of the Royal College of Music, London, Revisited" in *Ars musica septentrionalis*, PU Paris-Sorbonne, 2011.

Vincent, J.M. *The Life of Henry the Eighth and History of the Schism of England*, trans. Kirwan Browne, E.G. C. Dolman, 1852.

Walters Schmid, S. "Anne Boleyn, Lancelot de Carle, and the Uses of Documentary Evidence", PhD dissertation, Arizona State University, 2009.

Warnicke, R.M. *Wicked Women of Tudor England: Queens, Aristocrats, Commoners*. Palgrave Macmillan, 2012.

Weir, A. *Mary Boleyn: 'The Great and Infamous Whore'*. Vintage, 2011.

Wilkinson, J. *Anne Boleyn: The Young Queen To Be*. Amberley Publishing, 2011.

Mary Boleyn: The True Story of Henry VIII's Favourite Mistress. Amberley Publishing, 2009.

ACKNOWLEDGMENTS

This project initially started as a book about the women who influenced Anne Boleyn throughout her life. When I started researching the subject, I quickly realized that the noblewomen who surrounded Anne at the time when she was Queen Claude's maid of honour were immensely interesting and in need of introduction to a wider audience. This is how I decided to link their stories to those of their English counterparts. These extraordinary women captured my imagination and became a huge part of my life for over a year. I've read their letters and followed in their footsteps. This was an amazing journey.

Along the way, I encountered the most extraordinary generosity. I must thank Dr Lisa Urkevich, who so kindly sent me her article about Anne Boleyn's songbook and a copy of her dissertation. I must give thanks to Bruno Guignard from Bibliothèque Abbé-Grégoire in Blois, for answering my queries about the intriguing sketch of Queen Claude and her daughter Charlotte lying in state. I must also give a very special thank you to my friend, historian Brigitte Laurent, who helped me with some translations from the original French. Without her help, this book would have been incomplete. To my friend Joanna for patiently listening to my impassionate rants about women I was writing about. A special thank you to my copyeditor Jennifer Quinlan, who always makes sure that my manuscripts are impeccable.

Last but not least, I must thank my husband, without whose help and encouragement this book would not have been possible. He often gave up his own time to listen to me read aloud from the manuscript, allowing me to share my passion with him. From the bottom of my heart, thank you.

ABOUT THE AUTHOR

Sylvia Barbara Soberton is a historical writer with a passion for English and French history. She is the author of the best-selling book *The Forgotten Tudor Women: Margaret Douglas, Mary Howard and Mary Shelton,* which examines the lives of three extraordinary women who had been overshadowed by their more famous counterparts. She speaks two foreign languages and enjoys following in the footsteps of the women she is writing about. Her goal is to bring history to life, concentrating on the lives of the extraordinary women who lived and ruled in sixteenth century Europe. If you would like to follow her updates, chat with Sylvia or share your thoughts about her books, you are invited to do so by visiting one of her Facebook pages:

https://www.facebook.com/FamousWomenoftheFrenchCourt

https://www.facebook.com/theforgottentudorwomen/

Printed in Great Britain
by Amazon